Political Science
and Political Theory

Social Science Lexicons

Key Topics of Study
Key Thinkers, Past and Present
Political Science and Political Theory
Methods, Ethics and Models
Social Problems and Mental Health

Political Science and Political Theory

Edited by Jessica Kuper

ROUTLEDGE & KEGAN PAUL
LONDON AND NEW YORK

First published in 1987 by
Routledge & Kegan Paul Limited
11 New Fetter Lane, London EC4P 4EE

Published in the USA by
Routledge & Kegan Paul Inc.
in association with Methuen Inc.
29 West 35th Street, New York, NY 10001

Set in Linotron Baskerville
by Input Typesetting Ltd., London SW19 8DR
and printed in Great Britain
by Cox & Wyman Ltd, Reading, Berks

Library of Congress Cataloging in Publication Data

Social science encyclopedia.   Selections.
  Political science and political theory.

  (Social science lexicons)
  Includes bibliographies and index.
  1. Political science.   I. Kuper, Jessica.
II. Title.   III. Series.
JA71.S6425   1987   320   87–4273

British Library CIP Data also available
ISBN 0–7102–1171–6

Contents

Contributor List

General Editor: Jessica Kuper

Bailey, F G	Dept of Anthropology, University of California, San Diego
Baum, Alan	Dept of Social Science, Middlesex Polytechnic, Enfield, Middlesex
Beiner, R S	Dept of Politics, University of Southampton, and Dept of Philosophy, Queen's University, Kingston, Ontario
Beyme, Klaus von	Dept of Political Science, University of Heidelberg
Birnbaum, Pierre	Dept of Political Science, University of Paris
Blondel, Jean	Pro-Vice-Chancellor, and Dept of Government, University of Essex
Boissevain, Jeremy	Dept of Anthropology, University of Amsterdam
Brown, Archie	St Antony's College, University of Oxford
Brubaker, Stanley C	Dept of Political Science, Colgate University
Brunner, Ronald D	Colorado Center for Public Policy Research, University of Colorado
Calhoun, Craig	Dept of Sociology, University of North Carolina at Chapel Hill
Canovan, Margaret	Dept of Politics, University of Keele
Cohen, Brenda	Dept of Philosophy, University of Surrey
Cook, Karen S	Dept of Sociology, University of Washington, Seattle
Curtice, John	Dept of Political Theory and Institutions, University of Liverpool
Deane, Phyllis	Emeritus Professor of Economic History, University of Cambridge

Denoon, Donald	Research School of Pacific Studies, Australian National University
Fawcett, Sir James, QC	Former President, European Commission of Human Rights, and Emeritus Professor of International Law, King's College, London
Francis, Wayne L	Dept of Political Science, University of Missouri, Columbia
Frey, Bruno S	Institute of Empirical Economics, University of Zurich
Friedman, Jonathan	Dept of Ethnology, University of Copenhagen
Galtung, Johan	International Peace Research Institute, Oslo
Goldstone, Jack A	Dept of Sociology, Northwestern University, Evanston, Illinois
Goodwin, Barbara	Dept of Government, Brunel University, Uxbridge, Middlesex
Hall, Thomas D	Dept of Sociology, University of Oklahoma, Norman
Halsey, A H	Dept of Social and Administrative Studies, University of Oxford
Hauschildt, Jürgen	Christian-Albrechts University, Kiel
Hewitt, Cynthia	EI Colegio de Mexico, Mexico City
Himmelweit, Hilde	Dept of Social Psychology, The London School of Economics and Political Science
Hirst, Paul	Dept of Political Science, Birkbeck College, University of London
Horvat, Branko	Dept of Economics, University of Zagreb
Humphreys, Sally	Dept of Anthropology, University of Michigan, Ann Arbor
Kalberg, Stephen	Center for European Studies, Harvard University

Kavanagh, Dennis	Dept of Political Science, University of Nottingham
Kourvetaris, George A	Dept of Sociology, N Illinois University, De Kalb, Illinois
Kroeber-Riel, W	Institute for Behaviour Research, University of Saarlandes, West Germany
Kumar, Krishan	Keynes College, University of Kent
Kuper, Adam	Dept of Human Sciences, Brunel University, Uxbridge, Middlesex
Lijphart, Arendt	Dept of Political Science, University of California, San Diego
Lyons, David	Cornell Law School, Cornell University
McLellan, David	Eliot College, University of Kent
Marsh, D C	Formerly of the University of Nottingham
Marvick, Dwaine	Dept of Sociology, University of California, Los Angeles
Meyer, Alfred G	Dept of Political Science, University of Michigan, Ann Arbor
Miller, David	Nuffield College, University of Oxford
Minogue, Kenneth	Dept of Government, The London School of Economics and Political Science
Moore, Sally Falk	Dept of Anthropology, Harvard University
Nelson, Michael	Dept of Political Science, Vanderbilt University, Nashville, Tennessee
Niemi, Richard G	Dept of Political Science, University of Rochester
Pasquino, Gianfranco	Dept of Political Science, University of Bologna
Payne, Stanley G	Dept of History, University of Wisconsin-Madigan
Philp, Mark	Oriel College, University of Oxford

Pinto-Duschinsky, M	Dept of Government, Brunel University, Uxbridge, Middlesex
Reynolds, P A	Vice-Chancellor, University of Lancaster
Rose, Hilary	Dept of Applied Social Studies, University of Bradford
Rosen, F	Dept of Politics, The London School of Economics and Political Science
Russell, Peter H	Dept of Political Science, University of Toronto
Scaff, Lawrence	Dept of Political Science, University of Arizona
Schaffer, Bernard	Formerly of the Institute of Development Studies, University of Sussex
Tarrow, Sidney	Dept of Government, Cornell University
Tournon, Jean	Dept of Political Studies, University of Grenoble
Twaddle, Michael	Institute of Commonwealth Studies, University of London
Walker, Jack L	Institute of Public Studies, University of Michigan, Ann Arbor
Wallis, Roy	Dept of Social Studies, The Queen's University, Belfast
Wiatr, Jerzy J	Dept of Political Science, University of Warsaw
Yolton, John W	Dean, Rutgers, The State University of New Jersey

Political Science

Although the study of politics is an ancient pursuit, it is only in the last few decades that the discipline of political science became truly established, not perhaps so much because the fundamental problems which had intrigued the authors of the past have been superseded or even radically changed, but because new political processes, new techniques of government and, above all, a greater variety of studies have broadened markedly the fields of inquiry.

Traditionally, political science was essentially concerned with the purpose, character, and organization of the State. The great classics, Hobbes and Locke in the seventeenth century, Rousseau in the eighteenth, for instance, were primarily preoccupied with determining the goals of civil society and describing the institutions which appeared best-suited to achieving these goals. In the nineteenth century, the tradition was developed and amplified as new political institutions were set up in most Western-European countries and in America: the main preoccupation of some of the most prominent political scientists of the period, the constitutional lawyers, was to elaborate the ways in which these institutions could be firmly established and thus give the modern State a stable organization.

While political science analysis was thus focusing on the organization of the State, it was doing so on the basis of a twofold concern which remains a fundamental distinction to the present day. On the one hand, thinkers had a normative or prescriptive purpose: they wished to present the general principles on which the organization of government *should* be based. For political science is in large part born out of the desire to 'improve' political life and thus to reflect on the goals of government which would be most appropriate to bring about the 'good life'. Of course, this type of inquiry necessarily reflects the values of the thinkers themselves. Most political scientists of the past undertook their inquiries because of deeply felt views about human nature in politics; these views consequently differed profoundly from one thinker to another, with the result that the models of society are often in sharp contrast. Hobbes, for example, started from the hypothesis that man is a beast to man, and that the function of political organization is to make more liveable a society which would otherwise be 'nasty, brutish, and short'; Locke and Rousseau, on the contrary, had a more optimistic view of human nature and basically believed that the ills of society came from malorganization rather than from defects inherent in individuals.

On the other hand, alongside a desire to present the goals for a better society, political scientists had also to devote their attention to the examination of the 'facts'; they had to assess what was wrong with a situation they wished to alter and explain why their proposals would achieve the desired results. Political science has thus always included a study of the 'objective' characteristics of government, as well as a prescriptive or normative inquiry. The great classical writers often described in detail the existing arrangements and their drawbacks; they compared institutions in one country with those of another. Similarly, nineteenth-century constitutional lawyers looked for workable arrangements relating to elections, the structure and procedures of parliaments, the relationships between executive and legislature, thereby relating the political goals to the reality.

Political science is, consequently, both concerned with what should be and with what is. This is one reason why some believe that the term 'science' should not be taken too literally in the context of the study of politics, as political science is more than a science in the normal sense of the word: it is both descriptive examination and prescriptive philosophy. Improvements are studied and presented in the form of arguments, rather than by the analysis of data alone.

Naturally enough, although political science does incorporate both aspects, some political scientists are more inclined in one direction than in the other. Especially in recent years, when the discipline grew rapidly and became increasingly specialized, the political philosophers (sometimes known, albeit wrongly, as political 'theorists' – because there are also other political theorists) and the students of the 'facts' of political life (occasionally referred to as empirical political scientists) have often clashed, each group claiming to be superior.

The Problem of Definition

For a very long period, extending to the end of the nineteenth century, political science studied the State. There seemed little need to go beyond this simple definition of the scope of the subject, as the State appeared paramount and other organizations seemed to depend on it; indeed, as years went by, the involvement of the State in the daily life of citizens appeared to be on the increase.

Yet, while the State was becoming more pervasive, governmental decisions were increasingly subjected to the pressure of many groups operating within the State. The growth of political parties, of trade unions, of employers' organizations and, indeed, of large numbers of other associations, was challenging, if not the legal sovereignty of the State, at least its practical supremacy. Political scientists in this century could clearly not confine their analyses to State institutions and to the goals of these institutions; they had to broaden their inquiries to include the bodies which were involved in the many pressures brought upon the State. Moreover, 'political' activities similar to those taking place within the State were occurring within other groups – in the life of the parties, of trade unions, and of pressure groups in general.

Thus political science ceased being concerned exclusively with the State and became more broadly conceived. For this to happen, the subject-matter of the discipline had to shift from a specific area of inquiry – the State – to an activity – politics. But what, then, is politics? From the 1920s, many political scientists tried to establish the basic features of the activity which they were studying. In the 1930s and 1940s, especially under the influence of Lasswell, the operative concept was power, as politics does indeed appear to be closely related to the ability of some men to induce others to act (Lasswell and Kaplan, 1950; Barry, 1976).

But this approach gradually gave way to a more flexible and wider definition, as the scope of politics seemed to go beyond power and include many instances of 'natural' obedience which could not easily be defined as uses of power, at least in the normal sense of the concept. Politics thus became viewed as the activity concerned with the elaboration and implementation of collective decisions, through a variety of mechanisms involving power, to be sure, but also legitimacy, automatic acceptance, and basic loyalty. The definition proposed by Easton in the 1950s was widely adopted and suggests that political activity relates to the 'authoritative allocation of resources' in a community (Easton, 1953).

Such a definition of politics is intellectually more satisfying than the one which relates the field of study to the activities of the State. The effect was to enable political scientists to broaden markedly the scope of their analyses. If, for instance, the study of politics is concerned with the pressures on the government to take a particular decision, it follows that political scientists should also be concerned with examining the features of such pressures and, in particular, with the bodies involved in these pressures. While constitutional lawyers mainly studied assemblies, executives or courts, modern political scientists found it natural, indeed necessary, to look at groups of all kinds, not only political parties, but also other pressure groups in the decision-making process such as trade unions, churches, employers' organizations and others.

The Concern with the Systematic Analysis of Reality and the Development of Behaviourism
In the course of their inquiries, political scientists became increasingly aware of the gap between what constitutions proclaimed and what actually occurred. For example, it was simply not the case that parliaments and even governments were able to exercise the 'sovereignty' which was said to be

theirs in liberal democratic systems: that sovereignty was in fact shared by the various groups involved in the decision process. Thus, not only was the scope of empirical inquiries broadened, but there was a disaffection from – and at times a rejection of – the analysis of legal and institutional devices; in its place the emphasis was on the 'true' reality of political life. The new school of thought which pressured for greater realism was called *behaviourism* (Dahl, 1963; Storing, 1962; Meehan, 1971).

The behavioural approach in political science, started in the United States, was widely adopted in the 1950s and 1960s, and later extended to many other academic centres. This approach seemed particularly appropriate at a time when, both in Eastern Communist States and in many parts of the Third World, the gap was increasing between constitutional formulas and the reality of government. Even in Western liberal democracies, the constitutional approach appeared inadequate since parties and interest groups had strikingly modified the characteristics of political life. Thus one major area of political science – the comparative analysis of political systems pioneered by Aristotle over 2500 years ago – benefited from the behavioural approach at a time when so many new systems of government emerged throughout the world.

Quantification, 'Positivism' and the Crisis of Behaviourism
Behaviourism was not only a demand for a more realistic approach to the study of politics: it also included two other claims that were to lead to many controversies and ultimately contributed to its decline in the 1970s. First, behaviourism became closely associated with a desire, in itself eminently justifiable but in practice often difficult to bring about, to give empirical studies a 'truly' scientific basis. It tried to ensure that conclusions were not drawn merely from a few examples or from impressionistic remarks, but were the result of systematic examination of facts. This new trend in political science was indeed paralleled by similar developments in other social sciences, especially in economics, psychology, and, though to a somewhat lesser extent, sociology. It advocated a systematic

presentation of the facts and the testing of hypotheses, in particular, the use of quantitative techniques. Many political scientists anxiously sought indicators that could be expressed numerically, and they achieved significant results in a variety of fields in which large masses of numerical data could be used. This was obviously the case in electoral studies, which for at least a decade was to be the leading area of development of quantitative political science. Helped by the increased sophistication of survey techniques, political scientists were able to do complex analyses of the relationship between voting patterns and social, economic, and psychological characteristics of electors, both at a given moment and over time.

But there were problems. Not all aspects of political life were as readily quantifiable as electoral behaviour: much of the life of governments and groups appeared at least *prima facie* to have to be described in a less 'rigorous' manner. Moreover, an undue emphasis on quantification might lead to an exaggerated reliance on some types of indicators, because they were quantified, and to the neglect of other aspects, such as cultural factors, not as easily amenable to mathematical treatment. Nevertheless, the quantification process increased in political science during the 1960s and 1970s: parties, interest groups, legislative activity, governmental structures, court pronouncements and certain aspects of the decision-making process were examined more rigorously; but it also became clear that the goal of general quantification was very distant.

Meanwhile, interest began to shift from the problem posed by quantification to the underlying philosophical implications of behaviourism. The supporters of the behavioural approach did not only wish to be more factual and realistic; they also wanted political science to become more scientific. They hoped to develop theories that could be tested systematically through hypotheses; these, in turn, needed the backing of a 'general theory'. This suggested a move towards a positivistic type of inquiry, which was to cause major controversies. Behaviourists pointed out that political science had so far been concerned almost exclusively with normative theories and with the detailed examination of specific situations. They argued that what was needed was a systematization of the data through the search for overall explanatory frameworks which would account for the wide range of political phenomena hitherto presented in an unconnected manner.

Such a goal was logical in the context of a move designed to improve the scientific character of the discipline. But it was at best premature, and it proved to be contentious. It was clearly impossible to elaborate general theories, akin to those in the natural sciences, that could effectively explain all varieties in political life. Some models were advanced, such as systems analysis or structural-functionalism, but these had at best the status of frameworks which might guide the scholar in his inquiries; they were not testable theories accounting for reality. But these models pointed to the interconnection between the many political institutions present in a 'system'; they showed the need to look for the role (or functions) of the various institutions (structures), as this role was not necessarily the same from 'system' to 'system'. But this scarcely amounted to a general theory.

The models also proved contentious as soon as they claimed to be more than a 'guide for research': they tended to emphasize – even overemphasize – the need for 'stability' and 'system maintenance' in the development of political life. Critics argued that, far from being 'scientific' and 'objective', these models were truly ideological in the manner of the normative theories of the classical writers of the past. Marxists were not alone in stressing the part played by values in the analyses which scholars undertake in a field such as political science where the ideas of the 'good society' cannot easily be disentangled from the examination of the 'facts'.

As a result of this conflict, fewer scholars believed it possible to establish rapidly (if at all) a body of general theory from which one could deduce characteristics of political life.

The nature of reality is too complex. This is one reason why in the 1970s more emphasis came to be placed on 'middle-range' analyses of political phenomena, that is, studies of one particular aspect of the political system such as party development, legislative behaviour, or governmental structure and activity. If a general theory is to emerge, this can only be after a long process, especially since political science is not, and cannot be, merely the study of what is, however this is defined: it is also the study of what ought to be. Norms and prescription are part of the study of politics, whether this is consciously recognized or not.

Such a recognition does not make political science 'unscientific'; but it has the effect of leading to the conclusion that political science has to develop, alongside the other social sciences, in its own special way. Ideology and values will always play a part in the analysis of politics. Perhaps a new form of scientific methodology needs to emerge if all aspects of the discipline are to be fully interconnected; meanwhile, progress will have to take place both through normative and through empirical analyses, with, where it proves useful, the help of quantitative techniques.

J. Blondel
University of Essex

References

Barry, B. (1976), *Power and Political Theory*, London.

Dahl, R. A. (1963), *Modern Political Analysis*, Englewood Cliffs, N.J.

Easton, D. (1953), *The Political System*, New York.

Lasswell, H. D. and Kaplan, A. (1950), *Power and Society*, New Haven.

Meehan, E. J. (1971), *The Foundations of Political Analysis*, Homewood, Ill.

Storing, H. (1962), *Essays on the Scientific Study of Politics*, New York.

Further Reading

Blondel, J. (1981), *The Discipline of Politics*, London.

Jouvenal, B. de (1963), *A Pure Theory of Politics*, Cambridge.

Sabine, G. J. and Thorson, T. L. (1973), *A History of Political Theory*, New York.

Seliger, M. (1976), *Ideology and Politics*, London.

See also: *political theory*.

Political Theory

Political theory is a subject which is more easily defined ostensively than formally. It is simple enough to point to the intellectual tradition which runs from Plato and Aristotle through to Marx, Mill and beyond, but less simple to point to the common elements in their thought which enable us to say that they were all in some sense engaged in the same enterprise. Perhaps the best approximation is to say that political theory is an attempt to understand political and social relationships at a high level of generality, and in the light of that understanding to advocate a certain practical stance towards them. At one extreme, a theory may portray existing relationships as the perfect embodiment of rationality and consequently recommend conserving them in their entirety; at the other extreme, a theory may highlight the gulf between existing institutions and rational principles, and describe in some detail an alternative social and political order which would better realize the principles in question. The way in which this common project has been carried out, however, has varied a great deal. Some theories have started from a conception of the human individual, and asked what political and social arrangements would best satisfy his needs and desires. Others have interpreted existing institutions as part of an overall pattern of historical development – either as the culmination of that pattern, or as a transient stage destined to be replaced by something higher. Others again have begun by asking what kind of knowledge is possible in political matters, and gone on to defend institutional arrangements which give people tasks in proportion to their capacity to carry them out. Political theorists have been just as diverse in their methods as they have in their practical conclusions.

Because political theory aims to be prescriptive as well as explanatory, questions inevitably arise about its relationship to the practical outlooks of ordinary men and women, especially those relatively systematic world-views often referred to as ideologies. Political theory is best seen as an attempt to render these outlooks more adequate by reflecting on their underlying assumptions – discarding assumptions that are untenable, and providing more solid foundations for those that remain valid.

It is differentiated from ideology by the fact that ideologies take for granted beliefs that political theory puts in question. Thus an ideology might incorporate the belief that social inequalities were the proper result of differences in individual merit. A political theorist would need to ask both about the extent to which the distribution of benefits in society actually corresponded to personal merit, and about the meaning of the notion of merit itself – say about the features in virtue of which one person could be described as more meritorious than another. It would be wrong, however, to harden this contrast into a rigid distinction. No political theorist is able to subject all of the beliefs that enter his theory to critical examination; some he has simply to take for granted. We may therefore refer to the ideological components of political theories, and say of a theory such as Locke's that it embodies elements of liberal ideology, or of Marx's that it embodies elements of socialist ideology. Indeed, we may wish to think of political theory as an activity that can be carried on at different levels, according to the extent to which received ideological beliefs are put in question. At the lowest level, there will be theories that are little more than the systematic expression of an ideology; at the highest level, theories that are very much more reflective, in the sense that a high proportion of their component beliefs have been subjected to critical examination.

In our own century, the very idea of political theory has been called into question by the widespread acceptance of positivism as a philosophical standpoint. Positivism denies that there is any logical connection between empirical propositions describing the world as it is and normative propositions telling us how we ought to act. Acceptance of this view implies that political theory as traditionally conceived rested on a mistake. The mistake was to combine explanations of social and political relationships with recommendations about how those relationships should be carried on. On the positivist view there are two distinct enterprises: political science, which aims at the empirical explanation of political phenomena, and political philosophy, which starts from certain political values such as democracy and equality and draws out their practical implications. Although, as we shall see later, this view is open to challenge, its popularity has been such that a distinction is often now drawn between three types of political theory:

(1) *Empirical political theory.* This term is commonly used to refer to the theoretical parts of political science. Political scientists are interested in describing and explaining particular political events, but they are also interested in developing broader explanatory theories which draw together a wide range of phenomena under a single heading. They have, for instance, tried to explain in general terms why revolutions occur, or why some democracies are dominated by two large parties while others generate many small ones. The issues that are considered are often similar to those addressed in the older tradition of political theory, but much greater use is typically made of quantifiable evidence. Thus someone seeking to produce a theory about the causes of revolution would characteristically begin by looking for correlations between the outbreak of revolutions and other phenomena, such as the extent of economic inequality in the societies under consideration.

(2) *Formal political theory.* This burgeoning field overlaps considerably with 'social choice theory', 'public choice theory', and so on. The approach here is to model a political system by assuming certain procedural rules and actors with designated goals, and then to investigate formally (on the assumption that each actor pursues his goals rationally) what the final configuration of the system will be. Two major applications are to collective decision procedures and to party competition in a representative democracy. In the first case, the theorist postulates a population each of whom has his own preferences as between a number of policies, and looks at how these preferences will be amalgamated into a 'collective choice' by various decision rules (such as majority voting). One well-known result of these investigations is Arrow's (1963) theorem, according to which *no* decision rule can simultaneously meet a number of reasonable-sounding conditions (such as that if each person prefers x to y, y should not be collectively chosen in preference to x). In the second case, the theorist again assumes a population with given policy preferences, and looks at how parties

will behave under a democratic electoral system on the assumption that each party's aim is to win the election and each voter's aim is to secure policies that correspond as closely as possible to his preferences. This application was originally developed by Antony Downs (1957), and has since been considerably elaborated.

(3) *Normative political theory.* In this branch of the subject, the theorist is directly interested in the justification of political standpoints and policies. There is, however, disagreement about how strong a form of justification is possible. For some theorists, influenced by positivism, justification ultimately ends in a commitment to one or other basic political value. The theorist's room for manœuvre is created by the fact that such values cannot be translated simply or immediately into policy. Thus someone may believe that his underlying commitment is to individual freedom, but this commitment does not, of itself, tell him whether he should be in favour (say) of a night-watchman state or an interventionist welfare state. The theorist's job, on this view, is to explore what the idea of freedom means, and then to apply it to practical issues, such as whether redistributive taxation reduces the freedom of the wealthy, or increases the freedom of the poor, or does both. The alternative view maintains that it is possible to go beyond this minimum programme and provide rational foundations for the basic values themselves. An important recent attempt in this direction can be found in the work of John Rawls (1972), who has tried to show that principles of distributive justice can be derived from the choices that rational individuals would make if they were ignorant of their personal characteristics and place in society. Although this attempt has not been judged a success on all sides, it has served as a landmark in the English-speaking world for those who believe that the more ambitious version of normative theory is feasible.

This distinction betwen types of political theory is useful as a labelling device, and it corresponds to a real division of labour in the academic community; but it is much more doubtful whether a rigid separation between the three enterprises can be sustained intellectually. Consider each pairing in turn:

(1) Normative theories necessarily rely on empirical research whenever they move from the most abstract kind of conceptual analysis to consider what various concepts and principles imply for the design of institutions and policies. It is impossible to say, for instance, whether democracy can be achieved through a scheme of parliamentary representation without having some understanding of how electoral systems operate. On the other hand, every empirical theory embodies normative assumptions. This is so because the concepts that are used to group phenomena together for explanatory purposes – concepts such as 'revolution', 'democracy' and 'social inequality' – embody assumptions about what is significant in human affairs, and which occurrences are relevantly similar and dissimilar. Thus a theory that attempts to specify the social conditions under which revolutions are likely to occur presupposes that the term 'revolution' picks out a set of events which are interesting to the social scientist and have important features in common.

(2) Formal and empirical theory also feed off each other. Although those engaged in formal analysis frequently deny that their assumptions are meant to be empirically realistic, the undertaking itself would not be worth engaging in unless there was some connection between the assumptions made and behaviour in the real world. Thus Downs's theory of democracy would be little more than an intellectual conceit if political parties were not as a matter of fact sometimes prepared to alter their policies in order to attract voters. Conversely, the models developed in formal analysis are an important source of explanatory theory. A full theory of party competition will almost certainly need to incorporate Downsian mechanisms – that is, it will need to recognize that parties are driven by their interest in winning elections to adopt policies that correspond to voters' preferences – alongside other factors in explaining party behaviour.

(3) Finally, formal theory both borrows from and contributes to normative theory. This can be seen most easily in the case of the theory of collective choice. The conditions that a theorist will lay down for an acceptable decision procedure will reflect his normative commitments. One such condition might be

political equality: each person's preference should have an equal chance of determining what the collective choice will be. Conversely, the results of formal analysis may have important normative implications. An upshot of Arrow's theorem, for instance, is that there is in general no simple 'best' procedure for making social choices; instead societies should be prepared to use different procedures in different areas of decision, depending on such factors as the likely configuration of individual preferences on a given issue.

All of this suggests that the older political theorists were right to see political explanation and political prescription as integrally related. It does not, however, mean that it is now easy to do political theory in the traditional way. Academic specialization has meant that most practitioners currently work in one small corner of the field; and those who try to present a synoptic view of political life are liable to be denounced as amateurs. But since political theory responds to a permanent intellectual need – the need to subject our everyday political attitudes and assumptions to critical questioning – one can safely predict that, in one form or another, the enterprise will continue.

David Miller
Nuffield College, Oxford

References
Arrow, K. (1963), *Social Choice and Individual Values*, New Haven.
Downs, A. (1957), *An Economic Theory of Democracy*, New York.
Rawls, J. (1972), *A Theory of Justice*, Oxford.

Further Reading
Barry, B. (1965), *Political Argument*, London.
Berlin, I. (1964), 'Does political theory still exist?', in P. Laslett and W. G. Runciman (eds), *Philosophy, Politics and Society*, Second Series, Oxford.
Connolly, W. (1974), *The Terms of Political Discourse*, Lexington, Mass.

Miller, D. and Siedentop, L. (eds) (1983), *The Nature of Political Theory*, Oxford.

Riker, W. H. and Ordeshook, P. C. (1973), *An Introduction to Positive Political Theory*, Englewood Cliffs, N.J.

Runciman, W. G. (1969), *Social Science and Political Theory*, Cambridge.

Weldon, T. D. (1953), *The Vocabulary of Politics*, Harmondsworth.

See also: *political science*.

Administration

Administration is an aspect of organizational institutionalization or establishment. Its job is to avoid crucial challenges so as to keep institutions going. The administrator can establish and maintain any organization by imposing a process of compartmentalization. This requires the establishment of four sets of rules: the rules of satisficing, simplication, simulation and jurisdiction. Following these rules means that administration keeps things going by finding satisfactory means, by admitting only selected data and labelled categories and case applicants, by not trying to deal with a chaos of raw and unordered life and, finally, by dealing only with certain issues, and then only in particular ways and via specified officials – not with anything by anyone in any way. Overall, there is a departmental line or philosophy, an agenda. In short, the job of administration is to control the agenda, and the formulation of data, and to determine what and who can enter the discussion about policy, and how the discussion is then conducted.

However disguised, administration is political, partly because keeping organizations going demands the management of endogenous relations, legitimation and the creation of loyalty, and more generally because it is an inescapable part of any state apparatus. Administration allows the balance in state politics to be tilted to organization rather than coercion, so that in consequence politicians kill people less often than they might otherwise.

Administration is not confined to modern political organizations, but however common, old and various, administration seems to require certain conditions:

(1) Administration does not work well where decision making is weakly ordered. It requires an interest in keeping the organization going, because of loyalty or organizational slack. The favoured administrative ecology fosters political, constitutional or consensual mutual adjustment, rather than economistic, market-like or warlike adaptations.

(2) The administrator works best where each case needs to be referred through the hierarchy for minuting about precedents. Where this sort of expert supervision is carried out, it creates steep and highly pyramidical organizations.

(3) Another condition of administration is the establishment of a distinction between administrators and political office-holders. The distinction has, not surprisingly, been variously pursued through the history of administrative reforms and administrative sciences and among political systems. The Westminster model is peculiar. It provides for an elected and partisan minister who is at once a member of a collectively responsible cabinet and an amateur and changing extrinsic chief of a specific type of administrative organization. However, there have been politically significant variations in ministerialization, in recruitment and formation, and in the professional and legal status of administrative performances as between the generalistic Oxbridge anglophonic ideal, the Napoleonic codification of schools, service and administrative law, and the American Jeffersonian ambivalence about spoils, appointments and business or academic careers.

Politics and administration, however, are always in a necessary alliance in order to secure resources, foster institutional legitimation, manage conflicts, facilitate the delivery of services, and invent policy themes. Therefore, administration is not quite bureaucracy in Palmerston's sense of government by appointed officeholders. Yet it is bureaucratic in the sort of organizations it institutionalizes, in those peculiar methods of work and, above all, in its justifications by equity of process rather than substantive outcomes.

While it is common, culturally specific and non-cosmopolitan, administrative behaviour always provokes similar concerns: as in the search for other ways of doing it, like pretences that there could be a development administration different from the (colonial) 'hearing cases and collecting taxes', however ill-served development could be if cases were unheard and taxes uncollected; and in sterile discussions about professional, scientific or technical status.

Administration is inescapably present save in the abundance of Utopia, but however instrumentally therapeutic, it is also exclusive, punitive, privileged and dominant. Consequently, it lends itself to a legalistic, depoliticized and reductionist treatment in Marxist, economistic or managerial traditions of analysis.

Bernard Schaffer
University of Sussex

Further Reading

Dunsore, A. (1978), *Implementation in a Bureaucracy: The Execution Process,* Oxford.

Ham, C. and Hill, M. (1983), *The Policy Process in the Modern Capitalist State,* Brighton.

Heclo, H. and Wildavsky, A. (1980), *The Private Government of Public Money,* London.

Schaffer, B. B. (1973), *The Administrative Factor,* London.

Simon, H. A. (1945), *Administrative Behavior,* New York (2nd edn in 1957).

See also: *bureaucracy; decision making; policy sciences.*

Anarchism

Anarchism is a political philosophy which holds that societies can and should exist without rulers. Anarchists believe that this will not, as is commonly supposed, lead to chaos – 'anarchy' in the popular sense – but on the contrary to an increase in social order. Anarchists see the state as the decisive source of corruption and disorder in the body politic. They point to many examples where people freely co-operate, without coercion, to achieve common purposes. Among traditional societies they find much to interest them in the 'ordered anarchies' of certain African tribes such as the Nuer, as well as in the workings of autonomous peasant communities such as the Russian *mir* and the self-governing cities of medieval Europe. In modern times they have hailed the anarchist experiments of the German Anabaptists of sixteenth-century Münster; the Diggers and Fifth Monarchists of the English Civil War; the popular clubs and societies of the French Revolution; the Paris Commune of 1871; the Russian soviets of 1905 and 1917; and the anarchist ventures in Catalonia and Andalusia during the Spanish Civil War.

Christ and Buddha have been claimed among earlier anarchists; and there were many social movements in both medieval Europe and medieval China which drew a fundamentally anarchist inspiration from Christianity and Buddhism. Religious anarchism continued into modern times with Tolstoy and Gandhi. But the modern phase of anarchism proper opens with the eighteenth-century Enlightenment, and can be traced equally from Rousseau's romanticism and William Godwin's rationalism. An early exponent was Godwin's son-in-law, the poet Shelley. Later advocates included the French socialist Proudhon, the German philosopher of egoism Max Stirner, the American individualist Thoreau, and the Russian aristocratic rebels Michael Bakunin and Peter Kropotkin. Anarchism was a strong current during the Russian Revolution and its immediate aftermath; the suppression of the Kronstadt rising in 1921 and the emasculation of the soviets signalled its defeat. But the ideas lived on, to surface not only in Spain in the 1930s, but in Hungary in 1956, and in Paris in 1968, where the student radicals achieved a dazzling blend of anarchism and surrealism.

Krishan Kumar
University of Kent

Further Reading
Joll, J. (1964), *The Anarchists*, London.
Miller, D. (1984), *Anarchism*, London.
Ritter, A. (1980), *Anarchism: A Theoretical Analysis*, Cambridge.
Woodcock, G. (1963), *Anarchism*, London.

Arendt, Hannah (1906–75)

Hannah Arendt was one of the outstanding students of politics of our century, making major contributions both as a political historian and as a political philosopher. Born in Germany in 1906, she attended the universities of Marburg, Freiburg and Heidelberg, where she completed a doctoral thesis on St Augustine under the supervision of Karl Jaspers. After fleeing Germany in the 1930s she worked with Zionist organizations in France, then moved to the United States where she lectured at many universities, principally the University of Chicago and the New School for Social Research in New York. She was the recipient of many distinguished prizes and honours for her contribution to contemporary thought and culture. She died in New York City in 1975.

Arendt first gained prominence as an analyst of the totalitarian form of government, with the publication in 1951 of her monumental three-part study, *The Origins of Totalitarianism*. Her most important philosophical work is *The Human Condition* (1958), in which she argues that there is a 'hierarchy within the *vita activa* itself, where the acting of the statesman occupies the highest position, the making of the craftsman and artist an intermediary, and the labouring which provides the necessities for the functioning of the human organism the lowest'. On the basis of her division of worldly activities into labour, work and action, Arendt affirms that freedom and autonomy can only be fully realized in the context of a politicized existence, and that only by fulfilling the public dimension of life can we give meaning to human affairs. This comprehensive theoretical understanding of politics is further developed in *On Revolution* (1963) and in the essays in *Between Past and Future* (1961; enlarged edition, 1968).

All of Hannah Arendt's works generated intense controversy, from her early writings on Zionism of the 1940s to her essays on the American republic of the 1960s and 1970s. The fiercest of these controversies was provoked by her book *Eichmann in Jerusalem* (1963), in which she argued that the real evil of Eichmann's deeds lay in the bureaucratic shallowness that allowed the monstrous to appear ordinary – Eichmann's mindless banality. This raises the question of whether thoughtlessness is somehow essential to political evil, or whether the active exercise of man's mental abilities actually makes us abstain from evil-doing, and it is to questions such as these that Arendt devoted her last, unfinished work on *The Life of the Mind* (posthumously published in 1978).

Ronald Beiner
University of Southampton and Queen's University,
Kingston, Ontario

Further Reading
Canovan, M. (1974), *The Political Thought of Hannah Arendt*, New York.
Hill, M. A. (ed.) (1979), *Hannah Arendt: The Recovery of the Public World*, New York.
Kateb, G. (1983), *Hannah Arendt: Politics, Conscience, Evil*, Totowa, N.J.
Young-Bruehl, E. (1982), *Hannah Arendt: For Love of the World*, New Haven.

Authority
Six distinctions must be drawn in any account of the concept of authority (Friedman, 1973; Lukes, 1978):

(1) The failure to explain the unity and order of social life and the compliance of subjects solely in terms of coercion and/or rational agreement opens a space for the concept of authority. Authority refers to a distinctive form of compliance in social life (see 2). Three accounts exist of the basis of this special compliance. One sees authoritative institutions as reflecting the common beliefs, values, traditions and practices of members of society (Parsons, 1960; Arendt, 1963); a second sees political authority as offering a co-ordination solution to a Hobbesian state of nature, or a lack of shared values (Hobbes, 1651); and a third view argues that although social order is imposed by force, it derives its permanence and stability through techniques of legitimation, ideology, hegemony, mobilization of bias, false consensus and so on, which secure the willing compliance of

citizens through the manipulation of their beliefs (Weber, 1978 [1922]; Lukes, 1978).

(2) What is special about the compliance B renders A which marks off authority from coercion and rational agreement? Coercion secures B's compliance by the use of force or threats; persuasion convinces B by appeal to arguments that an action is in B's interests, is, for example, morally right, or prudent; but B complies with authority when B recognizes A's right to command him in a certain sphere. B voluntarily surrenders the right to make compliance contingent on an evaluation of the content of A's command, and obeys because A's order comes from an appropriate person and falls within the appropriate range. Where authority exists there will be 'rules of recognition' (Hart, 1961) or 'marks' by which to identify those eligible to exercise it.

(3) We must also distinguish between *de facto* and *de jure* authority (Peters, 1967; Winch, 1967). *De facto* authority is evidenced whenever B complies with A in the appropriate manner; *de jure* authority exists where A has a right to B's compliance in a given area which derives from a set of institutional rules. That A has one form of authority in no way entails that he will also have the other.

(4) Many writers have referred to authority as 'legitimate power'. This may mean (i) that coercion is exercised by someone with *de jure* authority, although the coerced agent is not responding to A's authority; or (ii) that A's orders in fact produce this distinctive form of non-coerced deferential obedience (A thus has *de facto* authority) – this being in sharp contrast to cases where compliance is based on fear.

(5) Authority is thus a two-tier concept: it refers to a mode of influence and compliance, and to a set of criteria which identify who is to exercise this influence. For this influence to take effect it must be exercised 'within a certain kind of normative arrangement accepted by both parties' (Friedman, 1973). This normative arrangement may be a common tradition, practice or set of beliefs (Winch, 1967; MacIntyre, 1967), or it may be simply a common acknowledgment that some set of rules is required to avoid chaos. B's compliance with A's authority may

take two forms: it may be unquestioning (as with Weber's 'charismatic authority') or B may be able to criticize A's command, yet still complies because he recognizes A's right to command, even if he privately disagrees with its content.

(6) A further important distinction is that between being *an* authority and being *in* authority. The former concerns matters of belief; the latter concerns A's place in a normative order with recognized positions of *de jure* authority. When A is *an* authority, he is held to have, or successfully claims, special knowledge, insight, expertise, and so on, which justifies B's deference to A's judgement. When A is *in* authority, he claims, and is recognized as occupying, a special institutional role with a co-ordinate sphere of command (as with Weber's legal-rational authority (1978)). When B complies with A's judgement where A is *an* authority, B's compliance involves belief in the validity of A's judgement; whereas, when A is simply *in* authority, B may disagree yet comply because he recognizes A's *de jure* authority. Traditional and charismatic leaders are authoritative over belief and value; leaders in legal-rational systems are granted authority in certain spheres of action for convenience. Where A is *an* authority, his influence over B relies on B's continued belief in A's guaranteed judgement. Where A is *in* authority, he relies on B continuing to recognize that he fulfils a valuable co-ordination function. Both systems may face legitimation crises when B no longer believes A, or no longer believes that A successfully co-ordinates. However, both systems may seek to maintain B's belief through a variety of techniques: ideology, hegemony, mobilization of bias, and so on (Habermas, 1976 [1973]).

Mark Philp
Oriel College, University of Oxford

References
Arendt, H. (1963), 'What is authority', in *Between Past and Future*, New York.
Friedman, R. B. (1973), 'On the concept of authority in

political philosophy', in R. E. Flathman (ed.), *Concepts in Social and Political Philosophy*, New York.

Habermas, J. (1976 [1973]), *Legitimation Crisis*, London. (Original German edn, *Legitimations-problem im Spatkapitalismus*, Frankfurt.)

Hart, H. L. A. (1961), *The Concept of Law*, Oxford.

Hobbes, T. (1651), *Leviathan*, London.

Lukes, S. (1978), 'Power and authority' in T. Bottomore and R. Nisbett (eds), *A History of Sociological Analysis*, London.

MacIntyre, A. (1967), *Secularisation and Moral Change*, London.

Parsons, T. (1969), 'Authority, legitimation, and political action', in *Structure and Process in Modern Societies*, Glencoe, Ill.

Peters, R. S. (1967), 'Authority', in A. Quinton (ed.), *Political Philosophy*, Oxford.

Weber, M. (1978 [1922]), *Economy and Society*, 2 vols, eds G. Roth and C. Wittich, Berkeley and Los Angeles.

Winch, P. (1967), 'Authority', in A. Quinton (ed.), *Political Philosophy*, Oxford.

Bentham, Jeremy (1748–1832)

Jeremy Bentham was undoubtedly one of the most important and influential figures in the development of modern social science. His numerous writings are major contributions to the development of philosophy, law, government, economics, social administration and public policy, and many have become classic texts in these fields. To these subjects he brought an analytical precision and careful attention to detail which, especially in matters of legal organization and jurisprudence, had not been attempted since Aristotle, and he transformed in method and substance the way these subjects were conceived. He combined a critical rationalism and empiricism with a vision of reform and, latterly, radical reform, which gave unity and direction to what became Philosophic Radicalism. Although he was not the first philosopher to use the greatest happiness principle as the standard of right and wrong, he is rightly remembered as the founder of modern utilitarianism. Many of Bentham's writings were never published in his lifetime or were completed by various editors. The new edition of the *Collected Works* (1968 — in progress) will replace in approximately sixty-five volumes the inadequate *Works of Jeremy Bentham* (1838–43), edited by John Bowring, and will reveal for the first time the full extent and scope of Bentham's work.

Bentham is best known for some of his earliest writings. *An Introduction to the Principles of Morals and Legislation* (printed in 1780 and published in 1789) and *Of Laws in General* (not published until 1945) are important texts in legal philosophy and, together with his critique of William Blackstone's *Commentaries on the Laws of England* in the *Comment on the Commentaries* (published first in 1928) and *A Fragment on Government* (1776), represent major landmarks in the development of jurisprudence. The *Introduction to the Principles of Morals and Legislation* was also intended to serve as an introduction to a penal code, which was an important part of a lifelong ambition, never fully realized, of constructing a complete code of laws (latterly called the *Pannomion*). At this time Bentham also turned to economic questions which were to occupy him in various forms throughout his life. His first publication was the *Defence of Usury* (1787), a critique of Adam Smith's treatment of this subject in *The Wealth of Nations*.

From the outset of his career, Bentham was devoted to reform and especially to the reform of legal institutions. His attitude towards fundamental political reform developed more slowly. Although at the time of the French Revolution he was not part of the radical movement in England, he wrote numerous manuscripts in support of democratic institutions in France. He eventually reacted strongly against the excesses of the revolution, but earlier contacts, largely developed through Lord Lansdowne, and the publication of his *Draught of a New Plan for the Organisation of the Judicial Establishment of France,* led to his being made an honorary citizen of France. One important development of this period was his friendship with Etienne Dumont, the Swiss reformer and scholar, whose French versions of Bentham's works, especially the *Traités de législation, civile et pénale* (1802), were read throughout Europe and Latin America and earned for Bentham a considerable international reputation. Following the French Revolution much of Bentham's practical energies were devoted, in conjunction with his brother Samuel, to establishing model prisons, called Panopticons, in various countries. His main effort in England failed, and this failure, though ultimately compensated by the government, was one factor leading him to take up the cause of radical political reform. The influence of James Mill was perhaps the most important factor (there were many) in his 'conversion' to radicalism in 1809–10, and the publication of *A Plan of Parliamentary Reform* in 1817 launched the Philosophic Radicals in their quest for parliamentary reform. In the 1820s, though now in his seventies, Bentham resumed the task of codification and the construction of the *Pannomion* in response to requests from governments and disciples in Spain, Portugal, Greece and Latin America. In his massive, unfinished *Constitutional Code* (1822–), he set forth a theory of representative democracy which was a grand synthesis of many of his ideas and a classic of liberal political thought.

Frederick Rosen
The London School of Economics
and Political Science

Further Reading
Halévy, E. (1901–4), *La Formation du Radicalisme Philosophique*, 3 vols, Paris.
Hart, H. L. A. (1982), *Essays on Bentham: Jurisprudence and Political Theory*, Oxford.
Hume, L. J. (1981), *Bentham and Bureaucracy*, Cambridge.
Rosen, F. (1983), *Jeremy Bentham and Representative Democracy*, Oxford.
See also: *Mill; utilitarianism.*

Bureaucracy

Agreement as to when and how the word bureaucracy was invented is widespread and precise. 'The late M. de Gornay . . .' notes Baron de Grimm, the French philosopher, in a letter dated 1 July, 1764, 'sometimes used to . . . invent a fourth or fifth form of government under the heading of *bureaucratie*.' Within a very short time, the physiocrat economist's word entered the international language of politics: the Italian *burocrazia*, the German *Bureaukratie* (later *Bürokratie*), and the English 'bureaucracy' (Albrow, 1970).

Agreement about what the word means, however, could hardly be *less* widespread or precise. In political debate, writes Martin Albrow, ' "bureaucracy" has become a term of strong emotive overtones and elusive connotations'. Social scientists have been no more precise. 'Sometimes "bureaucracy" seems to mean administrative efficiency, at other times the opposite. It may appear as simple as a synonym for civil service, or it may be as complex as an idea summing up the specific features of modern organizational structure. It may refer to a body of officials, or to the routines of office administration' (Albrow, 1970).

This confusion may be more apparent than real. From the plethora of definitions, two stand out: bureaucracy as rule by officials, and bureaucracy as a particular form of organization. Even these meanings, though distinct, are not unrelated.

Rule by officials was Vincent de Gornay's intention when, in the style of 'democracy' and 'aristocracy', he attached the Greek suffix for rule to the French word 'bureau', which already included 'a place where officials work' among its definitions. It also was the meaning of Harold Laski when he defined bureaucracy in the 1930 *Encyclopaedia of the Social Sciences* as 'A system of government the control of which is so completely in the hands of officials that their power jeopardizes the liberties of ordinary citizens,' and of Harold Lasswell and Abraham Kaplan (1950), who defined it in *Power and Society* as 'the form of rule in which the élite is composed of officials'.

Twentieth-century heirs to de Gornay's definition of bureaucracy have characteristically shared his observations on 'bureaumania' – the spread of bureaucracy – as well. They regard rule by officials to be the most prevalent form of government in modern society. Some have traced this rise to officials' organized concentration of expert knowledge. Others, such as Robert Michels (1962), have explained it in terms of the imperatives of large-scale organization itself: 'Who says organization, say oligarchy.'

Most modern authors of the de Gornay school have also inherited his displeasure with what he called the 'illness' of bureaucracy. Yet their shared distress belies the polarity of their diagnoses. Sometimes bureaucracy is looked upon as 'intolerably meddlesome', 'a demanding giant', 'an oppressive foreign power', and sometimes as 'timid and indecisive', 'flabby, overpaid, and lazy'. The same critics often seem to regard bureaucracy as both aggressive and passive. Laski, for example, having identified bureaucracy as a form of rule that 'jeopardizes the liberties of ordinary citizens', adds in the next sentence that: 'The characteristics of such a regime are a passion for routine in administration, the sacrifice of flexibility to rule, delay in the making of decisions and a refusal to embark upon experiment.'

In all cases, however, officials tend to be judged by subscribers to this first definition as the real power in any political system in which the ranks of officialdom are large. It was this view that Max Weber (Gerth and Mills, 1946) challenged in the early part of the twentieth century, with arguments that set the stage for the development of bureaucracy's second definition, as a particular form of organization.

To Weber, those who equated large numbers of officials with rule by officials sometimes confused appearance and reality. They saw official orders given and obeyed, and assumed from this that officials were wielding independent power. In truth, Weber argued, orders were more likely obeyed because their recipients believed that it was right to obey. Not power *per se*, but 'authority' – power cloaked with legitimacy – was at play. In modern society, such authority characteristically was 'legal' rather than 'charismatic' or 'traditional' in nature: an official's orders were considered legitimate when he was seen to be acting in accordance with his duties as defined by a written code of laws, including statutes, administrative regulations, and court precedents.

As Weber conceived it, bureaucracy was the form of organization best suited to the exercise of legal authority. If legal authority calls for 'a government of laws and not of men', bureaucracy may be thought of as 'an organization of positions and not of people'. Bureaucratic organizations consist of offices whose powers and duties are clearly defined, whose activities are recorded in writing and retained in files, and whose arrangement in relation to one another is hierarchic. Offices are filled on the basis of 'merit', as measured by diplomas, examinations, or other professional qualifications. Officeholders occupy, but in no sense own, their positions or the powers, duties, and other resources that go with them. Their personal relationships with the organization are defined by contracts that specify salary and career structure.

'Rule by officials' and 'a particular form of organization' are very different understandings of bureaucracy. But they also are related: as this history has shown, one definition was formed in reaction to the other. There may even be grounds for reconciling, if not fusing, the two.

Weber, for example, seemed most provoked by the connotations that were usually attached to the 'rule by officials' definition – the easy assumption that wherever officials proliferated, they governed. He was right in seeing that this assumption was often made, but one would be wrong in thinking it necessarily must be made. One can think of bureaucracy as a form of government without assuming that it is the most prevalent form of government.

Conversely, it is not uncommon for those who define bureaucracy in organizational terms to be concerned about rule by officials, either as dangerously efficient (a 'demanding giant') or as hopelessly inefficient ('flabby, overpaid, and lazy'). For Weber's part, he warned in one of his most widely remembered passages of the potential power of bureaucracy at its most efficient:

Under normal conditions, the power position of a fully developed bureaucracy is always overtowering. The 'political master' finds himself in the position of the 'dilettante' who stands opposite the 'expert', facing the trained official who stands within the management of administration. This holds whether the 'master' whom the bureaucracy serves is a 'people' . . . or a parliament . . . a popularly elected president, a hereditary and 'absolute' or a 'constitutional' monarch (Gerth and Mills, 1946).

Other social scientists who basically accept Weber's definition of bureaucracy direct their concerns about bureaucratic power to the inefficiency of such organizations. Robert Merton (1952), for example, notes the danger, inherent to any rules-bound organization, that the rules will become ends in themselves, blinding officials to the organization's service functions and making them resistant to change. In the same spirit, Michel Crozier (1964) describes bureaucracy as 'an organization that cannot correct its behaviour by learning from its errors'.

Michael Nelson
Vanderbilt University

References
Albrow, M. (1970), *Bureaucracy*, New York.
Crozier, M. (1964), *The Bureaucratic Phenomenon*, London.
Gerth, H. and Mills, C.W. (1946), *From Max Weber: Essays in Sociology*, New York.
Laski, H. (1930), 'Bureaucracy', in *Encyclopaedia of the Social Sciences*, Vol. 3, New York and London.
Lasswell, H.D. and Kaplan, A. (1950), *Power and Society: A Framework for Political Inquiry*, New Haven.
Merton, R. (1952), 'Bureaucratic structure and personality', in R. Merton (ed.), *Reader in Bureaucracy*, Glencoe, Ill.
Michels, R. (1962 [1911]), *Political Parties*, New York.
See also: *administration; authority; Weber.*

Burke, Edmund (1729–97)

Edmund Burke, the British statesman and political theorist, was born in Dublin in 1729. He came to London in 1750 and soon acquired a reputation as a philosopher and man of letters. In 1765, he was elected to the House of Commons, acting as party secretary and chief man of ideas to the Whig connection led by the Marquis of Rockingham. He wrote voluminously, and the eloquence he brought to expressing a high-minded but by no means unrealistic view of political possibilities has never been surpassed. He could bring out the universal element in the most parochial of issues.

Burke's enduring importance in articulating a political tendency is particularly evident in the *Reflections on the Revolution in France* (1790) and subsequent late works in which he defended his criticism of the Revolution against fellow Whigs who had welcomed it as an act of liberation from an odious Bourbon absolutism. Attacked as one who had betrayed the cause of liberty, Burke agreed (in the *Appeal from the Old to the New Whigs*) that consistency was the highest virtue in politics, but proceeded to theorize its complex nature. In supporting the American colonists, he argued, he was in no way committed to support every movement which raised the banner of liberty, for in his view the Americans 'had taken up arms from one motive only; that is, our attempting to tax them without their consent . . .' (Burke, *Appeal*, Vol. III). Real political consistency must take account of circumstances, and cannot be deduced from principles. And it was in terms of the contrast between historical concreteness and abstract principle that Burke interpreted the challenge posed by the revolutionaries in France.

The revolutionaries were, Burke argued, amateur politicians attempting to solve the complex problems of French society with a set of theories or what he called 'metaphysic rights'. They believed that an ideal rational constitution, in which a republic guaranteed the rights of man, was suitable for all societies. This belief constituted a revelation which stigmatized most existing beliefs as prejudice and superstition, and all existing forms of government as corrupt and unjust. On Burke's historical understanding of the specificity of different societies, the beliefs and practices of any society revealed their character; indeed, properly understood, they revealed a kind of rationality much more profound than the propositional fantasies of revolutionaries. To condemn what whole societies had long believed as merely mistaken was in the highest degree superficial. Society is a delicate fabric of sentiments and understandings which would be irreparably damaged if subjected to the butchery of abstract ideas. Burke judged that, as the revolutionaries discovered that the people were not behaving according to the rationalist prescriptions, they would have increasing recourse to violence and terror. At the end of every prospect would be found a gallows. He predicted that the outcome would be a military dictatorship.

Burke's genius lay in breaking up the conventional antitheses through which politics was then understood. He had never been, he wrote, 'a friend or an enemy to republics or to monarchies in the abstract' (Burke, 1855, *Appeal*, Vol.III), and this refusal to take sides on an abstractly specified principle became a dominant strain in conservatism. The real clue to wisdom in politics lay not at the level of high principle but of low and humble circumstance. This was the level of actual human experience, and at this level, there was not a great deal that governments could achieve, and most of what they could was to prevent evils rather than promote goods. No stranger to paradox, Burke insisted that one of the most important of the rights of man is the right to be restrained by suitable laws. Again, Burke was prepared to agree that society was indeed a contract, but he instantly qualified this conventional judgement by insisting that it was a contract of a quite sublime kind, linking the living, the dead and those yet to be born. It is in these hesitations and qualifications of conventional wisdom to which he was impelled by the excitements of his time that Burke's contribution to political understanding lies.

More philosophically, Burke adapted to political use the empiricist doctrine that the passions, especially as entrenched in and shaped by social institutions, are closer to reality than the speculations of philosophers, and especially of *philosophes*. His defence of prejudice threw down a gauntlet to the superficial rationalism of his opponents, and has sometimes been seen as expressing an irrationalism endemic to conservative thought. It is, however, an argument about the relations between reason and passion similar to that of Hegel, though in a quite different idiom.

Burke's political judgement is a conservative modification of the English political tradition and covers many areas. On the nature of representation, for example, he argued that the House of Commons was not a congress of ambassadors from the constituencies. His defence of the place of parties in British politics contributed to the acceptance and development of party government, however limited in intention it may have been (Brewer, 1971). In the indictment of Warren Hastings, he stressed the trusteeship of power and property which was never far from his thoughts. But in all his political writings, Burke wrote to the occasion, and it is perilous to generalize about him too far. His personal ambitions required manoeuvring in the complex world of late eighteenth-century politics which have led some writers (for example, Namier, 1929, and Young, 1943) to regard him as little more than a silver-tongued opportunist. This is to do less than justice to the suggestiveness of his prose and the momentousness of the occasions to which he so brilliantly responded.

Kenneth Minogue
London School of Economics
and Political Science

References

Burke, E. (1855), *Works,* London.

Brewer, J. (1971), 'Party and the double cabinet: two facets of Burke's thoughts', *The Historical Journal,* XIV.

Namier, L. (1929), *The Structure of Politics at the Accession of George III,* London.

Young, G.M. (1943), *Burke* (British Academy Lecture on a Mastermind), London.

Further Reading

Canovan, F. P. (1960), *The Political Reason of Edmund Burke,* North Carolina.

Cone, C. (1964), *Burke and the Nature of Politics: The Age of the French Revolution,* Lexington, Mass.

Macpherson, C. B. (1980), *Burke,* Oxford.

O'Gorman, F. (1973), *Edmund Burke,* London.

Parkin, C. (1956), *The Moral Basis of Burke's Political Thought*, Cambridge.

Stanlis, P. J. (1958), *Edmund Burke and the Natural Law*, Ann Arbor.

See also: *conservatism*.

Capitalism

The term capitalism relates to a particular system of socioeconomic organization (generally contrasted with feudalism on the one hand and socialism on the other), the nature of which is more often defined implicitly than explicitly. In common with other value-loaded concepts of political controversy, its definition – whether implicit or explicit – shows a chameleon-like tendency to vary with the ideological bias of the user. Even when treated as a historical category and precisely defined for the purpose of objective analysis, the definition adopted is often associated with a distinctive view of the temporal sequence and character of historical development. Thus historians such as Sombart, Weber and Tawney, who were concerned to relate changes in economic organization to shifts in religious and ethical attitudes, found the essence of capitalism in the acquisitive spirit of profit-making enterprise and focused on developments occurring in the sixteenth, seventeenth and early eighteenth centuries. Probably a majority of historians have seen capitalism as reaching its fullest development in the course of the Industrial Revolution and have treated the earlier period as part of a long transition between feudalism and capitalism. Marxist historians have identified a series of stages in the evolution of capitalism – for example, merchant capitalism, agrarian capitalism, industrial capitalism, state capitalism – and much of the recent debate on origins and progress has hinged on differing view of the significance, timing and characteristics of each stage. Thus Wallerstein (1979), who adopts a world-economy perspective, locates its origins in the agrarian capitalism that characterized Europe of the sixteenth, seventeenth and eighteenth centuries; while Tribe (1981), who also takes agrarian capitalism as the original mode of capitalist production, sees the essence of capitalism in a national economy where production is separated from consumption and is co-ordinated according to the profitability of enterprises operating in competition with each other.

Whatever the historical or polemical objective of the writer, however, his definition is likely to be strongly influenced by Karl Marx, who was the first to attempt a systematic analysis of the 'economic law of motion' of capitalist society and from whom most of the subsequent controversy on the nature and role of capitalism has stemmed. For Marx, capitalism was a 'mode of production' in which there are basically two classes of producers: (1) the capitalists, who own the means of production (capital or land), make the strategic day-to-day economic decisions on technology, output and marketing, and appropriate the profits of production and distribution; and (2) the labourers, who own no property but are free to dispose of their labour for wages on terms which depend on the numbers seeking work and the demand for their services. This was essentially the definition adopted, for example, by non-Marxist economic historians such as Lipson and Cunningham and by Marxists such as Dobb.

Given this perspective, it is primarily the emergence of a dominant class of entrepreneurs supplying the capital necessary to activate a substantial body of workers which marks the birth of capitalism. In England, and even more emphatically in Holland, it can be dated from the late sixteenth and early seventeenth centuries. Holland's supremacy in international trade, associated with its urgent need to import grain and timber (and hence to export manufactures) enabled Amsterdam to corner the Baltic trade and to displace Venice as the commercial and financial centre of Europe. The capital thus amassed was available to fund the famous chartered companies (Dutch East India Company, 1602, West India Company, 1621) as well as companies to reclaim land and exploit the area's most important source of industrial energy – peat. It also provided the circulating capital for merchants engaged in the putting-out system whereby they supplied raw materials to domestic handicraftsmen and marketed the product. Specialization within agriculture drew the rural areas still further into the money economy, and the urban areas supplied a wide range of industrial exports to pay for essential raw material imports.

Dutch capitalists flourished the more because they were subject to a Republican administration which was sympathetic to their free market, individualist values. In England, where similar economic developments were in progress in the sixteenth and early seventeenth centuries, the rising class of capitalists was inhibited by a paternalistic monarchical government bent on regulating their activities for its own fiscal purposes and power objectives and in terms of a different set of social values. The Tudor system of State control included checking enclosures, controlling food supplies, regulating wages and manipulating the currency. The early Stuarts went further in selling industrial monopolies and · concessions to favoured entrepreneurs and exclusive corporations and infuriated the majority whose interests were thus damaged. The English capitalists carried their fight against monopolies to the Cromwellian Revolution. When the monarchy was restored in the 1660s, the climate of opinion had been moulded by religious, political and scientific revolution into an environment which favoured the advancement of capitalism and laid the foundations for its next significant phase – the Industrial Revolution.

Orthodox economic theorists eschew the concept of capitalism – it is too broad for their purposes in that it takes into account the social relations of production. Modern economic historians adhering to an orthodox framework of economic theory also tend to avoid the term. They do, however, recognize a significant aspect of capitalism by emphasizing the rational, profit-maximizing, double bookkeeping characteristics of capitalist enterprise; and in the post-Second World War debates on economic development from a backward starting-point, there has been a tendency to regard the emergence of this 'capitalist spirit' as an essential prerequisite to the process of sustained economic growth in non-socialist countries. (See, for example, Landes, 1969; North and Thomas, 1973; Morishima, 1982.)

The modern debate on capitalism in contemporary advanced economies has revolved around its being an alternative to socialism. Marxist economists follow Marx in seeing capitalism as a mode of production whose internal contradictions determine that it will eventually be replaced by socialism. In the aftermath of the Second World War, when the governments of most developed countries took full employment and faster economic growth as explicit objectives of national economic policy, there was a marked propensity for the governments of capitalist economies to intervene actively and extensively in the process of production. At that stage the interesting issues for most Western economists seemed to be the changing balance of private and public economic power (see Shonfield, 1965), and the extent to which it was either desirable or inevitable for the increasingly 'mixed' capitalist economies to converge towards socialism. In the late 1960s and 1970s, when the unprecedented post-war boom in world economic activity came to an end, Marxist economists were able to point confidently to the 'crisis of capitalism' for which they found evidence in rising unemployment and inflation in capitalist countries; but non-Marxist economists had lost their earlier consensus. The economic debate on capitalism is now taking place in a political context which is relatively hostile to state intervention; and those economists who believe that the 'spirit of capitalism', or free private enterprise, is the key to sustained technological progress and that it is weakened by socialist economic policies, seem to carry more conviction than they did in the 1950s and 1960s.

Phyllis Deane
University of Cambridge

References

Dobb, M. (1946), *Studies in the Development of Capitalism*, London.

Landes, D. (1969), *Prometheus Unbound*, Cambridge.

Morishima, M. (1982), *Why has Japan Succeeded?*, Cambridge.

North, D. C. and Thomas, R. P. (1973), *The Rise of the Western World*, Cambridge.

Shonfield, A. (1965), *Modern Capitalism*, London.

Sombart, W. (1915), *The Quintessence of Capitalism*, New York.

Tawney, R. H. (1926), *Religion and the Rise of Capitalism*, London.

Tribe, K. (1981), *Genealogies of Capitalism*, London.

Wallerstein, I. (1979), *The Capitalist World-Economy*, Cambridge.

Weber, M. (1930), *The Protestant Ethic and the Spirit of Capitalism*, New York. (Original German, 1922, Tübingen.)

See also: *socialism; world-system theory.*

Charisma

Charisma is one of the more contentious sociological concepts, in part because it has been absorbed into popular, or at least mass-media, usage in a considerably adulterated form. The term derives from a theological conception which referred to the divine gift of grace. Max Weber developed its sociological use by extending it to refer to the recognition in an individual leader by his followers of supernatural or superhuman powers or qualities of an exemplary kind or of transcendental origin.

Weber's formulation gave rise to ambiguities. On the one hand, it could be argued that the nature of charisma inhered in the powers or qualities displayed by the individual, and thus was to be explained primarily in terms of the personal psychological attributes of the leader. On the other hand, it could be argued that the character of charisma lay in the recognition extended by the following, and thus was to be explained primarily in terms of the social psychological features of the interpersonal relationship between leader and followers. Common usage bears elements of both approaches, identifying the charismatic figure as one who displays personal attractiveness or forcefulness of a kind which leads to great popularity or popular devotion. However, this is quite antithetical to Weber's central thrust.

Weber sharply contrasts charisma with forms of authority deriving from tradition and from rationalistic or legal considerations. The charismatic leader is one who breaks with tradition or prevailing legal norms, and demands obedience on specifically irrational grounds of devotion as God's Prophet, the embodiment of transcendental forces, or as possessor of supernatural powers. Conventionally elected leaders, or heirs of an established tradition, cannot therefore be construed as charismatic because of their attractiveness or popularity or even both.

The following of a charismatic leader offers its obedience and devotion in virtue of the mission upon which it believes the leader to be engaged and the transcendental forces which he manifests. But it may require periodically to be reassured of the possession of those powers, demanding signs of the miraculous as the price of commitment.

The charismatic leader operates through a body of disciples or other personally devoted inner circle rather than an established administrative staff. Often – especially in the case of religious charisma – it may consist of members of the leader's immediate household, living in an intimate and emotionally-laden communal relationship with him. They receive their appointment not on the basis of technical expertise, but rather because of the intensity of their devotion or willingness to subordinate themselves to the leader's will. They are commissioned to carry out that will on an *ad hoc* basis. There is no administrative routine, or any such routine is short-lived, constantly disrupted by the intervention and revelation of the leader. The economic basis of the movement is irregular and founded on booty or free-will offerings. Decision making is erratic and inspirational.

Charisma is inevitably a precarious form of authority. Max Weber maintained that it could exist in its pure form for only a relatively brief period. In the course of time it tends to become transformed into a less spontaneous or less unpredictable form of leadership, toward traditionalism or rational-legal authority. Such a development appears to be an ineluctable consequence of perpetuating the movement's mission or of spreading it beyond an immediate, local band of disciples. Endurance over time or wider spread is likely to introduce the need for mechanisms of co-ordination, supervision and delegation. In consequence there will arise increasing impersonality and routine and the desire for greater stability and predictability on the part of officials.

The problem of succession often accelerates the process of routinization. The charisma of the founder is vested in another by virtue of hereditary succession or a ritual of consecration. Thus, such forms as 'hereditary charisma' or 'charisma of office' become an intervening step in the transformation of authority in a traditionalistic or rational-legal direction.

Roy Wallis
Queen's University of Belfast

Further Reading
Weber, M. (1947 [1922]), *The Theory of Social and Economic Organization*, London. (Part 1 of *Wirtschaft und Gesellschaft*, Tübingen.)
Willner, A. (1984), *The Spellbinders: Charismatic Political Leadership*, New Haven.
Wilson, B. (1975), *The Noble Savages: The Primitive Origins of Charisma and its Contemporary Survival*, Berkeley and Los Angeles.
See also: *Weber*.

Coalitions

Coalitions are collections of people who band together to accomplish some goal. As such, they are the stuff of which group decision making – especially what we think of as politics – is made.

Work on coalitions is both empirical and theoretical, two traditions which are now merging, each one informing the other. The empirical approach consists of establishing which individuals or groups work together, usually in some institutional setting. Thus, for example, there are studies of coalition making in the formation of cabinet governments, in electorates, legislatures, the judiciary, the military and so on, as well as in nongovernmental structures. The formation of alliances – though usually not referred to as coalitions – is yet another example. All forms of government require coalitions to obtain and retain power – whether the coalitions are groups who supported the election of those in power or groups that support the suppression of those who are not. Coalitions are ever changing, very quickly in some circumstances and more slowly in others.

Theoretical work on coalitions deals with the following: (1) the size of winning coalitions; (2) the basis on which coalitions form; (3) the distribution of 'pay-offs' among members of the winning coalition; and (4) the duration of the coalition.

Some of the most exciting work focuses on the size of winning coalitions. William Riker argued that in cases of complete information, coalitions would form that were of minimal winning size such that subtraction of one member would result in the coalition losing. The logic is simply that the pay-off to the coalition needs to be split up among fewer members. In situations with incomplete information, coalitions would be somewhat larger but would still tend toward minimal size.

A considerable volume of work has followed up on Riker's ideas. Some of it has expanded the theory, showing, for example, that in threatening situations there may be incentives for forming large coalitions. Similarly, the theory has been altered slightly to take account of situations in which actors (e.g., political parties) are of unequal sizes. Extensive empirical work has been done to try to support or refute the 'size principle'. Not surprisingly, the great uncertainty in social situations makes it difficult to know how small coalitions must be to confirm the minimal winning theory. Thus no one can agree about whether or not the theory is confirmed. What can be said is that Riker clearly recognized a force – that towards minimizing the size of coalitions just so long as they remain winning – that is of fundamental importance, even though in the real world it does not always operate to the same degree that it does in abstract situations.

Other work attempts to specify coalition formation by the characteristics of various possible outcomes, for example, those that are undominated, in the sense that the players in the winning coalitions could not guarantee that they would be better off by defecting from them. As with Riker's work, such theories often do not predict that a particular coalition will form but only that one of a set of coalitions will form. Experimental evidence has not shown one solution to be uniformly superior to another.

Coalition theories have been less successful in predicting

exactly which coalitions will form and the basis on which co-operation will be established. In a three-person situation, it is usually apparent why two should coalesce against one (the minimal winning size idea), but it is less readily apparent why any particular pair would join together. The most frequent hypothesis is probably that the specific coalitions that form depend on shared values. Thus, for example, if there are three political parties – one liberal, one moderate, and one conservative – one might well predict that the liberal and moderate parties, or the moderate and conservative parties, would more readily coalesce than the liberal or conservative parties. But a variety of other factors such as friendship or past experiences may also contribute to which individuals or groups coalesce.

One reason that prediction of specific coalitions is difficult is that it is not always clear just what the pay-off is to coalition members. Indeed, it may very well be that different coalition members are rewarded with different kinds of pay-offs. In a cabinet situation, for example, one party may obtain legislation that it thinks is important, another will receive visibility that will help it in the next election campaign, and yet another will achieve useful recognition for one of its leaders.

Coalition theory is also less successful with respect to specifying how pay-offs are divided among members of a winning coalition. That is, theories are often quite explicit about pay-offs, but in experiments players sometimes use simple rules such as equal pay-offs to all members. Most studies, however, find that pay-offs are weighted in favour of the larger coalition members.

A criticism of most coalition theories is that they are relatively static rather than dynamic. Simple observation and reasoning tells us that notions like trust ought to be very important when the same situation is faced repeatedly, as in legislative voting situations. Yet these notions are the most difficult to specify theoretically. Therefore, perhaps the weakest area of coalition theory is with respect to repeated 'plays'.

Richard G. Niemi
University of Rochester

Reference
Riker, W. H. (1962), *The Theory of Political Coalitions*, New Haven.

Further Reading
Holler, M. (ed.) (1983), *Coalitions and Collective Action*, Würzburg.
See also: *committees; decision making*.

Committees

The most notable committees are those that help govern nations – cabinet committees, legislative assemblies, party committees, and higher courts. But there are also boards of directors of corporations, labour union councils, state or provincial assemblies, and city councils, all of which are involved in governance. The term committee normally refers to a face-to-face group of people who arrive at a decision through some means of polling member opinions. The types of committees mentioned above have a firm institutional grounding and will have well-defined means of voting the issues that come before them. Their decisions have a semi-binding nature to them, perhaps subject to appeals or approvals elsewhere.

In contrast, there are many committees that are no more than advisory in nature, acting as a source of information for an administrator, a supervisor, or even a larger organization. For a larger organization, advisory committees offer a division of work, specialization, and economies of scale. For a single administrator or supervisor, advisory committees offer balanced judgement and a diversification of information sources beyond the ordinary chain-of-command. The growth of the seemingly infinite variety of committee organization and function has in many ways marked a decline in the traditional efficient chain-of-command method of conducting business. In a purely practical sense, technology has made it easier for committees to function effectively. Duplicating services and electronic transmission have made it more convenient to share information and communication and to arrange for meetings. Transportation advances have also facilitated the convening of committees.

The study of committees has progressed in two directions: in the study of single committees and in the study of committee systems. The study of single committees has concentrated on the justification of their use and voting strategies of members (for example, Black, 1958), or on the substantive decision-making norms of very important groups. Recently there has been increased attention given to committee systems, primarily in relation to legislatures. An eight-nation study of committee systems in national legislatures was completed in 1979 by Lees and Shaw, which tried to determine the significance of the various committee systems in relation to other decision-making foci. The study confirmed, for example, as others suspected, that committee systems have the most central role in US legislatures, while political parties have a weaker role.

The organizers of committee systems are faced with several decisions – how to divide up the subject matter; how many committees; how many members on each committee; how many committee assignments per member; how much authority to delegate; and whether or not to have subcommittees within committees. In representative bodies, small committees sacrifice representativeness, yet they may be necessary under a heavy agenda. The US Congress and state legislatures legislate through committees, and in Congress, the committees legislate through subcommittees. In other words, in the latter case, the subcommittees debate the subject before the committees deal with it. In Britain, India, and Canada, the issues are debated on the floor before they are assigned to committee. In essence, committee systems are becoming complex forms of organization, and serve as an ample challenge in future theories of decision making.

Wayne L. Francis
University of Missouri, Columbia

References
Black, D. (1958), *The Theory of Committees and Elections*, Cambridge.

Lees, J. D. and Shaw, M. (eds) (1979), *Committees in Legislatures*, Durham, NC.

Further Reading
Barber, J. (1966), *Power in Committees*, Chicago.
Francis, W. L. (1982), 'Legislative committee systems, optimal committee size, and the costs of decision-making', *Journal of Politics*, 44.
See also: *decision making*.

Communism

Communism connotes any societal arrangement based on communal ownership, production, consumption, self-government, perhaps even communal sexual mating. The term refers both to such societies and practices and to any theory advocating them. Examples of the former can be found in religious orders throughout history and in radical communities, from the sixteenth-century Anabaptists to the contemporary 'counterculture'; and the most famous example of advocacy of communism may well be the regime proposed for the guardian caste in Plato's *Republic*.

In the middle of the nineteenth century, the most radical schools of the growing socialist movement, including that of Marx and Engels, called themselves communists in order to dissociate themselves from other, allegedly less consistent, socialist groups. Hence when reference is made to that period, communism often is synonymous with the system of ideas developed by Engels and Marx, even though they often used the terms 'communism' and 'socialism' interchangeably. Communism in this sense connotes the sum-total of Marxist doctrines; hence it is the Marxist critique of capitalism and liberal theory and the project for the proletarian revolution, though at times it connotes specifically the ultimate goal of that revolution – the society visualized as emerging out of it, which is dimly foreseen as a society without property, without classes or a division of labour, without institutions of coercion and domination. The precise features of this society are not delineated in the writings of Marx and Engels, and among Marxists there are controversies about the degree of residual alienation and oppression (if any) that one ought to expect in the communist society of the future. Some of the hints Marx and Engels themselves gave come from their notion of a primitive communism allegedly prevailing among the savage early ancestors of the human race.

Among the earliest followers of Engels and Marx, the term fell into disuse; most Marxists around the turn of the century called themselves Social-Democrats. The term was revived after the Russian Revolution of 1917 by V. I. Lenin, who renamed his faction of the Russian Marxist movement the 'Communist Party' and compelled all those parties who wished to join the newly-created Third (or Communist) International to adopt the same designation, so as to dissociate themselves from the Social-Democratic parties. As a consequence, communism since then connotes that interpretation of Marxism which considers the ideas and actions of Lenin and his Bolshevik faction to be the only correct interpretation of Marxism, and the sum-total of parties that subscribe to this interpretation.

Leninism is characterized by the insistence that meaningful social change can come only through revolution, while reforms threaten to corrupt the oppressed. Further, it implies the application of Marxism to countries where capitalism is underdeveloped, hence the development of flexible political strategies, including the mobilization of peasants and ethnic minorities for revolution. Foremost, it insists on the need for a 'vanguard party' of revolutionaries-by-profession to whom correct knowledge of the laws of history and politics ('consciousness') is attributed. Within the party and its numerous auxiliary organizations designed to mobilize the working class and its presumed allies, the vanguard is expected to ensure the prevalence of enlightened 'consciousness' over blind passion by a combination of mass initiative and bureaucratic control that Lenin called 'democratic centralism'. Finally, Leninism implies the accumulated experience of the Russian Communist Party in governing their country. Communism thus connotes the theory and practice of rule by communist parties.

Although the leaders of ruling communist parties have generally refrained from claiming that the systems they were ruling were communist, it has become customary in the Western world to refer to them as communist systems. Communism thus refers to any society or group of societies governed by communist parties.

The mature form of communist rule was developed in the USSR under the rule of J. V. Stalin. Hence communism since the 1930s has become synonymous with Stalinism or Neo-Stalinism. This is a system in which the communist party proclaims itself the enlightened leadership and claims authority to speak for the entire nation. It enforces this claim through control over all organizations and associations, all forms of communication, education, and entertainment, individual appointments and careers. The chief aim of these systems is rapid economic growth through crash programmes of industrialization, carried out through a centralized command economy. Communism in its Stalinist form thus is a species of entrepreneurship.

Contemporary communist societies thus bear no resemblance to the vision of communism sketched by Marx and Engels or even to that provided by Lenin in his unfinished work, *The State and Revolution*. Yet the memory of that vision lingers and has repeatedly led to attempts within communist parties to define alternatives to Leninist and Stalinist theories and practices. Contemporary communism therefore is not one single orthodoxy, but an ever growing cluster of orthodoxies and heresies, all of them backing up their arguments by reference to Engels and Marx, yet fiercely contending with each other.

Alfred G. Meyer
University of Michigan

Further Reading
Claudin, F. (1975), *The Communist Movement: From Comintern to Cominform*, London.
Daniels, R. V. (ed.) (1965), *Marxism and Communism: Essential Readings*, New York.

Kolakowski, L. (1978), *Main Currents of Marxism*, 3 vols, Oxford.

Meyer, A. G. (1984), *Communism* (4th edn), New York.

Rosenberg, A. (1967), *A History of Bolshevism*, New York.

See also: *socialism*.

Conservatism

Conservatism is the doctrine that the reality of any society is to be found in its historical development, and therefore that the most reliable, though not the sole, guide for governments is caution in interfering with what has long been established. Clearly distinctive conservative doctrine emerged in the 1790s, in reaction to the rationalist projects of the French revolutionaries, and its classic statement is to to found in Edmund Burke's *Reflections on the Revolution in France* (1790). Burke's historical emphasis was itself the outcome of deep currents in European thought, currents rejecting abstract reasoning as a method for understanding the human world. The sheer flamboyance of Burke's rhetoric was necessary to bring conservatism into the world, however, since the doctrine in its purest form consists of a few maxims of prudence (concerning the complexity of things and the wisdom of caution) which, in the intellectualist atmosphere of the last two centuries, make a poor showing against the seductive philosophical pretensions of modern ideologies. These competing doctrines claim to explain not only the activity of politics, but man and his place in the universe. Burke himself thought that this wider picture was supplied for us by religion, and thus he was prone to extend the reverence appropriate to divine things so that it embraced the established institutions of society. This fideist emphasis, however, ought not to conceal the fact that conservatism rests upon a deep scepticism about the ability of any human being, acting within the constraints of a present consciousness, to understand the daunting complexities of human life as it has developed over recorded time.

Conservatism construes society as something that grows, and conservatives prefer pruning leaves and branches to tearing up the roots. The latter view is taken by radicals who believe that nothing less than a revolutionary transformation both of society and of human beings themselves will serve to save us from what they believe to be a deeply unjust society. Generically, then, all are conservative who oppose the revolutionary transformation of society. Specifically, however, conservatism is one of three doctrinal partners, each of which may plausibly claim centrality in the European political tradition. One of these is liberalism, constituted by its allegiance to liberty and the values of reform, and the other is constitutional socialism, whose fundamental preoccupation with the problem of the poor leads it to construe all political problems as issues of realizing a truer community. Modern politics is a ceaseless dialogue between these three tendencies and movements.

Conservatism in this specific sense emerged from a split in the Whig party in late eighteenth-century Britain, and it was only in the 1830s, when the present nomenclature of each of the three doctrines crystallized, that Tories began calling themselves 'conservatives'. This name failed to catch on in other countries, most notably perhaps the United States, where 'conservative' until recently connoted timidity and lack of enterprise. From the 1960s onwards, however, the tendency of American liberals (predominantly but not exclusively in the Democratic Party) to adopt socialist policies has provoked a reaction which calls itself 'neo-conservative' in testimony to its adherence to many classical liberal positions.

Since it is conservative doctrine that political parties must respond to changing circumstances, it would be not merely futile but paradoxical to discover a doctrinal essence in the changing attitudes of any particular Conservative party. Nevertheless, conservatism is not merely a doctrine but a human disposition, and many conservative temperaments have influenced the British Conservative Party, whose response to the successive problems of the modern world may give some clue to conservatism. Under Disraeli it organized itself successfully to exploit successive nineteenth-century extensions of the franchise, and its electoral viability has since largely depended upon the allegiance of the figure known to political scientists as the 'Tory workingman'. In the latter part of the nineteenth century, it rode a tide of imperial emotion and economic protection and stood for the unity of the United Kingdom against attempts to grant self-government to Ireland. Between the two World Wars, Baldwin saw it as the task of the Party to educate an electorate, now enjoying universal suffrage, in the responsibilities of power. After Attlee's creation of the Welfare State from 1945 to 1951, Churchill and Macmillan found conservative reasons for sustaining a welfarist consensus, but since 1976, Mrs Thatcher and a dominant wing of the Party identified the expense of the welfare state in its present form as one of the emerging problems of politics.

A principle of conservation offers little substantive guide to political action, and is vulnerable to the objection brought by F. A. Hayek: 'By its nature, it cannot offer an alternative to the direction we are moving' (*The Constitution of Liberty*, 1960). It is a mistake, however, to identify conservatism with hostility to change; the point is, rather, the *source* of change. It is characteristic of all radicals to seek one big change, after which a perfected community will be essentially changeless. On this basis, they often seek to monopolize the rhetoric of change. Liberals consider it the duty of an active government to make the reforms that will dissipate social evils. While refusing to erect limitation of government into an absolute principle, conservatives tend to think that, within a strong framework of laws, society will often work out for itself a better response to evils than can be found in the necessary complexities of legislation, and worse, of course, in the simple *dictat* of the legislator. Conservatism is, in this respect, a political application of the legal maxim that hard cases make bad law. It is thus a central mistake to think of conservatism as mere hostility to change. It poses, rather, the issue of where change should originate.

Like all political doctrines, conservatism is loosely but importantly associated with a particular temperament, a view of the world. It is characteristic of the conservative temperament to value established identities, to praise habit and to respect prejudice, not because it is irrational, but because such things anchor the darting impulses of human beings in solidities of custom which we often do not begin to value until we are already losing them. Radicalism often generates youth movements, while conservatism is a disposition found among the mature, who have discovered what it is in life they most value. The ideological cast of contemporary thought has provoked some writers to present conservatism as if it contained the entire sum of political wisdom; but this is to mistake the part for the whole. Nevertheless, a society without a strong element of conservatism could hardly be anything but impossibly giddy.

Kenneth Minogue
London School of Economics and Political Science

Reference
Hayek, F. A. (1960), *The Constitution of Liberty*, London.

Further Reading
Kirk, R. (1953), *The Conservative Mind*, Chicago.
Oakeshott, M. (1962), *Rationalism in Politics*, London.
Scruton, R. (1980), *Meaning of Conservatism*, London.
See also: *Burke; liberalism; radicalism.*

Constitutions and Constitutionalism

The constitution of a state is the collection of rules and principles according to which a state is governed. In antiquity the most important function of a constitution was to determine who should rule. The criterion which served as the basis for assigning political power reflected the ethos of the society. Thus each constitutional form exercised a moulding influence on virtue; the good citizen was a different being in an oligarchy, a democracy and an aristocracy (Aristotle). Although modern constitutions are far more complex, still the rules they establish for acquiring and exercising governmental power will usually embody the underlying norms and ideology of the polity.

The constitution of the modern nation state contains three main elements: (1) It establishes the principal institutions of government and the relationships among these institutions. These institutions may be structured on traditional Western lines of a division of executive, legislative and judicial responsibilities. The constitutions of one-party states gives greater emphasis to the structures of the governing party, while those based on theocratic principles assign a dominant position to religious offices and institutions. (2) Constitutions provide for a distribution of governmental power over the nation's territory. In a unitary state, local units of government are established as agencies of the central government. The constitution of a federal state assigns power directly to central and local levels of government. (3) Constitutions provide a compendium of fundamental rights and duties of citizens including their rights to participate in the institutions of government. Some constitutions emphasize economic and social rights as much, if not more, than political and legal/procedural rights.

In most countries there is a single document called 'The Constitution' which contains most of the significant elements of the constitutional system. But this is not the only form in which the rules of a constitution may be expressed. They may also take the form of ordinary laws such as statutes or decrees, judicial decisions or well-established customs and conventions. The United Kingdom is distinctive in that it does not have a document known as the Constitution; all of its constitutional rules are expressed more informally as statutes, judicial opinions, customs and conventions. Since the American Revolution the worldwide trend has been very much towards the codification of constitutional norms. New states established in the aftermath of revolution, the withdrawal of empire and world war have relied on a formal constitutional text to set out their basic governmental arrangements. However, even in these new nations, statutes, judicial decisions and conventions usually supplement the formal constitution.

A country may have a constitution but may not enjoy constitutionalism. Constitutionalism is a political condition in which the constitution functions as an effective and significant limit on government. Where constitutionalism characterizes a regime, the constitution is 'antecedent' to government, and those who govern are constrained by its terms. The constitutional rules of such a regime are not easily changed – even when they are obstacles to policies supported by leading politicians. Thus, constitutional government is said to be 'limited

government' (Sartori, 1956). The limits imposed by a constitution are sometimes said to embody a 'higher law' – the
enduring will of a people – which constitutes the basis of a
legitimate check on the will of governments representing transient majorities (McIlwain, 1947; Corwin, 1955).

Constitutionalism may be maintained by the practice of
judicial review, whereby judges with a reasonable degree of
independence of the other branches of government have the
authority to veto laws and activities of government on the
grounds that they conflict with the constitution. Constitutionalism may also be manifest in a formal amendment process that
requires much more than the support of a dominant political
party or a simple majority of the population to change the
formal constitution. The British situation demonstrates,
however, that neither of these practices is a necessary condition
for constitutionalism. In that country the most important
constitutional precepts are maintained and enforced more informally through well-established popular attitudes and the
restraint of politicians (Dicey, 1959).

The reality of constitutionalism depends on whether there
are political forces genuinely independent of the government of
the day powerful enough to insist on the government's observance of constitutional limits. Critics of those liberal democracies
that claim to practise constitutionalism contend that in reality
the constitutions imposing constitutional limits (e.g. the
judiciary or the opposition party) are not independent of
government, because they are controlled by social or economic
interests aligned with the government. On the other hand,
defenders of these regimes may point to occasions on which the
maintenance of constitutional rules has forced political leaders
to abandon major policies or even to abandon office (e.g. US
President Nixon in the Watergate affair).

In countries that have formal 'written' constitutions, whether
or not they practise constitutionalism, the constitution may
serve an important symbolic function. Constitutions are often
employed as instruments of political education designed to
inculcate public respect for political and social norms. A constitution may also be a means of gaining legitimacy, both intern-

ally and externally, for a regime. This is a primary function of constitutions in communist states (Brunner, 1977). The development of codes of fundamental human rights since the Second World War has prompted many states to include such rights in their domestic constitutions in order to ingratiate themselves in the international community.

Peter H. Russell
University of Toronto

References

Andrews, W. G. (1961), *Constitutions and Constitutionalism*, Princeton.

The Politics of Aristotle (1948), trans. by E. Barker, Oxford.

Brunner, G. (1977), 'The functions of communist constitutions', *Review of Socialist Law*, 2.

Corwin, E. S. (1955), *The 'Higher Law' Background of American Constitutional Law*, Ithaca, N.Y.

Dicey, A. V. (1959), *Introduction to the Study of the Law of the Constitution*, 10th edn, London.

Friedrich, C. J. (1950), *Constitutional Government and Democracy*, New York.

McIlwain, C. H. (1947), *Constitutionalism: Ancient and Modern*, revised edn, Ithaca, N.Y.

Sartori, G. (1956), 'Constitutionalism: a preliminary discussion', *American Political Science Review*, 56.

See also: *human rights*.

Corporatism

Corporatism, whether corporate, clerical or Fascist in origin, is an ideology of organization which assumes that a variety of parties will co-operate on the basis of shared values. Corporativism (also called neo-corporatism or liberal corporatism) presupposes, on the contrary, the existence of fundamental conflicts which, however, need not produce organizational disruption but can be mediated with the help of the state. The concept first appeared in Scandinavian writings after the Second World War (Heckscher, St Rokkan), but was only made generally known by Schmitter (1979, 1981). However, functional equivalents of the concept, labelled 'organized capitalism', can be traced back to Hilferding (1915) in the social democratic debate in Germany and Austria. The concept was thus developed in countries where state sponsorship of trade unions had a certain tradition, but where unions had achieved positions of considerable power.

In recent years, corporatism has been greatly extended. Left-wing theorists invoke it to explain how – despite expectations – through successful manipulation, crises did not come to a head, and class struggles were not exacerbated. More conservative scholars embraced neo-corporatism as a solution to what was termed the problem of 'ungovernability' (Schmitter, 1981). Ungovernability in modern democracies was widely thought to be a consequence of the overburdening of the system of communication. There was also said to be a weakening of legitimacy, from the point of view of the citizen. Schmitter pointed rather to the inadequate co-ordination of interests and of demands by state agencies. Corporatism offered itself as an alternative to the syndicalist view that a multitude of uncoordinated and sharply antagonistic groups confronted one another. In countries where the ideas of a social contract is undeveloped – as in Italy – or where a kind of 'bargained corporatism' is beginning to crystallize – as in Britain (Crouch, 1977) – the notion of corporatism has been rejected by the unions.

Where strategies of negotiation and conflict are in a more differentiated fashion, it is often apparent that the possibilities of neo-corporatism have been overestimated. Great strides have been made in spatial planning, health policies and to some extent in education (Cawson, 1978); but where many economic interests are involved, it seems that pluralist market models are more effective in articulating interests. Where ideologically founded alternatives are in question, as in environmental policy, negotiated settlements and compromise proposals tend to meet with strong opposition.

Klaus von Beyme
University of Heidelberg

References
Cawson, A. (1978), 'Pluralism, corporatism, and the role of the state', *Government and Oppositions*, 13.
Crouch, C. (1977), *Class Conflict and Industrial Relations Crisis. Compromise and Corporatism in the Policies of the British State*, London.
Schmitter, P. C. (1979), 'Still the century of corporatism?' in P. C. Schmitter and G. Lehmbruch (eds), *Trends Towards Corporatist Intermediation*, Beverly Hills.

Further Reading
von Beyme, K. (1983), 'Neo-corporatism. A new nut in an old shell', *International Political Science Review*.
Lehmbruch, G. and Schmitter, P. C. (eds) (1982), *Pattern of Corporatist Policy-Making*, Beverly Hills.

Corruption

In its most general sense, corruption means the perversion or abandonment of a standard. Hence it is common to speak of the corruption of language or of moral corruption. More narrowly, corruption refers to the abandonment of expected standards of behaviour by those in authority for the sake of unsanctioned personal advantage. In the business sphere, a company director is deemed corrupt if he sells his private property to the company at an inflated price, at the expense of the shareholders whose interests he is supposed to safeguard. Lawyers, architects and other professionals are similarly guilty of corruption if they take advantage of their clients to make undue personal gains.

Political corruption can be defined as the misuse of public office or authority for unsanctioned private gain. Several points about the definition should be noted. (1) Not all forms of misconduct or abuse of office constitute corruption. An official or a government minister who is merely incompetent or who betrays government secrets to a foreign power for ideological reasons is not generally considered corrupt. (2) Legislators and public officials in most countries are entitled to salaries and other allowances. Corruption occurs only when they receive additional *unsanctioned* benefits, such as bribes. In practice, it is frequently hard to draw the line between authorized and unauthorized payments and, in any case, this will change over time and will be drawn differently in different countries. A benefit regarded as a bribe in one country may be seen as normal and legitimate in another. Legal definitions of corrupt practices are only an imperfect guide since benefits forbidden by law are often sanctioned by social custom, and vice versa. The boundaries of accepted behaviour can be especially difficult to determine in countries affected by rapid political and social change. (3) *Electoral corruption* needs to be defined differently from other forms. Whereas most political corruption involves the abuse of public office, electoral corruption is the abuse of the process by which public office is won.

Common forms of corruption are bribery, extortion (the unauthorized extraction of money by officials from members of the public) and misuse of official information. Bribery need not consist of a direct payment to a public official. 'Indirect bribery' may take the form of a promise of a post-retirement job, the provision of reduced-price goods, or the channelling of business to a legislator or to members of his family.

Corruption was a serious problem in biblical and classical times, and was found in most periods of history. Cases of judicial corruption were particularly frequent. By the 1960s, an influential school of 'revisionist' political scientists nevertheless presented an optimistic view about the decline of corruption in advanced Western democracies (see Heidenheimer, 1970). Some of the 'revisionists' maintained that corruption did not present as grave a problem as previous writers had suggested. In many newly independent nations, where corruption was supposedly rampant, the practices condemned by Western observers as corrupt (for example, making payments to low-level officials for routine services) were accepted as normal by local standards. Moreover, some forms of corruption, far from damaging the process of social and economic development, could be positively beneficial. Bribery enabled entrepreneurs (including foreign companies) to cut through red tape, thereby promoting the economic advance of poor nations. Corruption was seen as a transitory phenomenon, which was likely to decline as economic and social progress was achieved. The general trend was to be seen, it was argued, in the history of Britain and the United States. In Britain, electoral corruption, the sale of titles and government jobs, and corruption relating to public contracts had been rife until the nineteenth century. The introduction of merit systems of appointment to the civil service, the successful battle against electoral corruption and a change in public attitudes towards the conduct of government had led to a dramatic decline in corruption – a decline which coincided with the nation's economic development. Similarly, in the United States, corruption had been rampant in the late nineteenth and early twentieth centuries. This had been a period of intense economic and social change. As suggested by Robert Merton, the corrupt urban party machines, such as the Democratic Party organization in New York City (Tammany Hall) had provided avenues for advancement for underpriviliged immigrant groups. After the Second World War, full employment, the advance of education, the decline of political patronage and the growth of public welfare benefits combined to eliminate the deprivation that had previously led to corruption. A new civic culture replaced the former loyalties to family and to ethnic group. According to a common view, the party machine and the corruption that had accompanied it withered away.

This interpretation has recently come under challenge. Corruption is neither so benign in underdeveloped countries, nor is it so rare in advanced ones as previously thought. It is unrealistic to suppose that advances in education or in techniques of public administration, the development of a 'publicregarding ethos' or economic development can lead to the virtual disappearance of corruption. The growth of governmental activity and regulation in the modern state increases the opportunities and the temptations for corruption. Improvements in education need not lead to the elimination of corruption but to its perpetuation in new, sophisticated forms.

Revelations since the 1970s have led scholars to give increased attention to the contemporary problems of corruption in advanced democracies and in communist countries. In the

United States, the Watergate affair of 1972–4 led to a wave of investigations that resulted in hundreds of convictions for corruption, including that of Vice-President Spiro Agnew. Others convicted included the governors of Illinois, Maryland, Oklahoma and West Virginia. Rampant corruption was uncovered in a number of states including Florida, New Jersey, Pennsylvania and Texas. In Britain, the conventional view about the virtual elimination of corruption was shattered by several major scandals in the 1970s. The far-reaching Poulson scandal, involving local government corruption in the north of England as well as members of Parliament, erupted in 1972. Local government corruption was proved in South Wales, Birmingham and in Scotland, while in London senior police officers were imprisoned. Japan, Italy and Israel are among other economically developed coutries where there have been recent revelations about corruption. In the communist sphere, there have been academic studies as well as official campaigns against corruption in the Soviet Union, China and Poland. The wide scope of governmental activity and control in these countries leads to a correspondingly wide scope for practices to evade this control. Forms of corruption that have been the focus of attention in a number of countries include police corruption and bribery involving multinational corporations (for example, in the arms trade).

The definition, causes and effects of corruption and techniques of reform continue to be matters of controversy among sociologists and political scientists. What has been established beyond dispute is that political corruption is a widespread, pervasive and potentially serious phenomenon.

M. Pinto-Duschinsky
Brunel University, Uxbridge

References
Clarke, M. (ed.) (1983), *Corruption: Causes, Consequences and Control*, London.
Heidenheimer, A. J. (ed.) (1970), *Political Corruption: Readings in Comparative Analysis*, New York.

Decision Making

There are three definitions of decision making, each of which is associated with a specific analytical approach. (1) Decision making is a rational, cognitive process by which a choice is made among several alternatives. The assumption is that the individual is capable of ranking alternatives in a rational manner, and choosing accordingly. This definition is associated with normative decision-making theory. (2) Decision making is concerned with the behaviour involved in making a choice even if such behaviour is spontaneous, impulsive or habitual. Here decision making is not treated as a cognitive process. This view of decision making is associated with behavioural decision theory. (3) Decision making is the actual process of making a choice. Various phases are distinguished: the recognition of the problem; the search for information; the processing of information and consideration of alternatives; and the formulation of the final choice. This procedural view is associated with the theory of collective decision making.

There are two sorts of theories concerning decision making. One set seeks logical, non-behavioural explanations, provides a formal analysis, and portrays decision making in terms of axiomatic models (Raiffa, 1968). Empirical theories, in contrast, describe actual decision-making behaviour, and explain it with reference to behavioural hypotheses.

Decision Making in Social Science Theories

Individual decision making is generally analysed in terms of psychological or social-psychological approaches. The researcher must consider and distinguish two types of psychological variables. The A-variable relates to the human arousal system (emotions, motivations, goals, etc.). The K-variable is the cognitive system, which is concerned with the perception, processing and storage of information.

Some decision-making theories are weighted in favour of the A-variable – for example, the conflict decision-making model of Janis and Mann (1977), who argue that the decision-making process is determined by the extent of conflict, whether emotional or motivational. Stronger conflicts induce insecurity and distress, and may interrupt or delay the decision-making process, while the individual searches for alternative, less threatening, solutions. Other theories restrict themselves to the K-features, and analyse decision making as the outcome of human information processing. These cognitive approaches neglect the influence of emotional factors (Kozielecki, 1981). The key element of cognitive theory is the notion that human beings have a limited capacity to recognize and digest information presented to them, and that decision making follows subjective, 'psycho-logical' rules that are considerably different from the rules of objective logic (Nisbet and Ross, 1980). Given his cognitive limitations, the individual is obliged to simplify the complexities of decision making. He uses various strategies to this end, including the identification of key pieces of information, the application of stereotypes, and simple rules of elimination.

Personality traits and personal self-image are key variables in individual decision making. Willingness to take risks is significant. While many people have internalized standards of 'rational decision making', their actual behaviour frequently diverges from this ideal standard, although they may present rational explanations of non-rational behaviour. This illustrates one of the pitfalls of using verbal methods to uncover the processes of decision making.

Currently, cognitive approaches are usually preferred for the analysis and measurement of decision-making processes. The researcher tries to understand the way in which individuals process information and make decisions, using various methods, including information display matrices, and the observation and measurement of visual and other sensory cues. These methods have not, however, yielded a satisfactory account of the 'psycho-logic' involved in decision making.

Collective decisions made by groups or within organizations have been of particular interest to sociologists, political scientists and economists. The early economic approach was normative, and favoured an axiomatic theory of rational decision making (corresponding to definition 1, above). Social scientists of other kinds preferred a more complex and descriptive approach (corresponding rather to definition 3). Recent studies tend to combine these approaches, economists now distancing themselves from the use of a simple monetary calculus and input-output models, and paying more attention to descriptions of decision-making behaviour.

Collective decisions are produced by the interaction of several individuals, whose personal qualities and views affect the final outcome. Yet collective decision making is more than the sum of a series of individual decision-making processes. Collective decisions are necessary where one individual is not competent to make a decision alone (K-explanation), or when several people are in conflict about the desired goals (A-explanation). The participants in the decision-making process may have specialized functions, which enhance productivity, but since the co-ordination of these specialists requires planning and adjust-ment, collective decision making may be a long drawn-out process.

Ideal-types of various kinds can be found in the literature on decision making, but there is little empirical research concerning the kinds of decisions made by groups of interacting individuals, nor is it at all clear whether individual or collective decisions are the more efficient. Contingency theory does deal with this issue, and suggests that collective decision making is more likely to be successful when the issue is very complex. Conversely, less complicated decisions are more efficiently made by individuals. Complexity is measured with reference to relevance, risk, problems of conflict, the existence of precedents, time pressures, and so on.

Collective decision making is complicated by a number of problems that are absent from individual decision making:

(1) *Deciding upon the actual goal.* People may collaborate and yet have different goals, because of different motivations (A-variable), or different cognitive approaches (K-variable), or different roles and statuses. If a solution is to be agreed upon, goal conflict must first be reduced (by a goal formation process).

(2) *Problems of communication.* Communication is the key to gaining information about goals, contexts, and strategies. While

the process of communication may lead to distortion and delay, it can also increase rationality.

(3) *Co-ordination efforts.* Participants may make different types of contributions, and offer different perspectives on the issues. Some individuals take more initiatives, while others are more reserved. Information must be collected from various quarters and evaluated. Alternatives must be considered. A co-ordinator must steer the decision-making process, to ensure that it can be completed efficiently, effectively, and within a reasonable time.

(4) *Power problems.* Some individuals are more powerful and consequently more influential. Others will, to a greater or lesser extent, concur in the goals and methods of the more influential members of the group.

(5) *Negotiation difficulties.* Decisions are normally made after a process of negotiation has been completed. The outcome of these negotiations depends on collective learning over time, especially by key members of the group. The process is influenced by personality factors, communications, the formation of coalitions, techniques of negotiation and arbitration, and the tactics employed by the actors, including, for example, the use of threats or deception.

While empirical research into all forms of decision making is still limited, insights have been won which already suggest ways of improving the efficiency and effectiveness of decision making in general.

Werner Kroeber-Riel
University of the Saarland

Jürgen Hauschildt
Christian-Albrechts University, Kiel

References
Janis, I. L. and Mann, L. (1977), *Decision Making, A Psychological Analysis of Conflict, Choice, and Commitment*, New York.
Kozielecki, J. (1981), *Psychological Decision Theory*, Dordrecht.

Nisbet, R. and Ross, L. (1980), *Human Inference: Strategies and Short-Comings of Social Judgment*, Englewood Cliffs, N.J.
Raiffa, H. (1968), *Decision Analysis*, Reading, Mass.

Further Reading
Hill, P. H., Bedau, H. A. *et al.* (1979), *Making Decisions. A Multi-disciplinary Introduction*, Reading, Mass.
See also: *committees; policy sciences*.

Democracy

In the classical Greek *polis*, democracy was the name of a constitution in which the poorer people (*demos*) exercised power in their own interest as against the interest of the rich and aristocratic. Aristotle thought it a debased form of constitution, and it played relatively little part in subsequent political thought, largely because Polybius and other writers diffused the idea that only mixed and balanced constitutions (incorporating monarchic, aristocratic and democratic elements) could be stable. Democracies were commonly regarded as aggressive and unstable and likely to lead (as in Plato's *Republic*) to tyranny. Their propensity to oppress minorities (especially the propertied) was what Burke meant when he described a perfect democracy as the most shameless thing in the world.

Democracy as popular power in an approving sense may occasionally be found in early modern times (in the radical thinkers of the English Civil War, the constitution of Rhode Island of 1641, and in the deliberations of the framers of the American Constitution), but the real vogue for democracy dates from the French Revolution. The main reason is that 'democracy' came to be the new name for the long-entrenched tradition of classical republicanism which, transmitted through Machiavelli, had long constituted a criticism of the dominant monarchical institutions of Europe. This tradition had often emphasized the importance of aristocratic guidance in a republic, and many of its adherents throughout Europe considered that British constitutional monarchy with an elected parliament was the very model of a proper republic. This idea fused in the nineteenth century with demand to extend the franchise, and the resulting package came generally to be called 'democracy'.

It is important to emphasize that democracy *was* a package, because the name had always previously described a source of power rather than a manner of governing. By the nineteenth century, however, the idea of democracy included representative parliaments, the separation of powers, the rule of law, civil rights and other such liberal desirabilities. All of these conditions were taken to be the culmination of human moral evolution, and the politics of the period often revolved around extensions of the franchise, first to adult males, then to women, and subsequently to such classes as young people of 18 (rather than 21) and, recently in Great Britain, to voluntary patients in mental hospitals.

Democracy proved to be a fertile and effervescent principle of political perfection. Inevitably, each advance towards democracy disappointed many adherents, but the true ideal could always be relocated in new refinements of the idea. The basis of many such extensions had been laid by the fact that 'democracy' was a Greek term used, for accidental reasons, to describe a complicated set of institutions whose real roots were medieval. The most important was representation, supported by some American founding fathers precisely because it might moderate rather than reflect the passions of an untutored multitude. The Greekness of the name, however, continually suggests that the practice of representation is not intrinsic to modern democracy, but rather a contingent imperfection resulting from the sheer size of modern nations by comparison with ancient city states. In fact, modern constitutional government is quite unrelated to the democracy of the Greeks.

Although modern democracy is a complicated package, the logic of the expression suggests a single principle. The problem is: what precisely is the principle? And a further question arises: how far should it extend? So far as the first question is concerned, democracy might be identified with popular sovereignty, majority rule, protection of minorities, affability, constitutional liberties, participation in decisions at every level, egalitarianism, and much else. Parties emphasize one or other of these principles according to current convenience, but most parties in the modern world (the Fascist parties between 1918 and 1945 are the most important exception) have seldom failed to claim a democratic legitimacy. The principle of democracy was thus a suitably restless principle for a restless people ever searching for constitutional perfection.

Democracy is irresistible as a slogan because it seems to promise a form of government in which rulers and ruled are in such harmony that little actual governing will be required. Democracy was thus equated with a dream of freedom. For this reason, the nationalist theories which helped destroy the great European empires were a department of the grand principle of democracy, since everybody assumed that the people would want to be ruled by politicians of their own kind. The demographic complexities of many areas, however, were such that many people would inevitably be ruled by foreigners; and such people often preferred to be ruled on an imperial principle – in which all subjects are, as it were, foreigners – rather than on a national principle, which constitutes some as the nation, and the rest as minorities. In claiming to be democratic, rulers might hope to persuade their subjects that they ruled in the popular interest.

Democracy is possible only when a population can recognize both sectional and public interests, and organize itself for political action. Hence no state is seriously democratic unless an opposition is permitted to criticize governments, organize support, and contest elections. But in many countries, such oppositions are likely to be based upon tribes, nations or regions, which do not recognize a common or universal good in the state. Where political parties are of this kind, democratic institutions generate quarrels rather than law and order. In these circumstances, democracy is impossible, and the outcome has been the emergence of some other unifying principle: sometimes an army claiming to stand above 'politics', and sometimes an ideological party in which a doctrine supplies a simulacrum of the missing universal element. One-party states often lay claim to some eccentric (and superior) kind of democracy – basic, popular, guided and so on. In fact, the very name 'party' requires pluralism. Hence, in one-party states, the party is a different kind of political entity altogether, and the claim to democracy is merely window-dressing. This does not necessarily mean, however, that such governments are entirely without virtue. It would be foolish to think that one manner of government suited all peoples.

Democracy as an ideal in the nineteenth century took for granted citizens who were rationally reflective about the voting choices open to them. Modern political scientists have concentrated their attention upon the actual irrationalities of the democratic process. Some have even argued that a high degree of political apathy is preferable to mass enthusiasm which endangers constitutional forms.

Kenneth Minogue
London School of Economics and Political Science

Further Reading
Macpherson, C. B. (1973), *Democratic Theory: Essays in Retrieval*, Oxford.
Plamenatz, J. (1973), *Democracy and Illusion*, London.
Sartori, G. (1962), *Democracy*, Detroit.
Schumpeter, J. (1943), *Capitalism, Socialism and Democracy*, London.
See also: *elections; parties, political; representation, political.*

Dependency Theory

The dependency paradigm, which gained currency within the social sciences during the 1960s and continued to be very influential in the 1970s, can be characterized as an eclectic, historical structuralist perspective on spatially-bounded socioeconomic and political inequality. The concept of *dependence*, lying at the heart of the paradigm and implying a constant concern for elements of social interaction precluding autonomous development within certain subunits of a wider system, is sufficiently broad to allow application to a number of general problem areas, within varying disciplines, and to be utilized within somewhat dissimilar ideological parameters. One can therefore speak of dependency in several forms: (1) The dialogue on neo-colonial dependence developed by European and African social scientists from the 1950s onward, as they dealt with the continued lack of autonomy of recently freed colonial peoples through reference to the social and psychological legacy of colonial rule. (2) The analysis of unequal terms of international trade through which Latin American economists explained the continued underdevelopment of their region in the early post-war period, later supplemented by a more comprehensive treatment of the phenomenon of unequal exchange within a world capitalist system. (3) The elucidation of complexities in relations among classes and within state formations shaped by the specific requirements of interaction during an era of international monopoly capitalism, which, in contrast to interpretations by economists, placed primary emphasis not on understanding the nature of external domination, but rather on clarifying distinctive *internal* patterns of response. (4) The presentation of a comprehensive historical explanation for the development of capitalism in Europe, positing the systematic transfer toward hegemonic centres from societies whose form of insertion in the wider system assured the 'development of underdevelopment' outside core areas of capitalist accumulation, and the extension of this argument into the field of intranational socioeconomic relations, where underdeveloped regions were considered 'internal colonies' of more developed ones.

All of these approaches had in common a rejection of earlier liberal or functionalist 'dualism', which had posited the coexistence of two theoretically unrelated types of societies (whether 'traditional' and 'modern' or 'developed' and 'underdeveloped'), and a consequent insistence upon the dynamic interaction of all subunits within a world system. All also exhibited certain points of disagreement with earlier Marxist treatment of imperialism, which was considered too rigid a projection of the European experience. Specifically, dependency theories appended an additional concern to the Marxist emphasis on exploitation as a transfer of surplus value from one class to another, during the process of production. This was a concern with territorially-based transfers of surplus product from one geographical unit to another during the process of circulation. The way was thus left open for consideration of exploitative or asymmetrical relations within modern socialist or communist society (Nerfin, 1977), although analytical priority was consistently granted to explaining the unequal development of capitalism.

Theoretical heterogeneity within the paradigm was reflected in varying prescriptions for policy and conflicting predictions of the future course of world development. One current of thought upheld the possibility that an alliance between working class and bourgeoisie within peripheral societies could encourage autonomous development. A second discarded the viability of such an alliance, given the strategic international ties of any supposedly 'national' bourgeoisie, yet saw the likelihood of 'dependent development' in association with international capital. And a third predicted the development of the periphery only upon the qualitative transformation of socio-economic relations brought about by proletarian revolution on a world-wide scale.

Cynthia Hewitt de Alcántara
El Colegio de México

Reference
Nerfin, M. (ed.) (1977), *Another Development*: *Approaches and Strategies*, Uppsala.

Further Reading
Chilcote, R. (ed.) (1981), *Dependency and Marxism*: *Toward a Resolution of the Debate*, Boulder, Co.
Roxborough, I. (1979), *Theories of Underdevelopment*, London.
See also: *world-system theory*.

Distributive Justice
The term distributive justice has a long history reaching back to Aristotle (*Nicomachean Ethics*). More recent philosophical treatments of the topic abound and are mostly concerned with

specifying just or fair principles of distribution within a collectivity, typically a society. Whenever valued goods or resources
exist some mechanism of distribution arises, and the concern of
philosophers has been to examine the 'justness' of the resulting
distribution (and, sometimes, the fairness of the distribution
procedure itself). Rawls (1971), in a major philosophical treatise
on justice, identifies principles by which members of a society
properly distribute the 'benefits and burdens of social cooper-
ation'. For Rawls, the 'primary subject of justice is the basic
structure of society'.

All social systems evolve mechanisms for distributing valued
resources and for allocating rights, responsibilities, costs and
burdens. Theories of distributive justice specify the conditions
under which particular distributions are perceived to be just or
fair. The various conceptions of distributive justice proposed by
philosophers and social scientists include the conceptualizations
identified by Eckhoff (1974): (1) *objective equality* – equal
amounts to each recipient; (2) *subjective equality* – equal amounts
based on perceived need or 'deservingness'; (3) *relative equality*
– allocation based on the 'fitness' or 'deservingness' of the
recipient; (4) *rank order equality* – allocation according to the
status or positional rank of the recipient in the social system;
and (5) *equal opportunity* – the allocation of equivalent opportunities to obtain the valued outcome to each recipient. A
further distinction is often made between distributive justice
and retributive justice, which is identified most frequently as
involving judgements of the fairness of the allocation of punishments for activity not condoned by the collectivity.

Social scientists in the past three decades have conducted
empirical research to investigate commonly held conceptions of
distributive justice, and to examine the reactions of individuals
and groups to perceived injustice. Findings suggest that perceptions of inequity are linked to lower levels of productivity,
morale, and satisfaction, as well as to the formation of 'revolutionary' coalitions. In some experimental settings actors even
attempt to redistribute outcomes in a more equitable fashion,
but the generality of these results has not been established.
Recent survey research attempts to examine the perceived fair-

ness of the distribution of income in various countries. Robinson and Bell (1978), for example, report that in Great Britain and in the United States, those who benefit from the system of distribution define objective inequality as just, while those who do not benefit (the 'underdogs') define objective inequality as unjust. More research identifying the impact of general cultural, social and economic conditions on justice-related attitudes and behaviour is needed. Contributors to a recent volume by Lerner and Lerner (1981) attempt to specify how economic conditions of demand and supply affect preferences for particular distribution principles and the perceived justness of these principles. Greenberg (1981) has examined the impact of scarcity. Both the theoretical and policy implications of different distributions and distributional procedures for collective action and social change must be specified in subsequent research.

Karen S. Cook
University of Washington

References

Eckhoff, T. (1974), *Justice: Its Determinants in Social Interaction*, Rotterdam.

Greenberg, J. (1981), 'The justice of distributing scarce and abundant resources', in M. J. Lerner and S. C. Lerner (eds), *The Justice Motive in Social Behavior*, New York.

Lerner, M. J. and Lerner, S. C. (eds) (1981), *The Justice Motive in Social Behavior*, New York.

Rawls, J. (1971), *A Theory of Justice*, Cambridge, Mass.

Robinson, R. V. and Bell, W. (1978), 'Equality, success and social justice in England and the United States', *American Sociological Review*, 43.

Elections

In politics elections are a device whereby popular preferences are aggregated to choose an officeholder. Choice by elections is now almost inseparable from representative democracy. Some see the opportunity for choice at periodic elections as the key element of Western democracy (Schumpeter, 1942; Lipset,

1960). As of 1975, 33 states did not hold elections to choose political leaders. For other states the crucial question is: what sort of elections? A further 33 states allowed only one candidate for each office. These are 'consent' elections (Mackenzie, 1958). States which allow competitive elections and the possibility of replacing the government are largely Western.

Election systems provide guidelines on such matters as who votes and how, frequency of election, how votes are counted, who stands for office and so on. In the twentieth century, most states have granted the vote to all (with a few exceptions) adult resident citizens. Over time, the suffrage has been extended from estates to individuals, and in the twentieth century to large categories formerly excluded on grounds of race, sex and property qualifications. The change has also been to equality or 'one man one vote one value' (Rokkan, 1970).

In most states, responsibility for registering eligible voters lies with the government. A significant exception is the United States, where states leave registration to individuals. This partly explains why the turn-out in presidential elections since 1960 has averaged 60 per cent, compared to over 80 per cent in many Western states. But American voters have more opportunities to cast votes, in federal, state, local and primary elections, and in long ballots. At the other extreme, political and cultural pressures may produce remarkable turn-outs and verdicts, for example 99.9 per cent turn-out in East Germany in 1964.

Elections have several functions (Rose and Mossawir, 1967). These include: (1) designating, directly or indirectly, the government; (2) providing feedback between voters and government; (3) demonstrating public support for or repudiation of a regime: (4) providing a means for the recruitment of political leaders, and (5) making the government answerable to the electorate. Functions may differ in states which have elections without choice, where a party's hegemonic or monopolistic position makes the outcome a foregone conclusion (Hermet *et al*, 1978).

In some countries (Belgium, Italy, Denmark and the Netherlands, for example) it is not the election but the inter-party bargaining following the election which determines the composition of government. Where the party system provides a choice between alternative potential majorities, voters do have such a choice. The impact of elections on policies depends in part on a programmatic disciplined majority party being in government. Until recently, the British two-party system was admired for providing a model of 'responsible party government'. More direct popular verdicts on issues may be made through referendums.

The nature of the electoral choice in each state is shaped by three sets of factors: (1) The *object* of election, for example, to choose a constituency representative, party list or President. (2) The *party system*, or pattern of voting alignments (Lipset and Rokkan, 1967). In turn this is shaped by cleavages in society, the electoral system, and the manœuvres of élites. (3) The *electoral system*, particularly those provisions which aggregate votes and translate them into seats, that is, rules for counting and weighing votes.

A distinction may be drawn between the absolute majoritarian system, as in France, in which the 'winner' has to achieve at least half the votes; the plurality (first past the post) system in many English-speaking countries; the various forms of proportionalism, including the pure Proportional Representation in the Netherlands (where 0.67 per cent of the vote gives a group a seat in the legislature); and those that combine elements of different systems (for example, West Germany has P. R. for half the seats, subject to a party gaining at least 5 per cent of the vote).

Proportionalism was introduced at the turn of the century in divided societies to provide guarantees to minorities which felt threatened by universal suffrage or majority rule. Proportionalism furthers the goals of representativeness but, in the absence of a clear party majority, makes the choice of government less certain.

The British plurality system has usually achieved certainty in choice of the government while sacrificing representativeness. In October 1974 Labour had 51 per cent of the seats in the House of Commons with 39 per cent of the votes. The two systems maximize different values; most Western states have opted for proportionalism, subject to qualifications.

We lack a good typology of elections. One may distinguish between degrees of choice, which in turn depends on the number of effective parties and the prospects of turnover in government. The United States has two parties, the Netherlands and Denmark a dozen. Italy, Sweden and Norway have had very long spells of dominant one-party rule, and there has been only one change in France since 1958. In the United States, Key (1955) distinguished between elections which were *maintaining* (reflecting normal party loyalties), *deviating* (in which short-term factors produced a short-term surge or decline in support for the parties), and *realigning* (in which there is a long-term change in the balance of party strengths).

There are limits on the decisiveness of elections as authoritative arbiters of policy. Incumbents of the bureaucracy and judiciary, and leaders of powerful interests, who are not elected by the voters, constitute checks. At present 'votes count, resources decide' (Rokkan, 1966). The debate about the relative influence of socioeconomic factors or party political factors (and therefore elections) has not been conclusive. The influence of the government depends on the power centralization in society. In pluralist and market societies the government is only one decision maker among others, and competitive elections and majority rule are only two elements in representative democracy. Competitive elections do not ensure the political responsiveness of an élite; they have to operate in favourable conditions. There are alternative methods of facilitating popular choice and eliciting and demonstrating popular consent (for example, acclamation, seniority, rotation, and élite bargaining), but election is still the birthmark of a government claiming to be democratic.

Dennis Kavanagh
University of Nottingham

References

Hermet, G. *et al.* (1978), *Elections Without Choice*, Paris.

Key, V. O. Jr (1955), 'A theory of critical elections', *Journal of Politics*.

Lipset, S. (1960), *Political Man*, London.

Lipset, S. and Rokkan, S. (eds) (1967), *Party Systems and Voter Alignments*, New York.

Mackenzie, W. J. M. (1958), *Free Elections*, London.

Rokkan, S. (1966), 'Norway: numerical democracy and corporate pluralism', in R. Dahl (ed.), *Political Oppositions in Western Democracies*, New Haven.

Rokkan, S. (1970), *Citizens, Elections, Parties*, New York.

Rose, R. and Mossawir, H. (1967), 'Voting and elections: a functional analysis', *Political Studies*.

Schumpeter, J. A. (1942), *Capitalism, Socialism and Democracy*, New York.

See also: *democracy; parties, political; voting.*

Élites

The term élite is part of a tradition which makes modern social scientists uneasy. At the same time, its use facilitates historical and contemporary analysis by providing an idiom of comparison that sets aside institutional details and culture-specific practices, and calls attention instead to intuitively understood equivalencies. Typically, an adjective precedes the word 'élite', clarifying its aim (oligarchic élite, modernizing élite), or its style (innovating élite, brokerage élite), or its institutional domain (legislative élite, bureaucratic élite), or its resources base (media élite, financial élite), or the decisional stage it dominates (planning élite, implementing élite), or its eligibility grounds (birth élite, credentialed élite).

Two quite different traditions of inquiry persist. In the older tradition, élites are treated as exemplars: fulfilling some historic mission, meeting a crucial need, possessing superior talents, or otherwise demonstrating qualities which set them apart. Whether they stabilize the old order or transform it into a new one, they are seen as pattern setters.

In the newer approach, élites are routinely understood to be incumbents: those who are collectively the influential figures in the governance of any sector of society, any institutional structure, any geographic locality or translocal community. Idiomatically, élites are thus roughly the same as leaders, decision makers or influentials, and not too different from spokesmen, dignitaries, or central figures. This second usage is more matter-of-fact, less normative in tone.

Still, élites are seen by many as selfish people in power, bent upon protecting their vested interests, contemptuous of the restraints on constitutional order, callous about the needs of larger publics, ready to manipulate opinion, to rig elections, to use force if necessary to retain power. A conspiratorial variant worries those who fear revolutionary subversive élites: fanatical, selfless, disciplined, competent, and devoted to their cause; equally contemptuous of political democracy, constitutional order, or mass contentment; willing to exploit hatred and misery, to misrepresent beliefs and facts, and to face personal degradation and social obloquy. Whether to preserve old patterns of life or to exemplify new ones, élites are those who set the styles.

When most social scientists talk about élites, they have in mind 'those who run things' – that is, certain key actors playing structured, functionally understandable roles, not only in a nation's governance processes but also in other institutional settings – religious, military, academic, industrial, communications, and so on (Czudnowski, 1982, 1983).

Earlier formulations lacked this pluralist assumption. Mosca and Pareto (see Meisel, 1965) both presumed that a ruling class effectively monopolized the command posts of a society. Michels insisted that his 'iron law of oligarchy' was inevitable; in any organization, an inner circle of participants would take over, and run it for their own selfish purposes. By contrast, Lasswell's formulation in the 1930s was radically pluralistic. Élites are those who get the most of what there is to get in any instititionalized sector of society and not only in the governing institutions and ancillary processes of organized political life. At every functional stage of any decision process – indeed, in any relevant arena – some participants will be found who have sequestered disproportionate shares of those values, whether money, esteem, power, or some other condition of life which people seek and struggle for. They are the élite at that stage and in that context. For Lasswell (1977), the question whether a situation is fully egalitarian – that is, extends élite status to every participant – is an empirical question, not a conceptual one. Nor is there necessarily any insitutional stability. Macro-analysis of history shows periods of ascendancy for those with different kinds of skills, such as in the use of violence, propaganda, organization, or bargaining strategy.

The social formations – classes, communities, movements – from which élites derive are not fixed, either. Élites are usefully studied by asking which communities they represent or dominate, which classes they are exponents or products of, which interests they reflect or foreshadow, which personality types they are prone to recruit or to shunt aside, which circumstances of time and place (periods of crisis, tranquility, or transition) seem to provide missions and challenges for them.

Élites may change their character. Élite transformation has often been traced. Pareto saw vitality and decay as an endless cycle. Students of Third-World modernization often note the heightened tensions within a governing élite that accompany the shift in power from a revolutionary-agitational generation to a programmatic-executive generation. Specialized élites – engineers, soldiers, priests – have often served as second-tier élites, recruited in the service of a ruling class that continues to set a governing style but whose members lack the skills to cope with new and pressing problems. Some scholars hold that a true élite emerges when those who perform the historic mission – whether to bring change, adapt to change, or resist to the end – become convinced that only they can carry out the mission properly. Self-consciously, they come to think of themselves as superior by nature – for example, able to think like scientists or soldiers, willing to take risks like capitalists or revolutionaries (Thoenes, 1965).

For some centuries, the historical forces that have been shaping the institutions of modern, urban, industrial, inter-dependent, institutionally-differentiated societies have had a net effect that enlarges, democratizes and equalizes the life-chances for élitehood. Everywhere the political stratification system typically resembles a pyramid, reflecting the striking cross-national uniformity that only tiny fractions of a country's citizens have more than an infinitesimal chance of directly influencing national policy or even translocal policies. At the same time, fewer disadvantages linked to social status, educational attainment, geographic residence, cultural claims, age and sex attributes, or institutional credentials appear to operate nowadays as conclusively or comprehensively as in the past.

Viewed as incumbents, those who hold key positions in the governing institutions of a community are, collectively, the élite. They are the custodians of the machinery for making policy. Once a sector of society becomes institutionally differentiated, its ability to adjust to conditions on its own terms is likely to be seriously constrained. Even within its semi-autonomous domains, a custodial élite finds it hard to sustain a liaison network or co-ordinate sector-wide efforts (Field and Higley, 1980). Medical élites are typically locality-rooted. Military services feud with one another. Scientists are engrossed with specialized lines of inquiry. Commercial élites are fragmented. Industrial giants are rivals.

In the modern world, when élites are seen as housed within conventionally recognized establishments such as military, diplomatic, legislative, or party organizational structures, mid-élites and cadres are linked hierarchically to top élites and specialized to implement the specific public and system goals of their domains. When élites are viewed as the top talent in a vocational field – lawyers, academics, entrepreneurs, and so on – the élite structure is much more disjointed. Mid-élites are the source of eligible talent, engaged in tasks having no necessary articulation with what top élites do, but nonetheless tasks that train and test, groom and screen individuals who may in due course reach top élitehood in their field (Putnam, 1976).

Top élites in a custodial structure do not necessarily work well together. The structural complexity of legislatures is such that they typically have rather segmented power structures. In characterizing a military élite, the rivalries of services and branches, the geographic deployment and the generational gaps between echelons all must be acknowledged (Janowitz, 1960). The illusion of homogeneity about the administrative élite is dispelled when one looks closely (Dogan, 1975). Career services give some coherence to relatively autonomous fields, like police, fire, diplomacy, health. But in specific policy domains, clientele élites often dominate the picture (Armstrong, 1973).

Especially when talking about élites in rather amorphous fields of endeavour, the implications of structural disjunctions on the perspectives of those in top positions seem far reaching. Most communications élites are set at working odds with one another in the various media where their contacts and skills apply. At community levels, civic leaders rarely sustain close contacts with their counterparts in other localities.

Élites are studied both in context, in what can be called élite characterization work, and out of context, in what is referred to as élite survey work. There are two main genres of the former – namely, those in which élites are characterized by their mission or function, and those in which élites are seen in a custodial capacity, and characterized by the performance of the institutional processes they control. In a corresponding way, élite surveys – in which élites are taken out of context – also have two main genres: those in which the investigator is mainly interested in what élites think, in the acumen, loyalty, and ideological bent of mind typical of certain élite perspectives; and those which explore the recruitment of élite figures by looking at the changing opportunity structure, at social credentials, screening criteria, processes of sponsorship, grooming and socialization, and at those who are the gatekeepers, brokers, mentors who affect the *corsus honorum* of a career. In modern systematic survey work, it is customary at the outset to say how, when and where the élite status of those studied has been established, whether by reputation, position held, or process participated in. Interviews are then held, often rather long interviews, to learn their beliefs, perceptions, preferences and appraisals. Necessarily, in survey work, élites are not studied 'in action'.

Dwaine Marvick
University of California, Los Angeles

References

Armstrong, J. A. (1973), *The European Administrative Elite*, Princeton.

Czudnowski, M. N. (ed.) (1982), *Does Who Governs Matter?*, DeKalb, Ill.

Czudnowski, M. N. (ed.) (1983), *Political Elites and Social Change*, DeKalb, Ill.

Dogan, M. (ed.) (1975), *The Mandarins of Western Europe*, New York.

Eulau, H. and Czudnowski, M. (eds) (1979), *Elite Recruitment in Democratic Polities*, New York.

Field, G. L. and Higley, J. (1980), *The Professional Soldier*, Glencoe, Ill.

Lasswell, H. D. (1977), 'The study of political elites', in D. Marvick (ed.), *Harold D. Lasswell on Political Sociology*, Chicago.

Mosca, G. (1939 [1896]), *The Ruling Class*, ed. A. Livingston, New York. (Original Italian edn, *Elementi di Scienza parlamentare*.)

Putnam, R. D. (1976), *The Comparative Study of Political Elites*, Englewood Cliffs, N.J.

Thoenes, P. (1966), *The Elite in the Welfare State*, Glencoe, Ill.

See also: *leadership; political recruitment and careers.*

Equality

'We hold,' wrote Thomas Jefferson (1747–1826), 'these truths to be sacred and undeniable; that all men are created equal and independent . . .' No natural scientist *qua* scientist could do other than dismiss such a statement as either meaningless or empirically false. Equality for a mathematician is a concept of some complexity in relation, for example, to identity or correlation, but one of no moral significance. Social scientists by contrast are latecomers to a debate about equality which is unresolved because it adds to the mathematician's complexity the further complications of moral argument. Equality refers to the principles on which human society ought, as well as might, be based. Jefferson's was a moral declaration, not an empirical description. Social science attempts to explore the empirical validity of such declarations. The question is whether, and in what sense, social, political, and economic equalities are possible. The answer is tentative, requiring the determination of the origins of inequality, the significance of inequality, and the viability of action intended to establish equality. All three aspects are disputed.

Traditional discussion of the origins of inequality turned on a crude distinction between nature and society. Modern recognition of cultural evolution complicates that distinction and tends to substitute a more elaborate matrix out of the consequences of interaction between genetic and environmental influences. But in neither simple nor sophisticated discussion is there denial of natural inequalities, the Jeffersonian declaration notwithstanding. Men are not clones, and Mendelian genetics guarantees variation. Dispute, however, persists in important areas of scientific ignorance. For example, there is not adequate scientific evidence to settle the dispute between those who believe in the genetic basis of differences between ethnic or racial or class groups in educational attainment or performance in intelligence tests, and those who hold such differences to be socially created. Resolution of such disputes is, in principle, possible through the further advance of empirically tested theories of the interaction between heredity and environment.

Meanwhile dispute about the significance of natural differences continues its long history. Plato confidently argued from natural to political inequality. Hobbes in *Leviathan* (1934 [1651]), expressed the opposite view:

Nature hath made man so equall, in the faculties of body, and mind; as that though bee found one man sometimes manifestly stronger in body, or of quicker mind than another; yet when all is reckoned together, the difference between man and man, is not so considerable, as that one man can thereupon claim to himself and benefit, to which another may not pretend, as well as he.

Hobbes's formulation still defines the debate. Egalitarian claims, especially with respect to race and gender, are more strident now than they were in the seventeenth century, and we would now say that Hobbes was making empirical propositions from both genetics and sociology, the one referring to natural differences and the other (about claiming and pretending) referring to the social psychology of man's perceptions of social rights. But the central assertion is fundamentally about the values which ought to be reflected in the actual relations of men and women in society.

In this sense the debate, turning as it does on ethical priorities between such values as equality, liberty, and fraternity, may never be finally resolvable. There have been, to be sure, notable recent contributions to greater conceptual clarity as to the meaning of terms. John Rawls (1971) adopts the device of the 'original position' – an 'if so' story of the rational choices that might be expected from an individual contemplating different societies with known different equalities or inequalities of positions but an unknown placement for the contemplator – to illuminate the problems of value choice. Brian Barry (1973) takes the discussion further to demonstrate how a small adjustment to Rawls's social and psychological assumptions opens the possibility of a crucial shift of preference towards egalitarian rather than liberal forms of society. But no amount of conceptual clarification, sophisticated or erudite, solves the problem of evaluation.

The social sciences can, however, note the provenance of different priorities. One mundane but momentous perspective recurs down the ages – the recognition of mortality. Thus Horace (65–8 BC) wrote: 'Pale death kicks his way equally into the cottages of the poor and the castles of kings.' And James Shirley (1596–1666) reminds us that:

Death lays his icy hand on kings
  Sceptre and crown
  Must tumble down

And in the dust be equal made
With the poor crooked scythe and spade.

This attitude is integral to Christian social teaching, which dominated the evaluation of equality at least until the eighteenth century. It was not that natural inequalities between individuals were denied so much as deemed irrelevant in discussing the rights and wrongs of dictatorship or democracy, freedom or slavery. Christians were not only 'equal before the Cross' but, as the early Church Fathers insisted, would, if they eschewed sin, live like brothers without inequalities of property and power. Sin, since the fall of Adam, had created earthly inequality. Political inequality might be necessary to protect order and restrain evil, but it did not arise, as Plato had imagined, from natural inequality. Political inequality in Christian tradition must be endured but by no means implied a necessary respect or admiration for the rich and the powerful. On the contrary, position in the next world was typically held to be threatened by privilege in this. 'He hath put down the mighty from their seat and hath exalted the humble and meek,' says the Magnificat.

The break with Christian attitudes of submission to inequality dates from the eighteenth century, with the decline of religious belief and the beginnings of a secular optimism with respect to the possibility of social transformation. Egalitarianism as a movement is commonly associated with Rousseau. But Rousseau, though believing that the evils of unfreedom and inequality were socially created, was a remorseless pessimist. He held that freedom was impossible except in a community of equals, but held out no hope of social transformation towards equality. In this sense he was a child of Christianity, and if the early socialists (Fourier, Proudhon, Saint-Simon, Robert Owen, William Thompson) were his intellectual children they were also crucially different in entertaining the hope of progress. Modern egalitarianism derives from this form of sociological optimism, and it was encouraged by, if by no means identical with, either the Hegelian idealist or Marxist materialist theories of the inevitability of social transformation. Hegel's elaborate analysis of the relation between masters and slaves, and Marx's development of it into a prediction of the future history of the working class, hold out the possibility of a community of equals.

However, egalitarianism does not presuppose either the Hegelian or the Marxist theory of history. Its more fruitful contemporary discussion in the social sciences proceeds on assumptions of openness or voluntarism as opposed to necessitous history. These debates are the substance of the third aspect of the equality problem – the viability of deliberate social action aimed at reducing inequality. One theoretical approach deserves mention here because it avoids both liberal evolutionist determinism and the alternative Marxist historicism. This is T. H. Marshall's interpretation of the development of citizenship in advanced industrial societies (Marshall, 1950). He shows in the case of Britain how the basic equality of membership in a society, which is rooted in the civil rights established in the eighteenth century, was extended to include political rights in the ninctccnth century and certain social rights in the twentieth century, when citizenship and class have been at war as opposing principles of social distribution. Marshall's analysis also brings out the important truth that the forces which influence the distribution of life chances are neither mechanical nor irreversible. Class displaced feudal status with formal equality of market relations, as well as ushering in new inequalities of social condition. Citizenship promotes unequal rewards as well as equal rights, for example state scholarships to selective university admission and universal political franchise. More generally, it may be noted that no social goal, equality, efficiency, liberty, order or fraternity may be regarded as absolute. Public policies are perforce compromises aiming at optimal balance between desired ends.

Three illustrations of the limits to egalitarianism are prominent in recent writing in the form of arguments against the viability of egalitarian theory:

(1) This concerns the immutability of occupational hierarchy, postulating a *de facto* necessity for some jobs to be more distasteful, unrewarding, and injurious to health than others. Given that life chances are largely determined by the individ-

ual's occupation, a hierarchy of social advantage seems to be inescapable, and equality, as opposed to equality of opportunity, therefore unobtainable. But, egalitarians reply, a less inegalitarian society is not sociologically impossible. It is not difficult to imagine a wide range of counteracting social policies. Apart from progressive taxation and levies on wealth, there could be national service specifically designed to direct the advantaged to a period of distasteful labour. The obvious rejoinders are lodged in the name of liberty and economic efficiency, again emphasizing the relativist character of claims for any social principle. Value choice is always the nub of the issue.

(2) An illustration may be had from Christopher Jencks's *Inequality* (1972), which essentially argues the importance of educational reform as an instrument of egalitarianism and stresses the role of chance or luck in the unequal distribution of income and occupational status. Schooling explains only 12 per cent of the variance in American incomes. But Jencks's argument is flawed in that his evidence is about the distribution of individuals over a given structure of occupations and wages. The explanation of inequality of income accruing to jobs is not what would explain who happens to hold those jobs. Whether the inequality of the job structure is immutable remains an open question.

(3) Finally, there is the alleged obstacle of genetic differences between races and classes of which Jensen has been an oustanding proponent (Jensen, 1972). As to classes, and against Jensen's marshalling of the evidence from studies of twins reared apart, there is the opposed conclusion of Schiff (1982) from his studies of cross-class adopted children in France. As to race, it has to be said that we do not yet have the techniques or the data to measure definitively the genetic and environmental influences on race-IQ differences. Nor does the answer really matter, for there are more important issues of equality and justice in present-day society which do not have to wait upon further advances in the social sciences.

A. H. Halsey
University of Oxford

References
Barry, B. (1973), *The Liberal Theory of Justice*, Oxford.
Hobbes, T. (1934 [1651]), *Leviathan* (London Everyman edn, 1934).
Jencks, C. (1972), *Inequality*, New York.
Jensen, A. (1972), *Genetics and Education*, London.
Marshall, T. H. (1950), *Citizenship and Social Class*, Cambridge.
Rawls, J. (1971), *A Theory of Justice*, Cambridge, Mass.
Schiff, M. (1982), *L'Intelligence Gaspillée*, Paris.

Further Reading
Letwin, W. (ed.) (1983), *Against Equality: Readings on Economic and Social Policy*, London.
Runciman, W. G. (1966), *Relative Deprivation and Social Justice*, London.
Tawney, R. H. (1952), *Equality*, (4th rev. edn), London.
See also: *distributive justice*.

Evolutionism and Progress

Evolutionism is the label now commonly used for a current of thought which was strongly represented in the anthropology and sociology of the nineteenth century. Although it fed on biological analogies, it must be clearly distinguished from Darwinian thinking. Its inspiration came rather from the older tradition of Lamarckian evolutionary theory, which provided the main rival to Darwinian theory until well into the twentieth century. Key elements in this tradition were the beliefs that organisms were intrinsically bound to improve themselves, that changes were progressive and often radical and sudden, and that acquired characters could be transmitted genetically. Typically, the 'stages' of ontogeny, or the individual life history, were taken to exemplify the 'stages' of phylogeny, the developmet of a species.

Herbert Spencer, one of the most consistent exponents of the organic analogy in the social sciences, was perhaps the leading evolutionist in sociology, but these general ideas were taken for granted by authors as diverse as Marx, Freud and Durkheim, and they survived in some modern theories in anthropology (for example, Childe, 1951), in the psychologial theory of Piaget, in 'Whig' history, and so on. The 'evolutionist' assumptions were, however, directly in contradiction to the Darwinian theory of evolution by variation and natural selection, which did not assume the existence of any progressive line of change. On the contrary, Darwin (1859) stated emphatically that 'I believe in no fixed law of development' (*On the Origin of Species*).

Evolutionist theory in the social sciences should perhaps be regarded as part of a broader tradition of theories of 'progress', which represents the most deeply entrenched way of conceptualizing social history in the West. It has a particular appeal to 'progressive' radicals and utopians, while the mirror-image theory, that the trend of history is towards social and cultural decadence, is, on the other hand, associated rather with right-wing political theories and with religious revivalism. Whether the unit of perfectibility was assumed to be humanity or a particular civilization or 'race', the theory was so abstract and value-laden as almost to defy empirical reference. Nisbett (1980), nevertheless, argues that the faith in progress has been eroded by a widespread scepticism about the unique superiority of contemporary Western civilization.

Adam Kuper
Brunel University, Uxbridge

References
Childe, G. (1951), *Social Evolution*, London.
Nisbett, R. (1980), *History of the Idea of Progress*, New York.

Further Reading
Mayr, E. (1982), *The Growth of Biological Thought*, Cambridge, Mass.
Peel, J. D. Y. (ed.) (1972), *Herbert Spencer on Social Evolution*, Chicago.
Stocking, G. (1968), *Race, Culture and Evolution*, New York.

Factions

A faction is a coalition of individuals personally recruited by, or on behalf of, an individual in competition with another individual or coalition with whom he was formerly united. Factions compete for honour and/or the control of resources. The central focus of a faction is the leader who has recruited it. Ties between leader and followers are usually personal, although followers sometimes recruit others on behalf of their leader. Factionalism – the competition between factions for scarce resources or power – can take many forms and has been recorded in all parts of the world, although the most numerous and detailed descriptions come from India. Factions are fundamental political units and factionalism the most elementary political process.

The earliest interest in factions came from political scientists (Lasswell, 1931), while social anthropologists only became aware of their significance during the past few decades. Firth (1957) was the first to attempt to set out systematically some of their functions and structural characteristics. He treated them as informal counterparts of more formal political groupings, and noted that members were recruited according to structurally diverse principles. This approach was elaborated by Nicholas a decade later (1965), who viewed factions as essentially symmetrically organized conflict groups in balanced opposition to each other. Factionalism occurred in situations of rapid social change and was one of the processes of adjustment leading to a situation of dynamic equilibrium (Siegel and Beals, 1966). The study of factionalism during the following decades reflected more general theoretical changes in the social sciences. Those interested in factions abandoned notions of dynamic equilibrium and balanced opposition, fundamental to the structural-functional mode of analysis (Silverman and Salisbury, 1978).

Competing factions are asymmetrical, and recruitment of members, while structurally diverse, is not random. Sometimes it manifests a definite class bias. Factionalism can bring about change. It is not exclusively a product of changes in the wider society. Rival factions, far from being in balanced opposition, differ in respect to access to resources and strategy, internal organization, ideology, social composition and symbolism. Although the number of competing factions can vary, there are usually two. Often one is associated with the dominant power configuration in the community, focusing on the headman, chief, or dominant landlord. This coalition forms the establishment. It is usually conservative; it has access to a range of resources, including the most important cultural symbols, and it tends to be defensive and concerned with protecting its superior position. Aligned against this power bloc is a category of persons who are dissatisfied with the way in which those with superior power wield it. Although initially they may be merely disgruntled, they may later organize a rival coalition and compete for resources. They form the opposition faction. Opposition factions, if they persist over time, tend to develop a more tightly-knit organizational structure in order to compete effectively against their more powerful rival.

Because factionalism takes place in a social framework in which unity and consensus is generally regarded as an ideal, it is seen as divisive, a temporary unpleasantness, the details of which should not be discussed with outsiders. Factionalism is basic to most communities and an intrinsic part of political life. In many societies factions have become permanent ritual moieties or political parties, embellished with a range of cultural and symbolic trappings.

Jeremy Boissevain
University of Amsterdam

References
Firth, R. (1957), 'Introduction: factions in Indian and overseas societies', *British Journal of Sociology*, 8.
Lasswell, H. D. (1931), 'Faction', *Encyclopedia of the Social Sciences*, New York.
Nicholas, R. W. (1965), 'Factions: a comparative analysis', in M. Banton (ed.), *Political Systems and the Distribution of Power*, London.

Siegel, B. J. and Beals, A. R. (1966), *Divisiveness and Social Conflict: An Anthropological Approach*, Stanford.

Silverman, M. and Salisbury, R. S. (1978), *A House Divided? Anthropological Studies of Factionalism*, Dalhousie.

See also: *coalitions*; *leadership*.

Fascism

Of all the major terms in twentieth-century political usage, fascism has tended to remain one of the most vague. At the popular level, it has become during the past two generations little more than a derogatory epithet employed to denigrate a bewildering variety of otherwise mutually contradictory political phenomena. It has been applied at one time or another to virtually every single form of twentieth-century radicalism or authoritarianism, as well as many more moderate phenomena. More specifically, in terms of political regimes, there has developed since the 1930s a broad tendency to refer to any form of right-wing authoritarian system that is not specifically socialist as fascist. In this usage the Italian regime of Benito Mussolini is used as terminological prototype for all non-Marxist or non-socialist authoritarian systems, however they may differ from Italian Fascism or among themselves.

Rigorous scholarly and historical definition of fascism however, refers to the concrete historical phenomena of the European fascist movements that emerged between the two World Wars, first in the Italian Fascist and German National Socialist movements founded in 1919–20 and then among their numerous counterparts in many European countries. An adequate political and historical definition of fascism must define common unique characteristics of all the fascist movements in Europe during the 1920s and 1930s while at the same time differentiating them from other political phenomena. Such a criterial definition must specify (1) the typical fascist negations; (2) fascist doctrine and goals, and (3) the uniqueness of fascist style and organization.

The uniqueness of fascism lay in its opposition to nearly all the existing political sectors, left, right, and centre. It was antiliberal, anticommunist (as well as antisocialist in the social democratic sense), and anti-conservative, though willing to undertake temporary alliances with other groups, primarily rightist.

In their ideology and political goals, fascist movements represented the most intense and radical form of nationalism known to modern Europe. They aimed at the creation of a new kind of nationalist authoritarian state that was not merely based on traditional principles or models. Though fascist groups differed considerably among themselves on economic goals, they all hoped to organize some new kind of regulated, multiclass, integrated national economic structure, diversely called national corporatist, national socialist or national syndicalist. All fascist movements aimed either at national imperial expansion or at least at a radical change in the nation's relationship with other powers to enhance its strength and prestige. Their doctrines rested on a philosophical basis of idealism and voluntarism, and normally involved the attempt to create a new form of modern, self-determined secular culture.

Fascist uniqueness was particularly expressed through the movements' style and organization. Great emphasis was placed on the aesthetic structure of meetings, symbols, and political choreography, relying especially on romantic and mystical aspects. Fascist movements all attempted to achieve mass mobilization, together with the militarization of political relationships and style and with the goal of a mass party militia. Unlike some other types of radicals, fascists placed strong positive evaluation on the use of violence, and strongly stressed the masculine principle and male dominance. Though they espoused an organic concept of society, they vigorously championed a new élitism and exalted youth above other phases of life. In leadership, fascist movements exhibited a specific tendency toward an authoritarian, charismatic, personal style of command (the *Führerprinzip*, in German National Socialist parlance).

Radical rightist groups shared some of the fascists' political goals, just as revolutionary leftist movements exhibited some of their stylistic and organizational characteristics. The uniqueness of the fascists, however, lay in their rejection of the cultural and economic conservatism, and the particular social élitism of the right, just as they rejected the internationalism, nominal egalitarianism and materialist socialism of the left. The historical uniqueness of fascism can be better grasped once it is realized that significant political movements sharing all – not merely some – of these common characteristics existed only in Europe during the years 1919–45.

Fascists claimed to represent all classes of national society, particularly the broad masses. Marxists and some others, conversely, claimed that they were no more than the tool of the most violent, monopolistic and reactionary sectors of the bourgeoisie. Both of these extreme interpretations are not supported by empirical evidence. In their earliest phase, fascist movements drew their followers from among former military personnel and small sectors of the radical intelligentsia, in some cases university students. Though some fascist movements enjoyed a degree of backing from the upper bourgeoisie, the broadest sector of fascist support, comparatively speaking, was provided by the lower middle class. Since this was one of the largest strata in European society during the 1920s and 1930s, the same might also have been said for various other political groups. In both Italy and Germany, a notable minority of party members were drawn from among urban workers. In Hungary and Romania primary social backing came from university students and poor peasants, and there was also considerable agrarian support in some parts of Italy.

A bewildering variety of theories and interpretations have been advanced since 1923 to explain fascism. Among them are (1) theories of socioeconomic causation of various kinds, primarily of Marxist inspiration; (2) concepts of psychocultural motivation related to social psychology and personality and social structures; (3) the application of modernization theory, which posits fascism as a phase in modern development. (4) the theory of totalitarianism, which interprets fascism as one aspect of the broader phenomenon of twentieth-century totalitarianism; and (5) historicist interpretations, which attempt multicausal explanation in terms of the major dimensions of central European historical development in the early twentieth century.

The only fascist movements to establish independent regimes of their own were those of Benito Mussolini (1922–43) and Adolf Hitler (1933–45), and only in the latter case did the movement's leader achieve complete power over the state. The other countries in which fascist movements were strongest were Austria (Austrian National Socialists), Hungary (Arrow Cross), Romania (Iron Guard), and Spain (Spanish Phalanx). In general, fascism had most appeal in countries defeated or destabilized by the effects of World War I. Though fascist movements appeared in every single European country during these years (and also, very faintly, in the countries of the western hemisphere and Japan, paralleled by more vigorous expression in South Africa), very few of them enjoyed any degree of success. In nearly all countries antifascists were generally much more numerous than fascists. The extreme radicalism and calls to war and violence of the fascists limited their appeal, as did the nonrationalist, voluntarist nature of their doctrines. The great expansion of military power by Hitler's Germany was mainly responsible for the broader influence and historical importance achieved by fascism for a few years. Similarly, the complete defeat of Germany and Italy in the war condemned fascism to such total political destruction and historical discredit that all attempts at revival have enjoyed only miniscule support since 1945.

Stanley G. Payne
University of Wisconsin

Further Reading

Laqueur, W. (ed.) (1976), *Fascism: A Reader's Guide*, Berkeley and Los Angeles.

Larsen, S. U. *et al.* (eds) (1980), *Who were the Fascists: Social Roots of European Fascism*, Bergen-Oslo.

Payne, S. G. (1980), *Fascism: Comparison and Definition*, Madison.

See also: *nationalism*; *radicalism*.

Federalism

Federalism is a way of organizing a state so that there is a division of powers between general and regional governments each independent within a sphere (Wheare, 1946). The territory of a federal state is divided into units (for example, states, cantons, provinces, republics) which often coincide with distinctive geographic, cultural or historic divisions of the country. Many of the institutions of government are duplicated at the national and local levels with both levels of government exercising effective control over the same territory and population. Thus, the citizens of a federal state belong simultaneously to two political communities: for those functions which are constitutionally assigned to the local level of government, the relevant community is the citizen's particular state, canton, province or republic; for functions assigned to the national government, the entire nation is the relevant community.

In a true federal state, both levels of government derive their powers directly from the constitution and neither is able to eliminate the other's jurisdiction. In this way a federal state is distinguished from a unitary state with territorial sub-units (such as counties, departments, districts) that receive all of their powers by delegation from a central government. At the other extreme, a federal system of government should be distinguished from a confederation, or league of states, in which the central level of government receives all its powers from the member states and has no autonomous powers of its own.

The United States of America was the first modern nation-state to adopt a federal constitution. In the nineteenth century some of the new states of South and Central America (for example, Venezuela, Colombia, Argentina, Brazil and Mexico) were organized on federal lines. But federal constitutions have been of less enduring significance there than in Switzerland (1848), Canada (1867) and Australia (1901) which, along with the United States, are the countries which have been practising federal constitutionalism without interruption for the longest time. In the twentieth century many of the constitutions established in the process of world-wide political reorganization following the two World Wars have incorporated the federal principle. Federalism has been a feature of constitutions adopted by many of Britain's former colonies (among them, India, Pakistan, Malaysia, and Nigeria) (Watts, 1966). In Europe, it is prominent in the constitution of the Federal Republic of Germany and is provided for in the constitution of two communist states, Yugoslavia and the USSR.

The balance of power and of citizens' allegiance between the two levels of government is a dynamic element in the politics of a federal state. In some federations, the forces of centralization, especially when fostered by a single unified political party, may be so strong as to negate the autonomy of the local level of government. In others, the forces of decentralization may be such that they lead to the break-up of the federal state (as in the case of British West Indian Federation). For a federal system to endure, there must be significant independent political forces supporting each level of government.

Peter H. Russell
University of Toronto

References
Watts, R. L. (1966), *New Federation: Experiments in the Commonwealth*, Oxford.
Wheare, K. C. (1946), *Federal Government*, Oxford.

Further Reading
Bowie, R. R. and Friedrich, C. J. (1954), *Studies in Federalism*, Boston.
MacMahon, A. W. (ed.) (1962), *Federalism – Mature and Emergent*, New York.
Riker, W. H. (1964), *Federalism: Origin, Operation, Significance*, Boston.
See also: *constitutions and constitutionalism*.

Freedom

Freedom is the constitutive value of European political life, in that slaves, lacking freedom, must submit to a master, while free men, being equal in respect of being free, constitute for themselves a government which secures order by law, and not by the unchecked will of a master. It is on this basis that Europeans have always distinguished their civil societies from the despotisms of the Orient, in which (according to the account commonly given in Western political thought) all submit to a master.

Among the ancient Greeks, *eleutheria* was the adult condition in which a free male left behind the tutelage of childhood and took his place among fellow citizens in the public life of the *agora*, ruling and being ruled in turn. For the Romans, *libertas* was the quality of the free plebeian and corresponded to the *dignitas* of the patrician. The concrete reality of freedom for the Romans lay in their intense constitutionality, and their aversion, for many centuries after the expulsion of the Tarquins, to submitting themselves to a king. When the civic humanists of the medieval Italian cities revived the republican ideal, Julius Caesar stood as the man who extinguished freedom and gave Rome at last a master.

Medieval Europe, however, had its own indigenous sources of freedom, derived from both Christianity and from the practices of the barbarians who replaced the Romans. Regarding the situation in which one man rules another as sufficiently unusual to require justification (*omne potestas est a deo* was a common statement of the sentiment), they explored the forms of consent and the constitution of authority with great inventiveness: parliaments, juries, inquests, the principle of representation and much else in what we call 'democracy', descend from the civil experience of that period.

In early modern Europe, these monarchical institutions and the classical republican tradition of freedom supplied a joint inheritance, and by no means a harmonious one. In the monarchical tradition, freedom was essentially a condition sustained by public life but enjoyed within the private realm. It came to be defined as a set of rights, which could be distinguished as the civil rights of the subject and the political rights of the citizen. Freedom, argued Thomas Hobbes, is 'the silence of the law', and, in this tradition, freedom has always resided in the ability of individuals, as judges of their own best interests, to order their lives within a structure of rules which are clear, predictable and known to all. The republican tradition, by contrast, took freedom as the moral ideal which identified being fully human with participation in public life. The active citizen, thus understood, was self-determining in that he participated in making the laws under which he lived. This view ultimately rested upon ideal memories of the virtuous and public-spirited cities of the ancient world. From Montesquieu onwards, many writers have judged that modern freedom, which is individualistic, is quite different from the civic freedom of those earlier times, but the ideal of a truly participatory community has never lost its power to influence European thought.

It was Rousseau who most notably elaborated this latter view of freedom, with a clarity of mind which led him to the paradoxical implication that the citizen who has been compelled to abide by a law for which he is in principle responsible is being 'forced to be free'. In the extreme development of this view, a man can only properly be described as free when he acts virtuously, which seems, in terms of the modern view of freedom, to be self-contradictory. These two views of freedom are often discussed today, following Isaiah Berlin (1969), as the negative and positive view of freedom. The negative view tends to be strongly associated with Anglo-Saxon societies, while continental life is more receptive to the positive view.

The issue is important because the ideal of freedom has become the ratchet of European social and political development. Philosophers and politicians alike make use of slogans and images developed from the contrast between slave and freed. 'Man is born free and everywhere he is in chains' begins Rousseau's *Social Contract* (1762), while Marx and Engels end the *Communist Manifesto* (1848) by telling workers that they have nothing to lose but their chains. Hegel argued in his *Philosophy of History* (1837) that a universal freedom has been the great achievement of the modern Germanic world. In the despotisms of the East, he argued, one was free; among the Greeks and Romans, some were, but in modern Europe, all were free. And indeed, within a few decades of Hegel's death in 1831, slaves had been freed throughout European possessions, and also in the United States. Paradoxically, it was in exactly this period that a new type of politician arose – communist, anarchist, nationalist and so on – to proclaim that modern Europe was, contrary to all appearances, the most cunningly contrived system of domination the world had ever seen. This doctrine launched the idea of liberation. But whereas freedom and liberty refer to the removal of arbitrary interferences with the way an individual governs his life, liberation was the project of removing *all* conditions thought to frustrate human satisfaction. It stands for a vision of human life in which desire flows freely and uninterruptedly into satisfying action. This is a vastly more ambitious project than that of liberty, and has appealed to a correspondingly less sophisticated audience.

Kenneth Minogue
London School of Economics and Political Science

Reference
Berlin, I. (1969), *Four Essays on Liberty*, London.

Further Reading
Cranston, M. (1953), *Freedom: A New Social Analysis*, London.
Mill, J. S. (1859), *On Liberty*, London.
See also: *democracy; human rights*.

Government

The study of government lies at the heart of political science, but there is little unanimity within the discipline as to how it should be studied or as to the types or forms that exist. Indeed, the term itself has a multiplicity of distinct, if related, meanings. Only an overview of the confusion and controversy can be given here.

Following Finer (1974) we can discern four different meanings of the term 'government': (1) Government refers to the process of governing, that is, the authoritative exercise of power. (2) The term can be used to refer to the existence of that process, to a 'condition of ordered rule'. (3) By 'the government' is often meant the people who fill the positions of authority in a society or institution, that is, the offices of government. (4) The term may refer to the manner, method or system of government in a society, that is, to the structure and arrangement of the offices of government and the relationship between the government and the governed.

The existence of some institution of sovereign government is a distinguishing feature of the 'state'. The study of such sovereign governments has been a major preoccupation of political scientists. But not all governments are sovereign; any institution, such as a trade union, a church group or a political party, which has a formal system of offices endowed with the authority to make binding decisions for that organization, can be said to have a government. Equally, government (in the sense of ordered rule) may exist in the absence of the state. A number of anthropological studies have revealed the existence of certain societies in which conflict is resolved by various social processes without resort to the coercive powers of a formalized state. Indeed, in any society there are many social situations (such as a bus or theatre queue) where potential conflict over an allocative decision is avoided by a non-coercive social process.

Sovereign government in advanced societies is normally regarded as consisting of three distinct sets of offices, each set having a particular role: (1) The role of the *legislature* is to make the law. (2) The *executive* (also sometimes confusingly referred to as the government) is responsible for the implementation of the law and in most advanced polities has come to play a predominant role in the formulation of proposals for new laws. (3) The *judiciary*, meanwhile, is responsible for the interpretation of the law and its application in individual cases.

Classification Schemes: The precise arrangement of the offices of government varies from state to state. Ever since Aristotle, the study of government attempted to classify the varieties of governments according to different types. The purpose of such classification exercises has varied, and has included both a desire to make normative statements about the best type of government and positive statements concerning the behavioural implications of different governmental structures. But all the classification exercises have in common an attempt to produce conceptual categories that make it possible to make meaningful generalizations about government in the face of a bewildering variation in the ways governments are organized.

Classifications of government are legion, yet some common threads can be discerned. Classifications have tended to concentrate on two criteria: (1) The arrangement of offices, which is more narrow in conception. (2) The relationship between the government and the governed.

(1) The first criterion has produced two classification schemes which are in wide currency amongst political scientists, particularly amongst students of democratic government. (a) The first of these classification schemes is based on the relationship between the executive and the legislature. In a parliamentary system, the executive is dependent for its continuance in office upon maintaining the support of the legislature. Members of the executive are commonly also members of the legislature. While a prime minister may be the most powerful member of the executive, important decisions within the executive are usually made collectively by a group of ministers. In a presidential system, on the other hand, the executive is independent of the legislature. Members of the executive are not normally also members of the legislature, while the ultimate source of decision-making authority within the executive lies with one man – the president. (b) The second classification concentrates on the distribution of power between different levels of government. In a unitary state all authority to make laws is vested in one supreme legislature whose jurisdiction covers the whole country. While it may permit local legislatures to exist, they do so only on the sufferance of the main legislature. In a federal state, on the other hand, there exist local legislatures which have at least a measure of guaranteed autonomous decision-making authority. Both forms of government can be distinguished from a confederation, where a group of states combine for certain purposes but with each state retaining its sovereignty.

(2) Classifications based on the second criterion – the

relationship between the government and the governed – have commonly concentrated on the extent to which governments attempt to achieve their aims by coercion of their citizens rather than persuasion, and on the extent to which limits are placed on the legitimate authority of government. The precise formulation of classification schemes based on this criterion varies widely, but not uncommonly a distinction is drawn between, at one extreme, liberal democratic government and, at the other, totalitarian governments. Under liberal democratic government, government is seen as primarily responsive to the wishes of society, and clear limitations are placed upon its ability to coerce society or to mould it in any particular way. Totalitarian governments, on the other hand, have few limits placed upon them and are seen as instruments whereby society may be changed.

New Approaches
The study of government has changed considerably since the Second World War. Historically, the study of government grew out of the study of constitutional law. It was characterized by a concentration on the formal institutions of government and upon constitutional provisions, while individual countries tended to be studied in isolation rather than in comparative framework. However, under the influence of the behavioural revolution, scholars have paid increasing attention to how governments actually operate, to institutions outside the formal apparatus of the state but which play a vital role in its operation (such as political parties and pressure groups), and to explicitly comparative study. Particularly influential in the development of comparative study have been approaches derived from systems theory, especially structural-functionalism. These approaches have attempted to develop a conceptual language, based upon the functions that are performed within any society, that could be applied to the study of government in any country, including developing as well as advanced societies.

John Curtice
University of Liverpool

Reference
Finer, S. E. (1974), *Comparative Government*, Harmondsworth.

Further Reading
Almond, G. A. and Coleman, J. S. (eds) (1960), *The Politics of the Developing Countries*, Princeton.
Easton, D. (1965), *A Systems Analysis of Political Life*, New York.
See also: *administration; authority; constitutions and constitutionalism; power; state.*

Hobbes, Thomas (1588–1679)

Thomas Hobbes is one of the most important figures in the development of modern science and modern politics. As a contemporary of Bacon, Galileo and Descartes, he contributed to the radical critique of medieval Scholasticism and classical philosophy that marked the beginning of the modern age. But he alone sought to develop a comprehensive philosophy – one that treated natural science, political science and theory of scientific method in a unified system. He published this system in three volumes, under the titles *Body*, (1655) *Man* (1957), and *Citizen* (1642). In the course of his long career, Hobbes also published treatises on mathematics, on free will and determinism, on the English common law system, and on the English Civil War. Although his work covered the whole of philosophy, Hobbes made his greatest contribution to modern thought in the field of political philosophy. On three separate occasions, he presented his theory of man and the state; the most famous of his political treatises, the *Leviathan* (1651), is generally recognized as the greatest work of political philosophy in the English language.

In all branches of knowledge, Hobbes's thought is characterized by a pervasive sense that the ancient and medieval philosophers had failed to discover true knowledge, and that a new alternative was urgently needed. It is this sense that defines Hobbes as a modern thinker and gives his work its originality, verve and self-conscious radicalism. In natural science (metaphysics and physics), he rejected the Scholastic and Aristotelian ideas of 'abstract essences' and immaterial causes as nothing more than vain and empty speech. The nature of reality is 'matter in motion', which implied that all phenomena of nature and human nature could be explained in terms of mechanical causation. In the theory of science, Hobbes dismissed the disputative method of Scholasticism and classical dialectics as forms of rhetoric that merely appealed to the authority of common opinion and produced endless verbal controversies. The correct method of reasoning combined the resolutive-compositive method of Galileo and the deductive method of Euclidean geometry. By combining these, Hobbes believed that every branch of knowledge, including the study of politics, could be turned into an exact deductive science.

In political science proper, Hobbes was no less radical in his rejection of the tradition. He opposed the republicanism of classical antiquity, the ecclesiastical politics of medieval Europe, and the doctrine of mixed-monarchy prevalent in seventeenth-century England. All these doctrines, Hobbes claimed, were seditious in intent or effect, because they were derived from 'higher' laws that allowed men to appeal to a standard above the will of the sovereign. Hobbes blamed such appeals, exploited by ambitious priests and political demagogues, for the political instability of his times, culminating in the English Civil War. The solution he proposed was political absolutism – the unification of sovereignty in an all-powerful state that derived its authority not from higher laws but from *de facto* power and the consent of the people.

With these three teachings – mechanistic materialism, exact deductive science, and political absolutism – Hobbes sought to establish science and politics on a new foundation that would produce certain knowledge and lasting civil peace.

From the first, Hobbes's philosophical system generated controversy. In the seventeenth century, Hobbes was treated as a dangerous subversive by all who believed in, or had an interest in, the traditional order. Christian clergymen condemned his materialist view of the world as atheistic and his mechanistic view of man as soulless; legal scholars attacked his doctrine of absolutism for placing the sovereign above the civil laws; even kings, whose power Hobbes sought to augment, were wary of accepting the teaching that political authority rested on force and consent rather than on divine right (Mintz, 1962). In the eighteenth and nineteenth centuries his defence of absolute and arbitrary power ran counter to the general demand for constitutional government. Hobbes has been treated more favourably in this century than ever before. Although some scholars have seen certain parallels between Hobbes's Leviathan state and twentieth-century tyrannies (Collingwood, 1942), most clearly recognize that Hobbes's 'enlightened despot', whose primary goal is to secure civil peace, is vastly different from the brutal and fanatical heads of totalitarian states (Strauss, 1959).

Such studies can be divided into several groups, each reflecting the perspective of a contemporary school of philosophy as it probes the origins of modernity. (1) Guided by the concerns of contemporary analytical philosophy, one group argues for the primacy of method and formal logic in Hobbes's system and views his politics as a set of formal rules which serve as utilitarian guidelines for the state (McNeilly, 1968; Watkins, 1965). (2) Another group has examined Hobbes's theory of 'political obligation' from a Kantian point of view. According to this interpretation, Hobbes's argument for obedience goes beyond calculations of utility by appealing to a sense of moral duty in keeping the social contract, and by requiring citizens to have just intentions (Taylor, 1938; Warrender, 1957). (3) Developed by Marxist scholars, a third interpretation uses Hobbes to understand the ideological origins of bourgeois society and to provide a critical perspective on bourgeois liberalism by exposing its Hobbesian roots (Macpherson, 1962; Coleman, 1977). (4) The fourth interpretation reflects the concerns of the natural law school. According to the foremost scholar of this school, Hobbes is the decisive figure in transforming the natural law tradition from classical natural right to modern natural 'rights'; Hobbes accomplished this revolution by asserting that the right of self-preservation, grounded in the fear of violent death, is the only justifiable moral claim (Strauss, 1936).

Robert P. Kraynak
Colgate University

References

Coleman, F. M. (1977), *Hobbes and America: Exploring the Constitutional Foundations*, Toronto.

Collingwood, R. G. (1942), *The New Leviathan*, Oxford.

Macpherson, C. B. (1962), *The Political Theory of Possessive Individualism*, Oxford.

McNeilly, F. S. (1968), *The Anatomy of Leviathan*, London.

Mintz, S. I. (1962), *The Hunting of Leviathan*, Cambridge.

Strauss, L. (1936), *The Political Philosophy of Hobbes*, Chicago.

Strauss, L. (1959), 'On the basis of Hobbes's political philosophy', in *What Is Political Philosophy?*, New York.

Taylor, A. E. (1938), 'The ethical doctrine of Hobbes', *Philosophy*, 13.

Warrender, H. (1957), *The Political Philosophy of Hobbes: His Theory of Obligation*, Oxford.

Watkins, J. W. N. (1965), *Hobbes's System of Ideas: A Study in the Political Significance of Philosophical Theories*, London.

Human Rights

Human rights are the rights and freedoms of all human beings, for 'les droits de l'homme' and 'die Rechte des Menschen' embrace women too.

I

Human rights are often called fundamental and universal. Fundamental can mean that there are rights which are inalienable in that there are no circumstances whatever in which they are to be denied; but, as we shall see, the number of rights of this character can be counted on the fingers of one hand: fundamental in this sense, then, is little more than rhetorical. A more realistic use of the term is to describe rights which are given priority in social policy, administration, and enactment of law: they are fundamental in a particular community because, often embodied in constitutional provisions, they not only can guide policy, but in fact override any administrative act or legislative enactment contrary to them. Those rights might also be loosely described as fundamental, which are in general practice to be exercised and respected – there is a presumption in favour of that – but they may still be restricted in special circumstances if that is in the common interest. Examples of these three kinds of fundamental rights may be given: of the first, prohibition of slavery; of the second, the equality of all before the law; and of the third, the freedom of the press.

Universality expresses an ideal, a goal, and not the present character of human rights. It is obvious that the recognition of particular rights and freedoms, and their observance, have varied greatly between cultures and over time, and they still vary; however, the growing interdependence of countries has led to the emergence of a common political objective: the gradual realization of minimum rules and standards of conduct and administration throughout the world.

But Edmund Burke (1729–97) expressed an important truth when, as a member of the British Parliament in 1775, he was pleading for conciliation with the American colonies, and said, 'All government, indeed every human benefit and enjoyment, every virtue and every prudent act, is founded on compromise and barter.' The European Convention on Human Rights adopts this balancing of rights. So Article 8 provides that:

(1) Everyone has the right to respect for his private and family life, his home and his correspondence.

(2) There shall be no interference (*ingérence/Eingriff*) by a public authority in the exercise of this right except such as is in accordance with the law (*prévue par la loi/gesetzlich vorgesehen*) and is necessary in a democratic society in the interests of national security, public safety (*la sûreté publique/die öffentliche Ruhe und Ordnung*), or the economic well-being of the country, for the prevention of disorder or crime, for the protection of health or morals, or for the protection of the rights and freedoms of others.

Further, the requirements of emergency are recognized, so Article 15 says:

(1) In time of war or other public emergency threatening the life of the nation any High Contracting Party may take measures derogating from its obligations under this Convention (*dérogeant aux obligations prévues . . ./welche die . . . vorgesehenen Verpflichtungen . . . ausser Kraft setzen*), to the extent strictly required by the exigencies of the situation (*dans la stricte mesure où la situation l'exige/den die Lage unbedingt erfordert*) provided that such measures are not inconsistent with its other obligations under international law.

(2) No derogation from Article 2 except in respect of deaths resulting from lawful acts of war or from Articles 3, 4(1) and 7 shall be made under this provision.

Article 15(3) requires that the Secretary General of the Council of Europe be kept fully informed of such measures.

Similar provisions are to be found in the International Civil and Political Rights Covenant.

II

Rights that are fundamental in the first sense suggested above, being inalienable in any circumstance, including national emergency, are limited in the European Convention to the prohibition of 'torture or inhuman or degrading treatment or punishment': Article 3, and of 'slavery or servitude': Article 4(1). While the right to life, and the principle of non-retroactivity of penalties and offences, are also not to be derogated from even in emergency, they are subject to specific exceptions in the Convention and so cannot be fundamental in the first sense. Rights and freeedoms that can be called fundamental in the second sense are protected in many national systems by constitutional provisions and procedures; while both national systems and the international instruments cover those that are fundamental in the third sense – in reality, with a balancing of rights: for example, how irresponsible can the press be in exercising its freedom of information; how far can a drunken father claim access to his children as a right of family life; are there limits to the right to strike; does the right to property protect the possession of assets acquired for the purpose of tax evasion? It is issues like these that are raised in individual applications to the European Commission of Human Rights and the UN Human Rights Committee.

III

In the balancing of human rights, there may be, first, permissible restrictions, illustrated above, the test of which is that they must be necessary for one or more of the stated purposes. Secondly, there is the principle of responsibility, stated, for example, in the Universal Declaration, Article 29(1): 'Everyone has duties to the Community in which alone the free and full development of his personality is possible.' There is a marked difference, in applying this principle, between what may be called the individualist and the collective approaches. If the European Convention is taken as expressing human rights, as conceived in Western Europe, individual rights predominate; the burden lies always on public authority to justify any restriction of them, and responsibilities are mentioned only for the press. The collective approach is vividly expressed in the USSR Constitution (1977). It contains a 'bill of rights', which is comprehensive and by any standards adequate, if read alone, for the exercise and protection of the rights of the citizen. But there follow statements of overriding social responsibilities: so 'Exercise of rights and freedoms shall be inseparable from the performance by a citizen of his duties . . .' and these include the duty 'to respect the rules of socialist society' (Article 59); 'to safeguard the interests of the Soviet state and contribute to the strengthening of its might and prestige' (Article 62); and 'to work conscientiously in his chosen socially useful occupation, and strictly to observe labour discipline' (Article 60). More generally it is 'for the purpose of strengthening and developing the socialist system' that citizens 'shall be guaranteed freedom of speech, the press, assembly, meetings, street processions and demonstrations' (Article 50).

IV

The exercise, observance and achievement of human rights and freedoms depends in the end on domestic arrangements in each country, though the international processes have influence.

There is first a distinction between means of direct enforcement, and progressive achievement of rights and freedoms, between what are sometimes called 'legal rights' and 'programme rights'. So under the Civil and Political Rights Covenant,

> Each State Party ... undertakes to respect and ensure (*à respecter et à garantir/zu achten ... und zu gewährleisten*) to all individuals within its territory and subject to its jurisdiction, the rights recognized. ...

While in the Economic, Social and Cultural Covenant,

> Each State Party ... undertakes to take steps individually and through international assistance and cooperation ... to the maximum of its available resources with a view to achieving progressively the full realization of the rights recognized ... by all appropriate means (*en rue d'assurer progressivement le plein exercise des droits/um nach und nach ... die volle Verwiklichung der ... Rechte zu erreichen*).

The Indian Constitution (1949) makes an analogous distinction between enforceable rights and directive principles. The international processes take many forms, but the principal alternatives are (1) the investigation and reporting of general situations, a method employed in the UN system; (2) the investigation of particular complaints brought by individuals or states with efforts to achieve a settlement: the European Commission of Human Rights deal with great numbers of individual applications (all but Greece, Malta, Cyprus and Turkey have recognized the right of individual petition) and some inter-state complaints, making a factual investigation and possibly a settlement; failing settlement it reports the case to the Committee of Ministers, expressing its *opinion* whether there has been a breach of the Convention. The Committee of Ministers has then to *decide* this issue, unless either the Commission or a Contracting

Party involved refer the case to the European Court of Human Rights. The functions of the UN Human Rights Committee are similar but its area of action is rather more limited than that of the European Commission; (3) the judicial process of determination in national courts, the European Court of Human Rights, and possibly other international courts.

James Fawcett
Member of the European Commission of
Human Rights (1962–84)

Further Reading
Bailey, S. (1972), *Prohibitions and Restraints in War*, Oxford.
Drzemczewski, A. (1983), *European Human Rights Convention in Domestic Law*, Oxford.
Lillich, R. and Newman, F. (eds) (1979), *International Human Rights and Problems of Law and Policy*, Boston.
Robertson, A. H. (1977), *Human Rights in Europe*, 2nd edn, Manchester.
Sieghart, P. (1983), *The International Law of Human Rights*, Oxford.
United Nations (1980), *UN Action in the Field of Human Rights*, New York.

Ideology
The concept of ideology is commonly traced back to the European Enlightenment and especially to Destutt de Tracy who is thought to be the first to use the term in print. There are, of course, earlier forms of the notion in, for example, Bacon's concept of 'idola' meaning 'impediment to knowledge'. The eighteenth-century development of the concept is closely linked to the French Encyclopedists' struggle against all forms of religious and otherwise traditional thought in the name of the new secular truth of science. But even if the term ideology is of modern European origin, the concept is quite probably more ancient. It appears, for instance, in the fifth-century Greek equivalent of the struggle between the 'Ancients and the Moderns', when representatives of the latter, champions of

science and civilization, attacked the old traditions and religion, in some cases attempting to explain scientifically the origin of ancient religious beliefs.

The concept of ideology reached its florescence in the great philosophical and social scientific systems of the nineteenth century. Comte criticized the negativism of the Enlightenment ideologists' attack on tradition and metaphysics, arguing that the forerunners of science had an important ordering function in society that would of necessity be maintained in the evolution of new mental systems (1901). What is reserved for the domain of purely intellectual activity in Comte is generalized to the entirety of mental production in society in Marx. Developing a line of thought descended from a group of critical students of Hegel referred to as the German ideologists, and especially well articulated in Feuerbach's materialist inversion of Hegel, Marx theorized that society's consciousness of itself was an ethereal self-mystification. Feuerbach's inversion of Hegel consisted in attempting to demonstrate the earthly foundations of metaphysics and religion. This he accomplished in his famous *The Essence of Christianity* (1957) in which he reduced the existence of religion to the fundamentally estranged character of human nature *in general*. Marx's critique of Feuerbach stressed the historicity of the so-called material basis of ideology as well as the notion that human nature is itself a historical product just as much as its ideological correlatives. He argued further that the estranged or alienated forms of consciousness were not mere intellectual reflections but forms of human practice that play an active role in the functioning and transformation of society itself. The practical aspects of ideology were seen to be directly associated with the structure of class domination.

Marx – and Engels – (1970) generalized the question of ideology from the realm of science versus tradition to that of real versus mystified social processes, thus encompassing questions of theory and questions of political control within the same framework. In this way the function as well as the content of the idea systems might be critically scrutinized.

Throughout the nineteenth and early twentieth centuries, the two aspects of the concept of ideology were elaborated upon. A broad array of terms seem to have been used in similar fashion: *Weltanschaung*, collective representation, sometimes even culture, all to capture the idea of the total mental life of society. In the work of Lukács and Mannheim there emerged a tradition of the sociology of knowledge that has been developed throughout the century, its most recent advocate being Habermas. This approach, heavily represented in the Frankfurt School of German sociology, has concentrated much of its effort on understanding the ideological basis of all forms of social knowledge including the natural sciences. In France, Durkheim and the *Année Sociologique* school elaborated the analysis of the relation between social structure and the organization of collective representations (religious, intellectual and otherwise) that are meant to reflect the former (Durkheim, 1965; Durkheim and Mauss, 1963). Their wide-reaching ethnological ambitions had important influences on the development of anthropology in France and Holland and more recently among British symbolists (Turner, 1967; Douglas, 1975). In the work of British functionalists there has been a concentration on the way in which ideology (religion and ritual) maintains social solidarity (Radcliffe-Brown), provides a 'charter' (Malinowski) for the social order, or otherwise prevents social disintegration (Gluckman).

In the more recent work of structural Marxists (for example, Althusser, 1971) a more extreme functionalism is evident, one where ideological 'apparatuses' are conceived as instruments that exist to maintain the coherence of a mode of production, a system of economic exploitation that itself generates its own self-maintenance by way of the production of appropriate mentalities, political structures and socialized subjects who are no more than the agents of the system.

Among both materialist and social determinist theoreticians, ideology has usually been assumed to be a locus in societal structure corresponding to patterns of thought and cognition, systems of values, religious organization, and so on, whose content is supposed in some way to reflect or, at the very least, to be a discourse upon a logically prior social structure.

Among cultural determinists and value determinists, often

referred to as idealists, the system of cultural categories or value orientations are said to determine or in some way provide the foundation for social action and organization.

Discussions of ideology have in classical social science been characterized by a pervasive dualism of idea/reality, ideology/practice, idealism/materialism. This mind/body dualism which has systematically conflated ideology and ideas, thought and meaning, has more recently been criticized. Theories of symbolic action (for example, Dolgin, Kemnitzer and Schneider, 1977); praxis theory (Bourdieu, 1977; Giddens, 1979), theories of ideo-logic (Augé, 1975), and theories of the imaginary construction of reality have all in different ways tried to overcome the dualism inherent in sociological and anthropological discourse (Berger and Luckmann, 1966). These approaches elaborate on the recognition that the organization of material praxis is symbolically constituted, just as the structure of meaning is the product of social practice. Works on the symbolism of power, the social functions of knowledge, the relation between culture and class (Foucault, 1977) have focused on the way in which symbolic practice organizes material realities. Anthropological analysis of the logic of category systems and their complex interpenetration with material practices has become an important area of theoretical discussion (Friedman, 1974; Barnett and Silverman, 1979).

Jonathan Friedman
University of Copenhagen

References

Althusser, L. (1971), 'Ideology and ideological state apparatuses', in *Lenin and Philosophy*, New York.

Augé, M. (1975), *Théorie des pouvoirs et idéologie*, Paris.

Barnett, D. and Silverman, M. (1979), *Ideology and Everyday Life*, Ann Arbor, Michigan.

Berger, P. and Luckmann, T. (1966), *The Social Construction of Reality*, New York.

Bourdieu, P. (1977), *Outline of a Theory of Practice*, Cambridge.

Comte, A. (1901 [1877]), *Cours de philosophie positive*, Paris.

Dolgin, J., Kemnitzer, D. and Schneider, D. (1977), 'As people express their lives, so they are . . .', 'Introduction', *Symbolic Anthropology*, New York.

Douglas, M. (1975), *Implicit Meanings*, London.

Durkheim, E. (1965 [1912]), *Elementary Forms of Religious Life*, New York (*Les Formes élémentaires de la vie religieuse*, Paris).

Durkheim, E. and Mauss, M. (1963), *Systems of Primitive Classification*, Chicago.

Feuerbach, L. (1957), *The Essence of Christianity*, New York.

Foucault, M. (1977 [1975]), *Discipline and Punish: The Birth of the Prison*, New York (*Surveiller et punir*, Paris).

Friedman, J. (1974), 'The place of fetishism and the problem of materialist interpretations', *Critique of Anthropology*, 1.

Giddens, A. (1979), *Central Problems in Social Theory*, Cambridge.

Marx, K. (1964), *Economic and Philosophic Manuscripts of 1844*, New York.

Marx, K. (1967 [1867]), *Capital*, vol. I, London.

Marx, K. and Engels, F. (1970), *Selected Works*, Moscow.

Turner, T. (1967), *The Forest of Symbols*, Ithaca, New York.

Further Reading

Feuer, L. (1975), *Ideology and the Ideologists*, Oxford.

Geertz, C. (1973), 'Ideology as a cultural system', in *The Interpretation of Cultures*, New York.

Gouldner, A. (1976), *The Dialectic of Ideology and Technology*, London.

Lichtheim, G. (1967), *The Concept of Ideology and Other Essays*, New York.

Imperialism

Imperialism has acquired so many meanings that the word ought to be dropped by social scientists, complained Professor Hancock (1950) several decades ago: 'muddle-headed historians in Great Britain and America use this word with heaven-knows how many shades of meaning, while Soviet writers are using it to summarize a theory and wage a war.' Alas, these errors continue. Autocratic rule over a diversity of otherwise roughly equal peoples goes back in time at least as far as the Indo-European Empire of Alexander the Great, but nowadays imperialism also means to Marxists the triumph of (mostly Western-European) monopoly finance capital over a still larger array of non-European peoples at the end of the nineteenth century, a very different kind of empire indeed. For some 'underdevelopment theorists', the term is simply synonymous with capitalism in general, not just its monopolistic stage. Demythologizing imperialism is therefore a rather slippery task.

Marxist theories of imperialism were first fleshed out during the first two decades of the century, principally in order to explain why the expected final collapse of capitalism was taking so long to happen. Later the outbreak of the First World War and the promptness with which European working peoples attacked one another rather than their bosses, added fresh urgency to thought. Nationalism, in retrospect, seems to have had something to do with this, as well as the autonomy of political choice at the time of outbreak of war from anything approaching economic rationality. But Marxist writers mostly looked elsewhere for explanations and for ammunition with which to pursue more sectarian concerns. Just before the war, Rosa Luxemburg provided in *Die Akkumulation des Kapitals* (1913) an analysis of imperialism which is still read respectfully today because of its pioneer probing of articulations between expanding capitalism and pre-capitalist social formations outside Europe. But during and after the 1914–18 War it was her advocacy of the mass revolutionary strike in order to speed up the final collapse of capitalism, otherwise given a new lease of life by imperialist expansion, that excited more immediate attention.

Marx himself had seen the expansion of capitalism outside its original heartlands as both a less important phenomenon and a more benign one than Luxemburg: it was a marginal matter, in at least two senses. Luxemburg, however, considered that capitalism could only survive if it continually expanded its territory. One problem with this view, as Mommsen (1981) has pointed out, is that 'Rosa Luxemburg's basic adherence to Marx's complicated and controversial theory of surplus value, which by definition accrued to capitalism alone, prevented her from considering whether, if the consumer capacity of the masses were increased, internal markets might not afford suitable opportunities for the profitable investment of "unconsumed" i.e. reinvestable, surplus value.' Another defect was that Luxemburg undoubtedly misunderstood the significance of the enormous rise in overseas investment at the start of the twentieth century. Along with Hobson before and Lenin subsequently, she assumed that it was closely associated with colonial annexations. In fact, as Robinson and Gallagher (1961) have reminded us, it diverged widely from it.   Hilferding had taken a slightly different view. In *Das Finanzkapital* (1910), he was more concerned to explain why capitalist crises had recently become less frequent (there had not been one since 1896), and he argued that free trade had been replaced by finance capital, whose dominance and ability to intervene with state help anywhere in the world had temporarily delayed the final catatrophe. But it was the British journalist and free-trader Hobson, with his wide array of attacks upon overseas investment and colonial annexations in *Imperialism* (1902), whom Lenin used most extensively in his own famous study of *Imperialism, The Highest Stage of Capitalism* (1917). This was written in order not only to explain the First World War but also to attack the reformism of Karl Kautsky, who had suggested that the coming final collapse of capitalism might be still further delayed by the emergence of an 'ultra-imperialism' stopping for the time being further intra-imperialist wars. In retrospect, Lenin's work on imperialism reads more like a tract than a treatise, but its subsequent importance was of course vastly increased by the success of Lenin's faction in seizing power in Russia in 1917; for many years afterwards it retained unquestionable status as unholy writ.

Shortly after the Russian Revolution, Lenin also latched onto one of the greatest uses of imperialism as political ideology, namely, as a weapon against non-communist empires. This tendency was continued by Stalin, who told the Twelfth Congress of the Russian Communist Party in 1923: 'Either we succeed in stirring up, in revolutionizing, the remote rear of imperialism – the colonial and semi-colonial countries of the East – and thereby hasten the fall of imperialism; or we fail to do so and thereby strengthen imperialism and weaken the force of our movement.' Such statements reversed Marx's original view that imperialism was good for capitalism but only of marginal importance in its development, and substituted a new conventional wisdom that (1) imperialism was bad news for all backward areas of the world, and (2) imperialism was of utterly central importance to the development of capitalism itself.

View (1) has been further popularized in recent years by the underdevelopment school associated with André Gundar Frank, and attacked recently by Warren (1981). View (2), on the other hand, has led to an oddly focused debate among historians over the colonial partition of Africa at the close of the nineteenth century, the 'theory of economic imperialism' being something of a straw man in this debate, as imperialism (on most Marxist views) did not arise until after the Scramble for Africa had taken place; and even after this date Lenin was clearly wrong about the direction of most overseas investment, let alone its political significance. Only in the case of South Africa (and possibly Cuba) is there even a plausible case for economic imperialism being identical with colonial annexation: the South African War indeed was popularly called 'les Boers contre la Bourse' in continental Europe at the time.

Other difficulties with Marxist views of imperialism derive from Lenin's use of Hobson's *Imperialism* (1902). Hobson was a very bitter critic of British overseas investment, but for very un-Marxist reasons. He was a free-trade liberal who saw colonial annexations and wars as a hugely expensive way of propping up the power and profits of a very small class of *rentier* capitalists, who pursued profit abroad to the detriment of investment at home. Only by manipulating the masses by appealing to their patriotism did this small class of capitalists get away with this (in his view) huge confidence trick and, ideally, social reform should increase the purchasing powers of the masses and thereby render 'imperialism' powerless. Lenin ignored Hobson's theories and simply used his facts. In retrospect, the 'facts' about the coincidence of overseas investment with colonial annexation appear very wrong-headed, his 'theories' much less so. Hobson's views on 'under-consumption' were later taken up and given some seminal twists by John Maynard Keynes, while his intuitions about connections between overseas annexations and metropolitan social structures were later taken up by Joseph Schumpeter and Hannah Arendt (for her analysis of the origins of Fascism).

Schumpeter wrote his essay *Zur Soziologie der Imperialismen* (1919) as an explicit attack upon Marxist theories of imperialism. Capitalism itself he considered to be essentially anti-imperialist in nature, and such monopolistic and expansionist tendencies characterizing pre-1914 capitalism he put down to the malevolent influence of an anachronistic militarism surviving from the European feudal past. Schumpeter defined imperialism as 'the objectless disposition on the part of a state to unlimited forcible expansion' (Schumpeter, 1951). The basic trouble with this particular formulation is that while the European colonial annexations of the late nineteenth and early twentieth centuries were certainly sometimes this, they were not always so. Similarly, while much European overseas investment in the late nineteenth century did not go to areas of European colonial annexation, sometimes it did. Furthermore, while 'the theory of economic imperialism' may well be a straw man as far as the debate about the causes of the Scramble for Africa is concerned, it would be absurd to suggest that the partitioners did not believe that there was *something* economically useful about Black Africa. Imperialism needs to be demythologized, not simply wished away.

Probably imperialism is best defined in some median manner. As the etymology of the word itself denotes, imperialism is closely concerned with empires and colonialism, but this is not necessarily always the case. In the Americas the Monroe Doctrine (1823) vetoed new formal empires by European countries – but not subsequent 'dollar diplomacy' by the US, sometimes supported by the overt use of force, sometimes with mere threats and unequal financial practices. Capitalism, too, is not necessarily linked with non-communist imperialism, but sometimes has been, especially in the many African and Asian colonial dependencies established during the second half of the nineteenth century. In these circumstances, imperialism is probably best separated analytically from both 'capitalism' and 'colonialism' and treated principally as the pursuit of intrusive and unequal economic policy in other countries supported by significant degrees of coercion.

Thus defined, imperialism as formal empire (or 'colonialism') may well be largely a thing of the past, except for strategic colonies (*colonies de position*). But imperialism as informal empire (or 'neocolonialism', to employ Nkrumah's terminology) probably has an assured future ahead of it – in both the non-communist and the communist-dominated worlds.

Michael Twaddle
Institute of Commonwealth Studies
University of London

References
Hancock, W. K. (1950), *Wealth of Colonies*, Cambridge.
Mommsen, W. J. (1981), *Theories of Imperialism*, New York.
Robinson, R. and Gallagher, J. (1961), *Africa and the Victorians*: *The Official Mind of Imperialism*, London.
Schumpeter, J. A. (1951 [1919]), *Imperialism and Social Classes*, Oxford. (Includes translation of *Zur Soziologie der Imperialismen*,)
Warren, B. (1981), *Imperialism: Pioneer of Capitalism*, London.
See also: *dependency theory; Third World; world-system theory.*

Interest Groups and Lobbying

Interest groups have been a part of political life in all the industrial societies of the Western world for more than a century, but the modern system began to take shape only in the late nineteenth century. The rapidly developing industrial economy spawned a great many new commercial and scientific specialties that served as the foundations for trade and professional societies. These new associations were meant to exercise control over unruly competition, provide forums for the exchange of information and the development of professional reputations, create knowledge about the latest methods or techniques in the field, and represent the occupational interests of their members before legislative committees or government bureaus. Membership in these groups waxed and waned with the fluctuations of the economy, and there were spurts of development during or immediately after wartime. A new set of linkages between government and the citizenry emerged, based squarely upon the rapidly growing occupational structure of the industrial society.

The number of interest groups has grown steadily throughout the twentieth century in all industrial societies, and the rate of increase has accelerated during the past twenty years. Most group theorists prior to the 1960s assumed that once individual citizens began to experience some social or economic problem, and became aware that they shared their difficulties with others, it would be perfectly natural for them to create a formal organization that would represent their joint interests before government. Individuals might be too poor or isolated from one another to act upon their shared beliefs, or they might not be sufficiently aroused to take the necessary pains. If they cared deeply enough, however, and events produced a sufficient amount of interaction with other affected individuals, theorists believed that eventually 'formal organization or a significant interest group will emerge and greater influence will ensue' (Truman, 1951). The process was thought to be more or less spontaneous, propelled by social disturbances arising from the growing complexity of the urban-industrial economy. Societies that did not impose unreasonable legal constraints upon the formation of associations could be expected to spawn interest groups in waves of mobilization and counter-mobilization until a form of equilibrium was achieved, only to be disturbed by further social or economic developments, setting off another round of mobilization.

A serious challenge to the idea that groups would organize spontaneously came in 1965 from Mancur Olson, who directly attacked the commonsensical assumptions at the heart of group theory about the natural inclination of citizens to take joint action in their collective interest. Olson showed that it would not be rational for self-interested individuals to take part in securing a collective benefit for a large group, even if they were aware they would be better off if the benefit were secured. It is the nature of collective benefits, like health insurance or public education, that they must be provided to everyone who meets universal standards of eligibility, so that any individuals out to maximize their own self-interest would refrain from making any contribution to the common effort, knowing that they would receive as much as everyone else in the group once the government began providing the benefit.

Olson believed that small groups might be able to induce their members to contribute to common objectives through peer pressure, but large groups could not be expected to act in their collective self-interest in most cases. The problem of the 'free rider' could be solved only if groups were able to provide tangible benefits as inducements directly to those who contributed to the common effort, or unless sanctions were employed, sometimes enforced by the courts – as with union shop agreements – that forced all potential group members to contribute to the common effort, whether they wanted to or not.

Olson's theory of public goods and individual incentives highlights the great obstacles facing those who wish to organize deprived elements of society. A balanced representation of group interests cannot be achieved from entirely voluntary political action when the marginal costs of participation differ so greatly among social groups, and where individual incentives to contribute to common goals are so weak. Some of these obstacles are lifted during periods of great political stress (Moe, 1980), and some can be overcome through the efforts of organizational entrepreneurs (Salisbury, 1969; Wilson, 1973), but there are limits to the impact individual leaders can have, no matter how energetic or clever they may be. Groups with large memberships that do not provide exclusive benefits or employ coercion to hold their members, usually attract mainly those with good educations and ample incomes for whom, presumably, the annual dues represent a painless way of amplifying their ideological views and of gaining a sense of involvement in the national political process (Berry, 1977; McFarland, 1976).

A great many new associations representing socially disadvantaged elements of the society have appeared in recent years in most Western democracies, but most have managed to remain in existence not through an outpouring of financial support from their members, but through the financial patronage of foundations, wealthy individuals, trade unions, or government agencies (Walker, 1983). Associations representing large social groupings, like consumers or the poor, that depend entirely on support from their members in response to mainly ideological appeals, typically have been short-lived.

Even though there has been an increase during the past two decades in the number of associations claiming to represent disadvantaged minorities, women, the mentally ill, children, or the elderly in most Western democracies, there is a natural tendency in democratic political systems for small, privileged economic or social minorities to present their case more effectively before government than large, unwieldy, disadvantaged groups pursuing broad collective interests. This imbalance in the system of advocacy provides intense minorities with an advantage when highly technical policy problems are being dealt with, when there is little conflict among the interests most directly involved in a policy area, or when policy problems are being resolved away from the glare of publicity mainly within public bureaucracies or government regulatory agencies (Hayes, 1982). Elected legislators can be relied upon to provide the representation required by large, vulnerable groups when there is a reasonable prospect that supporters of these interests can be reached through the mass media and convinced to vote in subsequent elections (Bauer *et al.*, 1963), but the problem of protecting the public interest from the selfish scramble of advocates for narrow interests remains one of the most pressing problems of democracy.

Democratic systems draw their legitimacy from widespead public acceptance of the procedures by which policy decisions are made. Citizens need not accept every rule or regulation, but they must remain convinced that the system is reasonably open, that legislators are striving to represent all the people equally, and that opportunities exist for citizens to organize and petition their leaders to reverse unfavourable decisions. Interest groups, therefore, perform an essential function in democratic government, but ironically, they also pose one of the most serious threats to the maintenance of public trust in democratic institutions. If large numbers of citizens become convinced that elected officials are incapable of advancing the public interest because of unreasonable pressures from advocates for narrow, special interests, the democratic system itself may begin to lose the essential legitimacy it requires to maintain peaceful debate and compromise. In order to manage this unavoidable dilemma of democracy, interest groups must be allowed to engage in vigorous forms of advocacy. But somehow enough balance must be maintained in the system – either through increasing the resources available to elected officials or by creating a balance of forces through subsidies for groups that are inherently diffi-cult to mobilize – so that the public will remain convinced that its system of government is both representative and fair.

Jack L. Walker
University of Michigan

References

Bauer, R. A., Pool, I. de Sola and Dexter, L. A. (1963), *American Business and Public Policy: The Politics of Foreign Trade*, New York.

Berry, J. M. (1977), *Lobbying for the People: The Political Behavior of Public Interest Groups*, Princeton.

Hayes, M. T. (1981), *Lobbyists and Legislators: A Theory of Political Markets*, New Brunswick.

McFarland, A. S. (1976), *Public Interest Lobbies: Decision Making on Energy*, Washington.

Moe, T. M. (1980), *The Organization of Interests*, Chicago.

Olson, M. Jr (1965), *The Logic of Collective Action*, Cambridge, Mass.

Salisbury, R. H. (1969), 'An exchange theory of interest groups', *Midwest Journal of Political Science*, 8.

Truman, D. B. (1951), *The Governmental Process*, New York.

Walker, J. L. (1983), 'The origins and maintenance of interest groups in America', *American Political Science Review*, 77.

Wilson, J. Q. (1973), *Political Organizations*, New York.

International Relations

In the most general sense, international relations have existed ever since men formed themselves into social groups, and then developed external relations with groups like themselves. Relationships were most frequently conflictual or warlike, although occasionally they were co-operative; but they took place in a system of anarchy and not within the framework of any political or legal or customary rules. These peculiar relationships were little considered by writers in the Western world before Machiavelli, but from the seventeenth century onwards international law (Grotius, Pufendorf, Vattel) and the problems of war and peace (Rousseau, Kant) began to attract attention. These historical origins, combined with the horror of the First World War, led to the subject's emergence as a policy-making, prescriptive and normative study: war was an intolerable evil, its recurrence must forever be prevented, and the duty of international relations scholars was to show how to achieve this. It was assumed that nobody could want war, so if states were democratic and governments were accountable to their peoples, and if the system's anarchy were ended (hence the League of Nations), war might be banished.

The diagnosis was too simple. The aspirations and actions of Hitler, Mussolini, the Japanese, and the Bolsheviks in Moscow showed the truth of the dictum of Morgenthau (1948) that peace and security is the ideology of satisfied powers. Scholars now turned their minds away from study of ways to achieve a supposedly universal goal to study of how things in the international arena in fact were. The modern subject of international relations was born. From the outset, though at first not explicitly, the subject was approached by different scholars from two different points of view. The first sought to establish why the significant units (or actors) on the international stage behaved in the ways they did: most such scholars saw states as the significant actors, and this branch of the subject became foreign policy analysis. The second group focused on the arena within which relations occurred, and was concerned to identify the mechanisms by which patterned relationships with a fair degree of stability and order were able to be maintained in conditions which, formally at least, were anarchical. The 1950s and 1960s saw a burgeoning of methodological experimentation and quasi-theoretical speculation, and a proliferation of journals. The behaviouralist revolution in the United States invaded international relations, as it did other social sciences, and a great debate with the so-called traditionalists raged through the 1960s and early 1970s, and is not yet concluded. But in the last decade, disappointment at the relative lack of success in the creation of theories with explanatory power for real-world problems has led to some redirection of attention towards substantive questions, to smaller-scale analyses and to theorizing over limited ranges of phenomena.

Foreign policy analysis is the branch of the subject in which most practical advances have occurred. Many conceptual frameworks have been developed, the most comprehensive probably being that of Brecher *et al.* (1969), but the central components of such frameworks are now widely agreed. States are conceived as having objectives of various kinds – political/security, economic, ideological. Objectives are not consistently compatible one with another, and a short-term objective may be inconsistent with a long-term goal. Objectives are ranked differently by different groups, organizations, and political leaderships within states, and rankings change over time. Explanation of policy-decisions thus requires understanding of political interplay and bureaucratic process. But the determination of policy is conditioned also by states' capabilities – economic, demographic, political, military – and by decision makers' perceptions of the comparative efficacy of their own capabilities as against those of the other state(s) with which they are dealing, all in the context of support relationships (alliances, economic aid) and of respective commitments elsewhere in the system. Most, if not all, relationships have elements of conflict and common interest, and are essentially of a bargaining character; but the conflictual element usually predominates, and the concept of power is thus central to the analysis. A check-list of such considerations affecting foreign policy decisions enables rudimentary comparisons of foreign policies to be made, but also makes possible greater awareness among policy makers of the likely consequences of their decisions. enable rudimentary comparisons of foreign policies to be made, but also makes possible greater awareness among policy makers of the likely consequences of their decisions.

The purposes of studies at the second or system level to determine the factors that make the stability of the system more or less probable, and the effect on international outcomes of the system's structure. Essential structural components are the number of significant units (or actors) in the system, the nature, quality and quantity of interactions among the units, the distribution of capabilities among them, and the degree to which realignment of relationships is easy or is constrained (a system that is ideologically highly polarized, for example, is relatively inflexible). Analysis at the system level is commonly more highly abstract than analysis of state behaviour: this makes possible theory construction of a more rigorous kind, but by the same token makes application of theory to the real world more difficult.

At both levels statistical and mathematical techniques are used, as well as more traditional methods relying on historical and verbally described data. The distinction between the levels is, of course, analytical only. To take just one example of interdependence: at the unit behaviour level the extent to which states are economically, militarily or ideologically interdependent will very greatly affect the policy choices that are open; at the system level the extent to which the realignment of units is impeded by their interdependence will fundamentally affect both outcomes and the stability of the system. Mention of interdependence calls attention to the fact that while states are widely accepted as still the most significant actors in the international arena, there are now many other actors, including intergovernmental organizations (the International Monetary Fund), and nongovernmental organizations (guerrilla groups, multinational corporations). The roles of these, in interplay with the behaviour of states, and as components of international systems, all form part – and some would say an increasingly important part – of the study of international relations.

P. A. Reynolds
University of Lancaster

References
Brecher, M., Steinberg, B. and Stein, J. (1969), 'A framework for research in foreign policy behaviour', *Journal of Conflict Resolution*, 13.
Morgenthau, H. J. (1948), *Politics Among Nations*, New York.

Further Reading
Carr, E. H. (1939), *The Twenty Years' Crisis 1919–1939*, London.
Holsti, K. J. (1977), *International Politics*, Englewood Cliffs, N.J.
Reynolds, P. A. (1980), *An Introduction to International Relations*, London.
Rosenau, J. N. (1971), *The Scientific Study of Foreign Policy*, Glencoe, Ill.
Smith, M., Little, R. and Shackleton, M. (1981), *Perspectives on World Politics*, London.
Waltz, K. N. (1979), *Theory of International Politics*, Reading, Mass.
See also: *peace; war*.

Judicial Process

As studied by contemporary social scientists, focusing primarily on liberal democracies, the judicial process is the complex of formal and informal operations by which tribunals adjudicate claims based on rules putatively authorized by the regime. The tribunals are differentiated and relatively autonomous from the rest of the polity, and typically do not initiate action, but respond when a claim fit for adjudication is presented to them through an adversarial presentation of evidence and argument. So defined, the judicial process is a relatively modern inquiry, dependent upon two intellectual developments: (1) The emergence of the ideal concept of a distinct judicial function performed by a distinct institution; and (2) the rise of a science of politics that emphasizes the informal processes over formal procedures of government and which, as applied to the study of the judiciary, questions the reality, attainability and intellectual sophistication of this conceptual ideal.

Although ancient and medieval political philosophers did distinguish a judicial function from other governmental functions, these distinctions were subordinated to a more fundamental one, that between legislation and politics. 'Legislation' was regarded by the ancients as an extraordinary event, subject at most to rare and cautious amendment, while politics encompassed deliberations and actions within the framework of this legislation. Viewing God as the ultimate legislator, medieval thinkers regarded virtually all governmental functions as aspects of the judicial function. Because the law was regarded as everlasting, yet the situations to which it was to be applied were ever-changing, the judicial function, both in ancient and medieval thought, included generous elements of practical wisdom and equity as essential supplements to the more literal terms of the law.

The more carefully defined and tightly circumscribed contemporary judicial function, performed by a specialized agency, arises concomitantly with the idea of law as the enactment of a sovereign legislator, or what students of political development call the shift of authority from a traditional to a constitutional basis. With authority to make law vested in a present institution having the capacity to change the law to meet new situations, the quasi-legislative character of the ancient and medieval judicial function would threaten to derange legislative authority and offend individual rights by effecting burdens and punishments retroactively. Ironically, this rigorous subordination of judgment to legislation also required the autonomy of the judiciary from the legislature, so that courts could be impartial to the parties before it and free from pressure to interpret the law other than as the legislature intended it at the time of enactment. From these conceptual and institutional developments there emerges, then, the idealized modern judicial function as one presupposing the existence of right answers at law, performed by a tribunal with sufficient autonomy to discern these answers in the resolution of disputes. We find numerous expressions of this ideal among theorists and jurists of liberal democracy; perhaps the most frequently quoted is that of Montesquieu, who held that judges were to be 'no more than the mouth that pronounces the words of the law, mere passive beings, incapable of moderating either its force or rigour'.

Influenced by evolutionary theory, jurists and social scientists during the late nineteenth and early twentieth centuries began shifting their focus from institutional forms and idealized purposes to the 'live forces' that were claimed to constitute the underlying reality. Those who called themselves 'realists' provided the most radical onslaught on the ideal judicial function by dismissing the ontological claim of 'right answers'. In most instances, within wide boundaries, they maintained, there was no right answer to be discovered, no measure by which to assess the claims of one judge's opinion over another; what really constituted the law were the psychological traits of the judge. A distinct but related movement, 'sociological jurisprudence', emphasized not only the creative character of the judicial function, but the need to consider both law and courts in the context of their larger political and social environments.

From this odd marriage of a judicial ideal, which is implicit in the theory and institutions of liberal democracy, and this realist assessment of that standard, is born the modern study of the judicial process. Bearing a greater likeness to its realist parent, it is predominantly an empirical inquiry. Central to its study are the following: the processes by which courts are staffed, the conditions of judicial tenure, and the effect of these on judicial decisions; how rules of procedure, both formal and informal, affect the definition and disposition of issues; the decision-making patterns of individual judges, the dynamics of collective decision making in juries and on appellate courts, patterns of interaction among the courts in appellate and federal systems; the impact and implementation of judicial decisions; and the comparative competence of judicial and nonjudicial branches of government for effecting social change. Normative inquiries focus on modes of legal interpretation and, especially regarding constitutional law, the propriety of judicial activism and restraint. A long promising, but as yet underdeveloped, area is the comparative study of the judicial process, including the study of systems other than those in liberal democracies.

Stanley C. Brubaker
Colgate University

Further Reading
Abraham, H. J. (1980), *The Judicial Process*, 4th edn, New York.
Horowitz, D. (1977), *The Courts and Social Policy*, Washington, DC.
Murphy, W. F. and Tanenhaus, J. (1972), *The Study of Public Law*, New York.
See also: *law*.

Law

Conceptions of what law is are culturally and historically specific. But legal 'theories' often claim for themselves a universalism that they do not really have. When scholars from the Western European legal tradition study the laws and legal institutions of other cultures, what they look for are norms and institutions that are either in form or function analogous to those in their own heritage. The category 'law' they proceed from is a Western cultural construct (Berman, 1983).

Many of the arguments about what law is or should be are organized around a single dichotomy: whether the basis of law is a moral consensus or a matter of organized domination. Law is sometimes interpreted as an expression of cultural values, sometimes as a rationalized framework of power. In ethnographic fact it is usually both. Separating the two absolutely creates a false opposition. Friedman (1975) has argued that 'the function of the legal system is to distribute and maintain an allocation of values that society feels to be right . . . allocation, invested with a sense of rightness, is what is commonly referred to as *justice*'. Society is thus anthropomorphized as a consensual entity having common values. But Friedman's more extended discussion indicates a clear awareness of social stratification, and sharp differences of interest and power. His social science approach tries to embrace both consensus and domination in the same analysis.

In the jurisprudence of the West there have been a number of competing scholarly paradigms of law. The four principal schools of thought with roots in the nineteenth century (and earlier) are conventionally designated: (1) natural law theory; (2) analytical jurisprudence (or legal positivism); (3) historical jurisprudence (or legal evolutionism); and (4) sociological jurisprudence. The various modern social science perspectives on law have been shaped by this intellectual history, as have modern works on jurisprudence and legal history. Current work is best understood in the light of earlier ideas.

(1) Natural Law Thinking

In its various forms this dominated Western ideas about justice through the eighteenth century, and has not fully disappeared, being perhaps most evident today in current arguments about universal human rights. It was once closely associated with the idea of divine law. Natural law theory postulates the existence of a universal, underlying system of 'justice' and 'right', which is distinguishable from mere human enactments, norms and judgments. The content of this natural law was thought to be discoverable by human beings through the exercise of reason. To be just, human laws should conform to natural law, but they do not always do so. Human law can be unjust.

(2) Legal Positivism

This was a nineteenth-century development that continues in new forms to the present, and attacked natural law thinking on the ground that it was unscientific, that it was grounded on a mythical entity, and that it confused law with morality. The notion was that only law *as it is* can be the subject of scientific inquiry, that the province of what law ought to be was not a matter for science, but for philosophers and theologians. It was Bentham's follower, John Austin, who first generated 'the science of positive law'. Austin's science was a 'conceptual jurisprudence' occupied with discovering the key doctrines and ideas actually used in the existing formal legal system.

Austin's most cited formulation is one in which law is treated as command, the source of law as 'the sovereign person or body' that sets it within a particular 'political society'. And, consistent with this position, Austin argued that international law was 'improperly so-called' because it was neither set nor enforced by a political superior. He invented a category, 'positive morality' to contrast with 'positive law' to accommodate the law-like quality of international law without having it disturb his model that associated law with sovereignty.

Later positivists were critical of Austin, and developed modifications. Hans Kelsen generated an analysis which he called 'the pure theory of law' in which he asserted that law consists of a hierarchy of norms to which sanctions are attached. The validity of lower-level norms is derived from higher norms, until ultimately at the top of the hierarchy is the 'basic norm' on which the whole structure depends. The effect of that basic norm is to require people to behave in conformity to the legal order. It defines the limits of that order.

Another major positivist critic of the Austinian perspective is H. L. A. Hart who also has reservations about the artificiality of Kelsen's idea of the basic norm, and proposes an alternative. Hart (1961) rejects a conception of law based on coercive order as one too much derived from the model of criminal law. He argues that in fact law does many more things than prohibit or command and punish. It also can empower persons to act, and can define the conditions under which such actions are legally effective. Hart points to three troublesome issues that frequently recur in the attempt to define the specifically legal and distinguish it from other domains: the relationship between law and coercive orders, between legal obligation and moral obligation, and the question whether law is to be understood as a set of rules. Plainly there are coercive orders, binding obligations and rules that are not matters of law, yet all three elements also are central to legal systems. How are these to be distinguished? Hart's resolution of this problem is to describe law as a set of social rules divided into two types: primary rules of obligation and secondary rules of recognition, change and adjudication. The secondary rules sort the legal from other rule orders. Since legal validity is established by formal criteria, according to Hart's definition, an immoral law can be legally valid. Original and elegantly formulated as Hart's discussion is widely acknowledged to be, it has been criticized for its exclusive focus on rules at the expense of other important dimensions of legal systems, particularly the fact that it is a formal internal definition that turns away from questions about the socioeconomic context, the institutional framework and cultural ideas that inform law in action. His is very much a formalist lawyer's definition, and emphatically not a sociological one. Much of the sociological perspective has emerged as a reaction against this kind of legal positivism.

(3) The So-Called Historical School
Here renamed evolutionist, this developed as another nineteenth-century reaction to natural law thinking. It is much more society-conscious and culture-conscious than positivism. In Germany this took the form of an almost mystical conception of the cultural unity of a people. This was coupled with the idea that there was an organic mode in which a people's inherent destiny unfolded over time. For Savigny, law was the expression of the spirit (*Volksgeist*) of a particular people, the notion of *Volksgeist* being ambiguously associated with race as well as culture. In this interpretation, custom was the fundamental form of law since it originated in the life of the people. Legislated law was only significant when grounded in popular awareness, a kind of codification and refinement of legal ideas already in the popular consciousness.

In England, Maine (1861) constructed a very different historical approach. He rejected Savigny's idea of the *Volksgeist* special to each people, and tried to generalize about the evolution of law and legal ideas in universal terms. Using comparative examples of the legal institutions of a few peoples, he endeavoured to show the sequential steps in the legal development of 'progressive' societies. His idea was that in the shift from kin-based to territorially-based polities, collective family property faded out and private individual property came in, that there was a change in the conception of certain wrongs which ceased to be treated as torts and came to be treated as crimes, and that much of the law affecting persons shifted from status to contract. Many of these generalizations have been criticized in later work, but the questions they raise remain issues of importance.

Marx, though only peripherally concerned with law, has had such a profound effect on social thought that his ideas about law must be taken into account in any review of these matters. He resists compartmentalization, but could be suitably placed within the historical school as his is a theory of sequential developments. Since in his model of history, class struggle is the principal dynamic of change, law is a dependent variable, not an independent force. In Marx's thought, the mode and relations of production constitute the 'base' of any social formation, and politics, law and ideology are part of the 'superstructure' of ideas and practices which maintain a given set of class relations. The state and law are seen essentially as instruments of class domination, and reflections of it. In the twentieth century, the expansion of the Welfare State, largely the product of legislation, has often been referred to in order to call into question some of these ideas of Marx's about law, but some Marxists see no contradiction in the matter and argue that what has happened is simply that class domination has taken new forms.

Marxist and neo-Marxist ideas are extremely important in the development of current critical legal theory. Marxist themes can be seen in the work of Abel (1982), Kennedy (1980), and Balbus (1977) among others. They interpret law as a mode of maintaining the inequalities inherent in capitalist economies, however seemingly ameliorative reformist laws sometimes appear on their face.

(4) The Sociological School
By contrast, from the start, this school was wedded to the idea that progress could be made to occur through legal reform. Today, a major species of legal sociology interprets law as the

means of solving social problems. Jhering thought of society as an arena of competing interests, and that the function of law was to mediate among them. The purpose was to produce 'the security of the conditions of social life' as a whole. The good of the whole was to come above special interests. Pound (1911–12) came to be very much influenced by Jhering's ideas as he considered the function of law in a democracy. He added his own conception that the task of law was one of 'social engineering'. In order that law achieve a scientifically informed efficacy in this role, he urged that sociological studies be made of any social field to be regulated, and also of the actual impact of existing legal institutions, precepts and doctrines.

Ehrlich, another member of the sociological school, stressed the gap between law on the books and the 'living law', the actual conventional practices of a people. For Ehrlich (1926 [1913]) social practice was the true source of viable law. This 'living law' could come to be embodied in formal statutes and decisions, but law that did not have that anchoring lacked the social vitality to be just and effective. Consequently Ehrlich exhorted lawyers and jurists to make themselves aware of existing social conditions and practices in order to bring formal law into harmony with society. This explains Ehrlich's broad definition of law as 'the sum of the conditions of social life in the widest sense of the term'. 'Law' included rules made and enforced by private associations. His was not a definition focused on 'government', but on 'society'.

Ehrlich's contemporary, Weber (1954 [1922]), conceived of law equally broadly. Law, he said, involved a 'coercive apparatus', the purpose of which was norm-enforcement within a community, corporate organization or an institution. Thus lawlike norms could be 'guaranteed' by a variety of social bodies, not only by the state, although the state differed from the others in having a monopoly on 'coercion by violence'. Weber made it clear that, despite the coercive apparatus, the motive for obedience to norms was not necessarily the existence of such a system of physical coercion. The motive could be 'psychological'.

In his models of government and society, his 'ideal types',

Weber identified the bureaucratic state with a 'legal order' of 'rational' rules. As he saw it, the evolution of law was marked by a movement from formal and substantive irrationality to rationality. In this sense rationality meant a logically coherent system of principles and rules. Legal irrationality was the use of means other than logic or reason for the decision of cases. Ordeals and oracles were examples of formal irrationality. Arbitrary decisions in terms of the personal predilections of the judge constituted substantive irrationality. In his ideal types Weber postulated a consistency between the type of overall political organization of a society (its mode of 'imperative co-ordination'), its values and ideology, and its type of legal system.

Weber's ideas continue to influence the work of theorists of law. One of the recent revisionist writers is Unger (1976), who borrows 'ideal types' from Weber and postulates a multiplicity of them in historical sequence. But not only do his types differ from Weber's, but he sees as the principal impetus to change an awareness of the dissonance between ideal and real in a particular social order. His is a very orderly, very personal vision. In his view, the problem of our time is the reconciliation of freedom and community.

Like Weber's, Durkheim's (1960 [1893]) legal theory had an evolutionary theme. He thought that primitive societies were held together by 'mechanical solidarity', a coherence produced by a homogeneity of culture and a sameness of all social units, while the cohesion of complex societies was one of 'organic solidarity' founded on the division of labour in society and a system of complementary differences. Associated with each of these was a type of law. He regarded punitive retribution as the mode of dealing with wrongs in primitive society, while restitutive justice was appropriate to repair many wrongs under conditions of 'organic solidarity'. While Durkheim's interpretation of law in primitive societies was quite wrong, as the anthropologist Malinowski (1926) later showed, the direction of his inquiry, the question to what extent law is an aspect of social cohesion, remains cogent.

Today, social scientists approach law with a distilled and selective recombination of many of these classical ideas of nineteenth-century and early twentieth-century scholars. They use these transformed paradigms in combination with new methods, new information and new preoccupations. These have been generated in a very much altered politico-economic setting. Statistical studies have become an essential concomitant in many analyses of law and its effect in mass society. Quantitative methods have also been applied to the study of legal institutions themselves, to the behaviour of courts, lawyers, and administrative agencies. Legal arguments and rationales are not taken at face value, but are studied as texts, both as they reveal and as they obscure values and interests. Economic dimensions and consequences have loomed increasingly large in the study and evaluation of legal norms. The costs of 'justice' and the nature of access to 'justice' have become major issues. The high-flown values that legal principles express are examined by legal economists in the light of their 'efficiency' and their social effect, not just their self-defined moral content.

Anthropologists have substantially enlarged the existing body of knowledge regarding the social order of non-Western societies, simple and complex. Ethnographic materials collected through direct observation have made plain the ways in which order is maintained without government in small-scale systems, and the way disputes are negotiated in oral cultures. These works are pertinent to the operation of subsections of large-scale, complex societies. A knowledge of such subsystems illuminates the peculiar relation between national laws and local practices in many parts of the world.

The importance and widespread existence of plural legal systems has been acknowledged in the post-colonial world as never before. All the theories founded on a notion that consensus and common values necessarily underlie all effective legal systems have been brought into question in the many instances in which power, rather than consensus, underpins particular laws. The role of law in relation to dissensus and conflict, cultural pluralism and class stratification is an increasingly urgent question for social theorists. The difference between the way law is conceived in the West and elsewhere has also become important as the greater interdependence of all countries is manifest. The question whether there are overarching commonalities that are or could be embodied in international law bears on everything from international commerce to the rights of refugees.

Variously conceived by the professions that generate, apply and enforce it, law is obviously quite differently approached by those who observe, analyse and teach it. Thus there is the law of lawyers and judges, of governments, of legislators and administrators, the formal legal system, its concepts and doctrines, its institutions and workings. In a related, but not identical, territory is the law of legal theorists and legal scholars and social scientists, many of them teachers. Beyond that is the way that the legal order impinges on ongoing social life.

Social scientists study all of this wide range, with a great variety of purposes and perspectives. Some are occupied with assembling information which will be the basis for proposed reforms. Others are engaged in trying to understand the relation between the actual workings of legal institutions and the self-explanations that form its ideology, without any immediate application in mind, rather with the idea of enlarging knowledge, and refining theory. In the broadest sense, one might say that there are two general streams of modern research. One is a social problems/social engineering approach that proceeds from the assumption that law is a consciously constructed instrument of control which has the capacity to shape society and to solve problems, an instrument which can itself be reformed and perfected towards this end. Research is seen to serve these practical purposes. In contrast is the social context approach which assumes that law is itself a manifestation of the existing structure (or past history) of the society in which it is found, and tries to know, understand or explain its form, content and institutions by showing contextual connections. Instead of just one 'social science approach' to law, there are many.

Sally Falk Moore
Harvard University

References

Abel, R. (1982), 'The contradictions of informal justice', in R. Abel (ed.), *The Politics of Informal Justice, Vol. I: The American Experience*, New York.

Balbus, I. D. (1977), 'Commodity form and legal form: an essay on the "relative autonomy" of the law', *Law and Society Review*, 571.

Berman, H. J. (1983), *Law and Revolution; The Formation of the Western Legal Tradition*, Cambridge, Mass.

Durkheim, E. (1960 [1893]), *The Division of Labour in Society*, Glencoe, Ill. (Original French edn, *De la Division du travail social*, Paris.)

Ehrlich, E. (1936 [1913]), *Fundamental Principles of the Sociology of Law*, tr. Walter L. Moll, Cambridge, Mass. (Original German edn, *Grundlegung der Soziologie des Rechts*, Munich.)

Friedman, M. (1975), *The Legal System, A Social Science Perspective*, New York.

Hart, H. L. A. (1961), *The Concept of Law*, New York.

Kennedy, D. (1980), 'Toward an historical understanding of legal consciousness: the case of classical legal thought in America 1850–1940', *Research in Law and Sociology*, 3.

Maine, H. (1861), *Ancient Law*, London.

Malinowski, B. (1926), *Crime and Custom in Savage Society*, London.

Pound, R. (1911–12), 'The scope and purpose of sociological jurisprudence', *Harvard Law Review*, 24 and 25.

Unger, R. (1976), *Law in Modern Society*, New York.

Weber, M. (1954 [1922]), *Max Weber on Law in Economy and Society*, ed. M. Feinstein, Cambridge, Mass. (Original German edn, *Wirtschaft und Gesellschaft*, Tübingen.)

Further Reading

Black, D. (1976), *The Behavior of Law*, New York.

Cain, M. and Hunt, A. (1979), *Marx and Engels on Law*, London.

Friedman, L. M. and MacCaulay, S. (eds) (1977), *Law and The Behavioral Sciences*, 2nd edn, Indianapolis.

Nader, L. and Todd, H. F. (eds) (1975), *The Disputing Process – Law in Ten Societies*, New York.
Nonet, P. and Selznick, P. (1978), *Law and Society in Transition*, New York.
See also: *judicial process*.

Leadership

Machiavelli, so Bertrand Russell said, produced in *The Prince* a 'handbook for gangsters'. That remark illuminates a fundamental confusion in studies of leadership. An objective analysis should describe and explain how leaders control their followers. Whether they use that control to achieve fame or infamy is, although obviously an important question, one that should be left to historians and other commentators.

There is in fact a mass of *apparently* dispassionate scientific investigation of the subject in sociology, social psychology and books about management. Most of these studies are limited. The effective leader is said to be 'group-oriented', 'fulfils group needs' and oils the wheels of human interaction. But that is only one style of leadership: it is egalitarian in its assumptions, manipulative at its strongest, and sometimes no more than the hypocritical claim of a leader to be only the mouthpiece for his followers. There are also leaders who do not read a consensus, but impose it: remote majestic men and women, objects of fear and reverence. Moreover, these small-group quasi-scientific investigations are often shallow. They rely too much on questionnaires and too little on behaviour. They are blind not only to deceit and bluff, but also to the essential characteristic of leadership, which is its mystique.

Followers can be bought, but the purchaser is not a leader; he is an employer. Domination can also be achieved by force. That can be one element in effective leadership; but not that alone, if only because the required concentration of sustained force is an impossibility. The right to dominate is voluntarily given to one who has the 'gift' of leadership; what Max Weber called 'charisma'. Weber saw charisma as one among other styles of domination, but in fact all effective leaders command some measure of devotion. In one way or another a leader must seem to be superhuman.

Sometimes leaders are officially declared gods, as with all Roman emperors from Augustus onwards. Sometimes the deification is a matter of image and metaphor, as when Nkrumah was called the 'Redeemer'. Sometimes it is no more than human attributes expanded beyond the normal: courage, perseverance, endurance and the like. One essential capacity combines ideas of effectiveness with flair, intuition or luck; an ability to come to the right decision in a manner that transcends rationality. In case after case, leaders, even those not overtly anti-intellectual, make clear that reason has its limits, that leadership is an art (not a science), and is a talent which some people have and others do not.

Since leaders in fact cannot work miracles, the study of leadership becomes the examination of strategies (including institutional arrangements) (1) for maintaining in the followers the illusion of a unique talent in the leader, and (2) for solving problems which the real world presents, or, failing solution, for imposing on the situation a definition which leaves unhurt the image of the leader's effectiveness.

F. G. Bailey
University of California, San Diego

Further Reading
Burns, J. M. (1978), *Leadership*, New York.
Gibb, C. A. (ed.) (1969), *Leadership*, London.
Machiavelli, N. (1950 [1513]), *The Prince*, New York.
See also: *charisma; decision making.*

Legitimacy

The discussion of legitimacy in social and political theory seems to confirm Hegel's dictum that theoretical reflection begins only when a practice has completed its development and become problematic. Questions about the moral worth or rightness of different forms of rule were present at the very beginning of systematic thinking about society. In *The Politics*, for instance,

Aristotle held that some constitutions were 'right' (those promoting the common interest of citizens), while others were 'perverted' (those serving only the particular interest of rulers), a distinction grounded in a teleological metaphysics. However, classical theory lacked an explicit language of legitimacy. That was to be an invention of modern thought, represented best in Rousseau's promise in the *Social Contract* to demonstrate how political authority could be rendered 'legitimate'. Rousseau's hypothetical argument resting on the *volonté générale* served as both an epitaph for the Aristotelian tradition and a warning about the contestability of legitimacy in the modern age. This shift from a metaphysical to a voluntaristic account prepared the way for the contribution of Max Weber, the greatest modern theorist of legitimacy.

All modern theory starts from the assumption that legitimacy has to do with the quality of authoritativeness, lawfulness, bindingness, or rightness attached to an order; a government or state is considered 'legitimate' if it possesses the 'right to rule'. Unfortunately, the definition begs the most crucial question: in what does 'right' consist, and how can its meaning be determined? Generally speaking, this question has been answered in two ways. One school of thought has argued with Weber (1968 [1922]) that, 'It is only the probability of orientation to the subjective *belief* in the validity of an order which constitutes the valid order itself.' According to this view, 'right' reduces to belief in the 'right to rule'. The presence of objective, external or universal standards for judging rightness grounded in natural law, reason or some other transhistorical principle is typically rejected as philosophically impossible and sociologically naive. In his sociology of legitimacy, Weber attempted to guard against the 'relativistic' consequences of such a conception by identifying four *reasons* for ascribing 'legitimacy' to any social order: tradition, affect, value-rationality and legality. This classification then served as the basis for his famous analysis of the 'pure types' of 'legitimate domination' (*legitime Herrschaft*): traditional, charismatic and legal-rational.

Recent scholars have argued about the logic, meaning and application of Weber's views. Some writers have sharply criticized the sociological approach generally for subverting a rational distinction between legitimate and illegitimate forms of rule; for failing to distinguish legitimacy from legality; and for confusing a distinction among belief elicited through coercion, habit or rational choice. (In what sense Weber may be guilty of these charges is a matter of dispute.) Underlying these criticisms from the second school of thought is the conviction, expressed particularly in the work of Jürgen Habermas, that a satisfactory theory of legitimacy must be philosophically grounded in such a way as to render possible a 'rational judgement' about the 'right to rule'. For Habermas (1975), grounds have been sought in a rather complex 'consensus theory of truth', where 'truth' signifies 'warranted assertability' under conditions of *ideal* 'communicative competence'.

Whether Habermas or others sharing his assumptions have provided a coherent philosophical grounding for the theory of legitimacy remains an open question. One difficulty with their attempt is that it comes at an awkward time, philosophically considered, for under the influence of Dewey, Wittgenstein and Heidegger, philosophy itself has begun to challenge the project of identifying foundations of knowledge which can be used to achieve definitive criteria of rationality. If this challenge succeeds, then it will become difficult to imagine any viable philosophical alternative to the Weberian typological approach.

In light of this impasse, the most recent work on legitimacy has proceeded in three directions: (1) Some theorists have moved towards developing a theory of *il*legitimacy, arguing that the real problems of the modern state lie with its essential lack of legitimacy. (2) Social scientists attracted to empirical theory have often dropped the term legitimacy altogether, hoping to avoid troublesome normative issues, and have instead looked only for quantifiable 'regime support'. (3) Probably the most innovative direction has been taken by those investigating processes and strategies of legitimation used by the state (particularly in the domains of science, technology, education and communication) to shore up sagging belief in its right to rule. Such diversification, whatever its eventual results, is a firm indication that the problem of legitimacy will remain centrally important in social and political theory, at least as long as the modern state-system remains intact.

Lawrence A. Scaff
University of Arizona

References
Habermas, J. (1975 [1973]), *Legitimation Crisis*, Boston. (Original German edn, *Legitimationsprobleme im Spätkapitalismus*, Frankfurt.)
Weber, M. (1968 [1922]), *Economy and Society*, New York. (Original German edn, *Wirtschaft und Gesellschaft*, Tübingen.)

Further Reading
Rogowski, R. (1974), *Rational Legitimacy: A Theory of Political Support*, Princeton, N.J.
Schaar, J. H. (1981), *Legitimacy in the Modern State*, New Brunswick.
See also: *authority; social contract; state; Weber.*

Liberalism

The belief that people can and that they should be free to determine their own destiny is certainly ancient and widely diffused. So widespread and vague an idea – a sentiment rather than a dogma – is almost impossible to study in time and space; all that can be observed is the variety of specific social propositions which arise from it.

Contemporary liberalism, in the sense of a series of social ideas belonging to a political tradition, often seeks its roots in the ideas of Levellers in Cromwell's coalition during the English Civil War of the seventeenth century; in the revolt of the American colonists a century later; and in Jacobin revolutionaries in France soon afterwards. Present-day liberals find the clear articulation of a range of liberal propositions in the philosophical writings of Rousseau and Locke, in the propaganda of Tom Paine, and in the economic analysis of Adam Smith. These classic expressions were antagonistic towards the essentially feudal political structures, which had more or less successfully administered agrarian societies in Western Europe but which floundered in the attempt to regulate increasingly urban and non-agricultural peoples and processes. Because of the structure of these historic conflicts, liberalism came to be rationalist and humanist, rejecting hereditary authority and supernatural sanctions on behaviour. Naturally, these ideas appealed most powerfully to individuals and groups who were themselves in conflict with the agrarian order, and to mercantilist regulation of trade. In the long run, as emergent capitalists and their allies took up the classic ideas, general arguments for freedom were transformed into specific requests for equality of economic opportunity.

In the two centuries since liberal ideas were most forcibly expressed, feudal state structures and social relationships have almost entirely disappeared and − at least in fully capitalist societies − many items of a formal liberal programme have been implemented. That list would include the election of legislators by adults, the control of the executive either by popular vote or by legislative supremacy, and a judiciary independent in day-to-day matters from intervention by other arms of government. If the mechanics of government have become more liberal, however, the spirit which animates these modern structures is very much more oppressive than Rousseau, or Paine, or Smith expected. With the logic of capitalist accumulation established as the most promising strategy for creating employment and revenue, the opinions of owners and managers of enterprises naturally carry heavy weight. Equality of political rights restrains, but it does not obliterate the unequal political, cultural and social influence of holders of economic power. In fully industrial societies, therefore, liberalism is close to the point of sterile exhaustion, defending (in the name of ancient revolutions against extinct oppressions) as great a degree of inequality as feudal states ever enjoyed. The actual justification for inequality is not the liberal procedures which restrain it, but rather the relatively high standards of health, education, income and consumption which have prevailed.

Outside the fully capitalist societies, the liberal sentiment confronts and is shaped by quite different circumstances. The French Revolution itself helped to clarify an alternative theory of liberation in the minds of some thoughtful revolutionaries. The alternative theory was less concerned with the survival or revival of feudal structures than with the significance of privately owned property as the source of inequality and oppression. If private ownership of productive property were the core problem, then collective ownership might represent a solution. These socialist ideas, gathered together and restated and developed by Marx and Engels later in the nineteenth century, provided an ideology of liberation – until they were taken over by successful revolutionary movements in Russia, Eastern Europe and China. Like liberalism, socialism could be applied as an ideology of government just as much as an ideology of revolt.

The great ideological struggles of the twentieth century have been dominated by liberal and socialist dogmas. Where capitalist development had not already occurred on a massive scale, socialist ideas have been more successful as ideologies of government than their liberal rivals. In those societies, therefore, liberal ideas retain their pristine revolutionary force, threatening to undermine party and bureaucratic controls.

However, most of the world's population live in societies which are neither fully capitalist nor controlled by socialist administrations. Like socialist societies, most Third-World governments are heavily bureaucratic; and the national bureaucracies are often directed by military officers or by narrow oligarchies. In these oppressive situations, even the formal programme of liberalism – equality before the law, a genuinely independent judiciary, regular elections on a wide franchise – would be revolutionary. In such circumstances, however, the prevalence of a grinding poverty and the daily struggle for survival leave little room even in the imagination for such seemingly abstract notions. For precisely the reasons which would render liberal procedures a revolution, they are unlikely to be realized.

In a programme of procedures, then, liberalism has probably run its course by the late twentieth century, almost as completely as anarchism. Where the programme has been implemented, it has grown sterile; elsewhere it seems unrealizable. But as a sentiment, infinitely adaptable to evolving oppressions and always opposed to them, it is still an idea which is cherished in every corner of the world. To look (and work) for the time where it becomes obsolete is not an unworthy aspiration.

Donald Denoon
Australian National University, Canberra

Further Reading
Brausted, E. K. and Melhuish, K. J. (eds) (1978), *Western Liberalism*, London.
Gaus, G. (1983), *The Modern Liberal Theory of Man*, London.
Minogue, K. R. (1963), *The Liberal Mind*, London.
See also: *conservatism*; *equality*; *Mill*; *socialism*.

Local Politics
Modern systems of local government emerged in the eighteenth and nineteenth centuries. Their units were the administrative units of former monarchies which were being transformed into modern nation-states. In the twentieth century, two new types of local political systems developed, both resulting from major political upheavals. The Soviet system of local government, based on the unification of representative- and executive functions, and also on the leadership of the Communist party on all levels of government, was first introduced in the USSR and then adopted in several other Socialist states. In the newly independent states of Asia and Africa, various forms of local government emerged, based on the adaptation of the administrative structures of former metropolitan countries, as well as on the precolonial local political institutions.

Because of the diversity of existing patterns of local government, it is difficult to find a common definition for all forms of local politics. Countries differ in the extent to which local politics are autonomous in relation to national government, in the degree to which local government controls economic and other aspects of life within the territorial limits of its jurisdiction, in the internal organization of local politics, the size of local subdivisions, and so on. Nevertheless, the basic characteristic of local politics is that it consists of political activities (1) conducted within territorially delimited units of subnational administration and (2) directed at meeting the needs of such communities.

Relations between national and local politics vary from strictly federal patterns, in which local political units can determine their own destinies, to strictly unitary systems, in which local units of administration are simply extensions of the national government, wholly subordinated to and dependent on it. In practice, existing local political systems occupy various places on this continuum, but the growing complexity of politics in the twentieth century has resulted in closer national-local linkages (Kjellberg and Teune, 1980).

Social science research on local politics has its roots in early twentieth-century American studies on local communities, some of which covered questions of political participation and local political power (see especially Lynd and Lynd, 1929; Lynd and Lynd, 1937). After the Second World War, local politics became one of the most fashionable subjects of political science (Robson, 1948; Banfield and Wilson, 1963). New empirical studies published in the US originally focused on the composition of local ruling elites (Hunter, 1953; Dahl, 1961), but the emphasis soon shifted to the broader issues of 'Who governs, where, when and with what effects?' (Clarke, 1968). This stimulated collaboration with sociologists and encouraged the uses of statistical methods.

After 1960, there was a growth in cross-national comparative research. A notable example was a comparison of local politics and local leadership patterns in India, Poland, the US and Yugoslavia in the late 1960s (Jacob *et al.*, 1971). In 1970, the International Political Science Association established a Research Committee on Comparative Study of Local Government and Politics in an effort to stimulate interest in comparative studies with special reference to participation and local government outputs. Interest in cross-national collaboration in this field is also evident in the activities of other international bodies. Today local politics studies can provide cross-national findings on the relationship between governmental structures and patterns of leadership and community performance and development.

Jerzy J. Wiatr
University of Warsaw

References

Banfield, E. C. and Wilson, J. Q. (1963), *City Politics*, Cambridge, Mass.

Clark, T. N. (ed.) (1968), *Community Structure and Decision-Making: Comparative Analyses*, San Francisco.

Dahl, R. A. (1961), *Who Governs?*, New Haven, Conn.

Hunter, F. (1953), *Community Power Structure*, Chapel Hill, North Carolina.

Jacob, P. E. *et al.* (1971), *Values and the Active Community*, New York.

Kjellberg, F. and Teune, H. (eds) (1980), 'Recent changes in urban politics: national-local linkages', *International Political Science Review*, 1.

Lynd, R. S. and Lynd, H. M. (1929), *Middletown*, New York.

Lynd, R. S. and Lynd, H. M. (1937), *Middletown in Transition*, New York.

Robson, W. A. (1948), *The Development of Local Government*, London.

Locke, John (1632–1704)

John Locke was born in 1632 at Wrington in Somerset. He entered Christ Church College, Oxford in 1652 where he received his MA in 1658. In that same year he was elected student of Christ Church; in 1660 he became lecturer in Greek; lecturer in Rhetoric in 1662, and censor of Moral Philosophy in 1664. From 1667 to 1681 Locke was physician and secretary to Anthony Ashley Cooper, Lord Ashley (later, First Earl of Shaftesbury). He was elected fellow of the Royal Society in 1668, and was secretary to the Lords Proprietors of Carolina from 1668 to 1675. In 1684, he was deprived of his appointment to Christ Church by royal decree. He lived in Holland from 1683 to 1689; was Commissioner on the Board of Trade from 1696 to 1700, and died at Otes (Oates) in the parish of High Laver, Essex in 1704.

Locke's *Essay Concerning Human Understanding* (1690) made a major contribution to psychology and to philosophical psychology. That work offered the outlines of a genetic epistemology, and a theory of learning. Locke's interest in children is reflected not only in his pedagogical work, *Some Thoughts Concerning Education* (1693), but in many passages of the *Essay* where he traced the development of awareness in children. The oft-quoted metaphor used by Locke to characterize the mind as a blank tablet should not blind us to the fact that the Lockean mind comes equipped with faculties, that the child has specific 'tempers' or character traits which the educator must learn to work with, and that human nature for Locke has basic self-preserving tendencies to avoid pain and seek pleasure. These tendencies were even called by Locke 'innate practical principles'. The innate claim his psychology rejected was for truths (moral and intellectual) and specific ideational contents.

Much of the *Essay* is occupied with discussing how we acquire certain ideas, with showing how a combination of physical and physiological processes stimulate and work with a large number of mental operations (for example, joining, separating, considering, abstracting, generalizing) to produce the ideas of particular sense qualities and many complex notions, such as power, existence, unity. One such complex notion is the idea of self or person.

The account of the idea of self – or rather, *my* idea of *my* self, for Locke's account of this notion is a first-person account – emerges out of a discussion of the question, 'Does the soul always think?' That question had been answered in the affirmative by Descartes. For Locke, not only was it empirically false that the soul always thinks; that question suggested wrongly that something in me (my soul), not me, thinks. *I* am the agent of my actions and the possessor of my thoughts. Moreover, all thinking is reflexive: when I think, I am aware that I am thinking, no matter what form that thinking takes (sensing, willing, believing, doubting or remembering). It is the awareness of my act of thinking which also functions in awareness of self. Consciousness appropriates both thoughts and actions. The self or person for Locke consists in that set of thoughts and actions which I appropriate and for which I take responsibility through my consciousness.

Appropriation is a fundamental activity for Locke. I appropriate my thoughts and actions to form my concept of self. The *Essay* details the appropriation by each of us of ideas and knowledge. Education is also an appropriation of information, but more importantly of habits of good conduct. Education is a socializing process. It takes place usually within the family, with a tutor (for Locke writes about the education of a gentleman's son). But the account of the socialization process extends to Locke's political writings, *Two Treatises on Government* (1690), where he discusses the family, duties parents have to their children and to each other (a marriage contract is part of his account of the family), and the rights and duties of citizens in a political society. The appropriation of land, possessions and eventually money by the activities of the person constitutes an early stage in Locke's account of the movement from the state of nature to a civil (political) society.

The political society, as the pre-political state of nature, is grounded in law and order; order is respect and responsibility to each other and ultimately to God whose law of nature prescribes these duties. Locke's law of nature is a Christianized version of that tradition. The individual laws which he cites on occasion prescribe and proscribe the actions sanctioned or denied by the liberal religion of his day. These laws differed little in content from those innate moral truths Locke attacked; it was not the truths he rejects, only the claim that they were innate. Locke's society is fairly slanted in favour of the individual: preservation of the person, privacy of property, tacit assent, the right of dissent. At the same time, the pressures towards conformity and the force of majority opinion are also strong. The structure of his civil society, with its checks and balances, its separation of powers, its grounding on the law of nature, is designed to achieve a balance between the rights and needs of the individual and the need for security and order. His views on toleration (which were expressed in a series of tracts), while directed mainly against religious intoleration, match well with his insistence that government does not have the right to prescribe rites, rituals, dress and other practices in religion. Locke's toleration did not, however, extend to unbelief, to atheism.

The methodology for acquiring knowledge recommended by Locke and illustrated in his *Essay* stressed careful observation. Both in the physical sciences and in learning about ourselves and others, it was the 'plain, historical method' (that is, experience and observation) which holds the promise of accurate knowledge, or sound probability. Knowledge was not limited to demonstrative, deductive processes. Truth claims were always open to revision through further reports and observations. These concepts of knowledge and this experiential method were extended by Locke to what was later termed (for example, by Hume) 'the science of man' or 'of human nature'. His detailed attention to his own thought processes enabled him to map the wide variety of mental operations and to begin the development of a cognitive psychology. His interest in children, throughout his life, led to observations and descriptions of their behaviour. He had many friends who had children, and lived for several years on different occasions with families who had several young children. The *Essay* uses some of these observations as the basis for a brief genetic learning theory, and his *Some Thoughts* contains many remarks and recommendations for raising children based upon his firsthand experience with children in their natural environment.

Locke's social theory grew out of his reading and (more importantly) out of these habits of observing people in daily life. In his travels in France and Holland, he often recorded details of activities and practices, religious, academic and ordinary. Where direct observation was not possible, he used the new travel literature for reports on other societies, other customs and habits. He had his own biases and preferences, to be sure, but with his dedication to reason and rationality, he seldom allowed emotions to affect his observations or his conclusions. He was an articulate representative of the Royal Society's attitudes in the sciences, including what we know as the social sciences.

John W. Yolton
Rutgers College

Locke's Writings:
Epistola de Tolerantia, Gouda, 1689.
Essay Concerning Human Understanding, London, 1690.
Further Considerations Concerning Raising the Value of Money, London, 1695.
Letter Concerning Toleration, London, 1689.
A Letter to Edward Lord Bishop of Worcester, London, 1697.
The Reasonableness of Christianity, as Delivered in the Scriptures, London, 1695.
A Second Letter Concerning Toleration, London, 1690.
Short Observations on a Printed Paper, Intituled 'For Encouraging the Coining Silver Money in England, and After, for Keeping it Here', London, 1695.
Some Considerations of the Consequences of the Lowering of Interest and Raising the Value of Money, London, 1692.
Some Thoughts Concerning Education, London, 1693.
A Third Letter for Toleration, London, 1692.
Two Treatises of Government, London, 1690.
Works, London, 1714, 3 vols.

Further Reading
Aaron, R. I. (1971), *John Locke*, 3rd edn, Oxford.
Colman, J. (1983), *John Locke's Moral Philosophy*, Edinburgh.
Cranston, M. (1957), *John Locke, A Biography*, New York.
Dunn, J. (1969), *The Political Thought of John Locke*, Cambridge.
Tully, J. (1980), *A Discourse on Property. John Locke and his Adversaries*, Cambridge.
Yolton, J. W. (1956), *John Locke and the Way of Ideas*, Oxford.
Yolton, J. W. (1970), *Locke and the Compass of Human Understanding*, Cambridge.

Machiavelli, Niccolo (1469–1526)

Machiavelli was a Florentine patriot, civil servant and political theorist. Entering the service of the Council of Ten which ruled republican Florence in 1498, he was sent abroad on diplomatic missions which provided much of the experience later to be distilled as advice on political and military skill. In 1512 the republic crumbled and the Medici family, who had long dominated Florentine politics, returned to power. Accidentally and unjustly implicated in a plot against them, Machiavelli was arrested and tortured. On his release he was exiled from the city, and retired to a small farm in Sant' Andrea, seven miles south of the city. The remainder of a disappointed life was devoted to writings, some of them intended to persuade the new rulers to restore him to the centre of affairs which he so dearly loved.

The Prince (1513), written soon after his downfall, was a short work of advice to princes, focused in its last chapter on the local problem of liberating Italy from foreign domination. Some writers (Spinoza and Rousseau most notably) have taken the work as a satire on monarchy, but it seems evidently a piece of self-advertisement in the service of ingratiation. Settling in to a life of exile, Machiavelli farmed, and wrote the *Discourses on the First Ten Books of Titus Livius* ([1532] 1950), a sequence of reflections on political skill, largely as exemplified in the Roman republic. His republican sympathies are evident in this work, but the frank discussion of ruthless and immoral options, for which he is notorious, is no less to be found here than in *The Prince*. By 1520 he had written on *The Art of War* and commenced *The History of Florence*. His comedy *Mandragola* is one of the classics of Italian literature. In 1525, the Medici regime was overthrown and a republic restored, but the new regime failed to employ him. He died in 1526.

Machiavelli criticized previous writers on politics for dealing with ideal and imaginary states, and claimed himself to deal with the 'effective truth' (*verita effettuale*) of politics. Situated firmly within the tradition of civic humanism, he was deeply preocuppied with the constitution of cities and the glory of heroes. His contribution to the unblinking realism of the period was to recognize that the heroes of statesmanship had not invariably followed the moral advice current in a Christian community, and indeed that some of the maxims conventionally pressed upon princes might well lead directly to their ruin. A prince must therefore know, he argued, how not to be good, and to use this knowledge according to necessity. Beyond that, however, he thought that those rulers who are in the process of consolidating their power must know how to dominate the imaginations of men. One who did was Cesare Borgia, a prince with whom Machiavelli dealt while serving the Florentine republic. Borgia had used one of his lieutenants, Ramirro da Orca, to pacify, with all necessary brutality, the newly conquered Romagna; he then had da Orca killed, and his body cut in two, and left in the piazza at Cesena, to satisfy the grievances and no doubt dominate the imaginations of the people. The ferocity of this spectacle, he wrote in chapter VII of *The Prince*, 'caused the people both satisfaction and amazement'. It is often said that Machiavelli believed in one kind of morality for private life, another for statesmen. Yet for all his cynicism, there is nothing actually relativist to be detected in his straightforward recognition of good and evil. Rulers are not accorded a different morality; they are merely construed as the guardians of morality itself and accorded a licence to violate moral norms when necessary. Transposed out of the idiom of advice to princes and into a characterization of the emerging modern state (of which Machiavelli was an acute observer), this became the idea of reason of state.

Machiavelli was very far from encouraging any sort of enormity. Statesmen are the creators of civilization, and their ambitions are without glory unless they serve the public good. Machiavelli talked with some diffidence of the proper use of cruelty in politics. The test of necessary cruelty is that it is economical, and this combination of utility with an ethic of honour was highly distinctive of his attitude. 'When the act accuses him, the outcome should excuse him,' wrote Machiavelli, in a passage often translated as 'the end justifies the means'. But Machiavelli is concerned not with moral justification but with the proper judgement to be made by subjects, and historians. From this technical point of view, religion is important because it binds men to commitments and intensifies their virtue. Machiavelli is deeply anticlerical in a Latin style, and often directly hostile to Christianity because its ethic of humility weakens governments and discourages a serious military ferocity. His admiration goes to the heroic actor in this world rather than to the pious devotee of the next.

The Machiavelli of the *Discourses* is less well known but more enduring. Here we find a conflict theory of society, with men struggling to hold states together against the tendencies of dissolution. Machiavelli bequeathed to later thinkers the classical idea that any enduring constitution must balance monarchic, aristocratic and democratic elements. To create and sustain such a state, in which mere private and familial preoccupations are transcended in the public realm of citizenship, is the supreme human achievement, but contains its own ultimate doom. For states create peace, and peace allows prosperity, and when men grow accustomed to peace and prosperity, they lose their civic virtue and indulge private passions: liberty, to use Machiavelli's terms, gives way to corruption. This tradition of thought, with its emphasis on citizenly participation, never ceased to be cultivated even in the absolute monarchies of early modern Europe, and became dominant from the time of the French Revolution onwards. It composes much of what the modern world calls 'democracy'.

The Machiavelli of popular imagination, however, has always been the exponent of the pleasures of manipulation, the supreme pornographer of power. Many revolutionary adventurers have found in him conscious formulae to cover what they were inclined to do by instinct. And in this role, Machiavelli has been remembered by social psychologists constructing a questionnaire to measure the manipulative tendencies of personality. Those who score high are called 'high machs', while less manipulative people are called 'low machs'.

Kenneth Minogue
London School of Economics and Political Science

Further Reading
Chabrol, F. (1958), *Machiavelli and the Renaissance*, London.
Hale, J. R. (1961), *Machiavelli and Renaissance Italy*, London.
Skinner, Q. (1981), *Machiavelli*, London.
Pocock, J. (1975), *The Machiavellian Moment*, Oxford.

Majority Rule

Majority rule as a political slogan was used effectively as a rallying cry in a very few societies, especially British colonies in Africa during the era of decolonization from the 1950s to the 1970s. Wherever entrenched interests sought to delay full independence or to build minority interests into the independence constitution, the slogan 'majority rule' mobilized popular (and populist) demands for the erosion of those interests. This usage reflected a short-term tactical need, rather than a strategic commitment to a particular style or substance of government. Accordingly, once the particular obstacles had been removed, the term disappeared from political rhetoric.

Outside this particular context, majority rule has been used surprisingly seldom. In other times and in other places, a popular struggle against foreign control has been expressed in nationalist terms, or in the language of class conflict. It may therefore be a measure of the fragile national sentiment, and the inchoate class configurations of British African colonies, which led to the use of this term in those situations. The precise ethnic character, and the class orientation, of the presumptive independent government, were not yet entirely clear while the process of decolonization was in train: accordingly, the populace was commonly mobilized for independence by populist and ill-defined appeals. Once the successor government was securely installed in office, and governing on behalf of the whole population with more or less credibility, continued use of the term 'majority rule' was either subversive or otiose. Conceivably, it could be resurrected in those countries where the military have superseded civilian administrations, or in South Africa where the White minority retains political power; but in these contexts popular political rhetoric is more commonly couched in terms of ethnicity or of social class, than of majority rule. In general, therefore, it is reasonable to consider the term exclusively as the relic of a quite specific era, and of narrowly defined social and political circumstances. Its essential vacuity has prevented it from making the transition from political slogan to the language of social analysis.

Donald Denoon
Australian National University
Canberra

See also: *democracy*.

Marx, Karl Heinrich (1818–83)

Marx was a German social scientist and revolutionary, whose analysis of capitalist society laid the theoretical basis for the political movement bearing his name. Marx's main contribution lies in his emphasis on the role of the economic factor – the changing way in which people have reproduced their means of subsistence – in shaping the course of history. This perspective has had a considerable influence on the whole range of social sciences.

Karl Heinrich Marx was born in the town of Trier in the Moselle district of the Prussian Rhineland on 5 May 1818. He came from a long line of rabbis on both his father's and his mother's sides. His father, a respected lawyer in Trier, had accepted baptism as a Protestant in order to be able to pursue his career. The atmosphere of Marx's home was permeated by the Enlightenment, and he assimilated a certain amount of romantic and early socialist ideas from Baron von Westphalen – to whose daughter, Jenny, he became engaged in 1835 and later married. In the same year he left the local gymnasium, or high school, and enrolled at the University of Bonn. He transferred the following year to the University of Berlin, where he soon embraced the dominant philosophy of Hegelianism. Intending to become a university teacher, Marx obtained his doctorate in 1841 with a thesis on post-Aristotelian Greek philosophy.

From 1837 Marx had been deeply involved in the Young Hegelian movement. This group espoused a radical critique of

Christianity and, by implication, a liberal opposition to the Prussian autocracy. Finding a university career closed to him by the Prussian government, Marx moved into journalism. In October 1842 he became editor, in Cologne, of the influential *Rheinische Zeitung*, a liberal newspaper backed by Rhenish industrialists. Marx's incisive articles, particularly on economic questions, induced the government to close the paper, and he decided to emigrate to France.

Paris was then the centre of socialist thought and on his arrival at the end of 1843, Marx rapidly made contact with organized groups of emigré German workers and with various sects of French socialists. He also edited the shortlived *Deutsch-französische Jahrbücher*, which was intended to form a bridge between nascent French socialism and the ideas of the German radical Hegelians. It was also in Paris that Marx first formed his lifelong partnership with Friedrich Engels. During the first few months of his stay in Paris, Marx rapidly became a convinced communist and set down his views in a series of manuscripts known as the *Ökonomisch-philosophische Manuskripte* (*Economic and Philosophic Manuscripts of 1844*). Here he outlined a humanist conception of communism, influenced by the philosophy of Ludwig Feuerbach and based on a contrast between the alienated nature of labour under capitalism and a communist society in which human beings freely developed their nature in co-operative production. For the first time there appeared together, if not yet united, what Engels described as the three constituent elements in Marx's thought – German idealist philosophy, French socialism, and English economics. It is above all these Manuscripts which (in the West at least) reorientated many people's interpretation of Marx – to the extent of their even being considered as his major work. They were not published until the early 1930s and did not attract public attention until after the Second World War; certain facets of the Manuscripts were soon assimilated to the existentialism and humanism then so much in vogue, and presented an altogether more attractive basis for non-Stalinist socialism than textbooks on dialectical materialism.

Seen in their proper perspective, these Manuscripts were in

fact no more than a starting-point for Marx – an initial, exuberant outpouring of ideas to be taken up and developed in subsequent economic writings, particularly in the *Grundrisse* (1857–8) and in *Das Kapital* (1867). In these later works the themes of the '1844 Manuscripts' would certainly be pursued more systematically, in greater detail, and against a much more solid economic and historical background; but the central inspiration or vision was to remain unaltered: man's alienation in capitalist society, and the possibility of his emancipation – of his controlling his own destiny through communism.

Because of his political journalism, Marx was expelled from Paris at the end of 1844. He moved (with Engels) to Brussels, where he stayed for the next three years. He visited England, then the most advanced industrial country in the world, where Engels's family had cotton-spinning interests in Manchester. While in Brussels, Marx devoted himself to an intensive study of history. This he set out in a manuscript known as *The German Ideology* (also published posthumously); its basic thesis was that 'the nature of individuals depends on the material conditions determining their production'. Marx traced the history of the various modes of production and predicted the collapse of the present one – capitalism – and its replacement by communism.

At the same time that he was engaged in this theoretical work, Marx became involved in political activity and in writing polemics, (as in *Misère de la Philosophie* (1847) (*The Poverty of Philosophy*), against what he considered to be the unduly idealistic socialism of Pierre Joseph Proudhon. He joined the Communist League, an organization of German emigré workers with its centre in London, for which he and Engels became the major theoreticians. At a conference of the league in London at the end of 1847, Marx and Engels were commissioned to write a *Manifest der kommunistischen Partei* (1848) (*Manifesto of the Communist Party*), a declaration that was to become the most succinct expression of their views. Scarcely was the *Manifesto* published when the 1848 wave of revolutions broke in Europe.

Early in 1848, Marx moved back to Paris, where the revolution had first erupted. He then went on to Germany where he founded, again in Cologne, the *Neue Rheinische Zeitung*. This widely influential newspaper supported a radical democratic line against the Prussian autocracy. Marx devoted his main energies to its editorship, since the Communist League had been virtually disbanded. With the ebbing of the revolutionary tide, however, Marx's paper was suppressed. He sought refuge in London in May 1849, beginning the 'long, sleepless night of exile' that was to last for the rest of his life.

On settling in London, Marx grew optimistic about the imminence of a fresh revolutionary outbreak in Europe, and he rejoined the rejuvenated Communist League. He wrote two lengthy pamphlets on the 1848 revolution in France and its aftermath, entitled *Die Klassenkämpfe in Frankreich 1848 bis 1850* (1850) (*The Class Struggles in France*) and *Der achzehnte Brumaire des Louis Bonaparte* (1852) (*The Eighteenth Brumaire of Louis Bonaparte*). But he soon became convinced that 'a new revolution is possible only in consequence of a new crisis', and devoted himself to the study of political economy to determine the causes and conditions of this crisis.

During the first half of the 1850s the Marx family lived in three-room lodgings in the Soho quarter of London and experienced considerable poverty. The Marxes already had four children on their arrival in London, and two more were soon born. Of these, only three survived the Soho period. Marx's major source of income at this time (and later) was Engels, who was drawing a steadily increasing income from his father's cotton business in Manchester. This was supplemented by weekly articles he wrote as foreign correspondent for the *New York Daily Tribune*. Legacies in the late 1850s and early 1860s eased Marx's financial position somewhat, but it was not until 1869 that he had a sufficient and assured income settled on him by Engels.

Not surprisingly, Marx's major work on political economy made slow progress. By 1857–8 he had produced a mammoth 800-page manuscript – a rough draft of a work that he intended should deal with capital, landed property, wage-labour, the state, foreign trade, and the world market. This manuscript, known as *Grundrisse* (or 'Outlines'), was not published until 1941. In the early 1860s he broke off his work to compose three large volumes, entitled *Theorien über den Mehrwert* (1861–3) (*Theories of Surplus Value*), that discussed his predecessors in political economy, particularly Adam Smith and David Ricardo.

It was not until 1867 that Marx was able to publish the first results of his work in Volume One of *Das Kapital*, devoted to a study of the capitalist process of production. Here he elaborated his version of the labour theory of value, and his conception of surplus value and exploitation that would ultimately lead to a falling rate of profit and the collapse of capitalism. Volumes Two and Three were largely finished in the 1860s, but Marx worked on the manuscripts for the rest of his life. They were published posthumously by Engels. In his major work, Marx's declared aim was to analyse 'the birth, life and death of a given social organism and its replacement by another, superior order'. In order to achieve this aim, Marx took over the concepts of the 'classical' economists that were still the generally accepted tool of economic analysis, and used them to draw very different conclusions. Ricardo had made a distinction between use-value and exchange-value. The exchange-value of an object was something separate from its price and consisted of the amount of labour embodied in the objects of production, though Ricardo thought that the price in fact tended to approximate to the exchange-value. Thus – in contradistinction to later analyses – the value of an object was determined by the circumstances of production rather than those of demand. Marx took over these concepts, but, in his attempt to show that capitalism was not static but an historically relative system of class exploitation, supplemented Ricardo's views by introducing the idea of surplus-value. Surplus-value was defined as the difference between the value of the products of labour and the cost of producing that labour-power, that is, the labourer's subsistence; for the exchange-value of labour-power was equal to the amount of labour necessary to reproduce that labour-power and this was normally much lower than the exchange-value of the products of that labour-power.

The theoretical part of Volume One divides very easily into three sections. The first section is a rewriting of the *Zur Kritik der politischen Ökonomie* (1859) (*Critique of Political Economy*) and analyses commodities, in the sense of external objects that satisfy human needs, and their value. Marx established two sorts of value – use-value, or the utility of something, and exchange-value, which was determined by the amount of labour incorporated in the object. Labour was also of a twofold nature according to whether it created use-values or exchange-values. Because 'the exchange-values of commodities must be capable of being expressed in terms of something common to them all', and the only thing they shared was labour, then labour must be the source of value. But since evidently some people worked faster or more skilfully than others, this labour must be a sort of average 'socially necessary' labour time. There followed a difficult section on the form of value, and the first chapter ended with an account of commodities as exchange-values, which he described as the 'fetishism of commodities' in a passage that recalls the account of alienation in the *Pariser Manuskripte* (1844) (*Paris Manuscripts*) and (even more) the *Note on James Mill*. 'In order,' said Marx here, 'to find an analogy, we must have recourse to the mist-enveloped regions of the religious world. In that world the productions of the human brain appear as independent beings endowed with life, and entering into relation both with one another and the human race. So it is in the world of commodities with the products of men's hands.' The section ended with a chapter on exchange and an account of money as the means for the circulation of commodities, the material expression for their values and the universal measure of value.

The second section was a small one on the transformation of money into capital. Before the capitalist era, people had sold commodities for money in order to buy more commodities. In the capitalist era, instead of selling to buy, people had bought to sell dearer: they had bought commodities with their money in order, by means of those commodities, to increase their money.

In the third section Marx introduced his key notion of surplus value, the idea that Engels characterized as Marx's principal 'discovery' in economics. Marx made a distinction between *constant* capital which was 'that part of capital which is represented by the means of production, by the raw material, auxiliary material and instruments of labour, and does not, in the process of production, undergo any quantitative alteration of value' and *variable* capital. Of this Marx said: 'That part of capital, represented by labour power, does, in the process of production, undergo an alteration of value. It both reproduces the equivalent of its own value, and also produces an excess, a surplus value, which may itself vary, may be more or less according to the circumstances.' This variation was the rate of surplus value around which the struggle between workers and capitalists centred. The essential point was that the capitalist got the worker to work longer than was merely sufficient to embody in his product the value of his labour power: if the labour power of the worker (roughly what it cost to keep him alive and fit) was £4 a day and the worker could embody £4 of value in the product on which he was working in eight hours, then, if he worked ten hours, the last two hours would yield surplus value – in this case £1.

Thus surplus value could only arise from variable capital, not from constant capital, as labour alone created value. Put very simply, Marx's reason for thinking that the rate of profit would decrease was that, with the introduction of machinery, labour time would become less and thus yield less surplus value. Of course, machinery would increase production and colonial markets would absorb some of the surplus, but these were only palliatives and an eventual crisis was inevitable. These first nine chapters were complemented by a masterly historical account of the genesis of capitalism which illustrates better than any other writing Marx's approach and method. Marx particularly made pioneering use of official statistical information that came to be available from the middle of the nineteenth century onwards.

Meanwhile, Marx devoted much time and energy to the First International – to whose General Council he was elected on its foundation in 1864. This was one of the reasons he was so delayed in his work on *Das Kapital*. He was particularly active in preparing for the annual congresses of the International and in leading the struggle against the anarchist wing of the

International led by Mikhail Bakunin. Although Marx won this contest, the transfer of the seat of the General Council from London to New York in 1872 – a move that Marx supported – led to the swift decline of the International. The most important political event during the existence of the International was the Paris Commune of 1871, when the citizens of Paris, in the aftermath of the Franco-Prussian war, rebelled against their government and held the city for two months. On the bloody suppression of this rebellion, Marx wrote one of his most famous pamphlets – entitled *Address on The Civil War in France* (1871) – which was an enthusiastic defence of the activities and aims of the Commune.

During the last decade of his life Marx's health declined considerably, and he was incapable of the sustained efforts of creative synthesis that had so obviously characterized his previous work. Nevertheless, he managed to comment substantially on contemporary politics in Germany and Russia. In Germany he opposed, in his *Randglossen zum Programm der deutschen Arbeiterpartei* (1875) (*Critique of the Gotha Programme*), the tendency of his followers Wilhelm Leibknecht and August Bebel to compromise with the state socialism of Ferdinand Lassalle in the interest of a united socialist party. In Russia, in correspondence with Vera Sassoulitch, he contemplated the possibility of Russia's bypassing the capitalist stage of development and building communism on the basis of the common ownership of land characteristic of the village council, or *mir*. Marx, however, was increasingly dogged by ill health, and he regularly travelled to European spas and even to Algeria in search of recuperation. The deaths of his eldest daughter and of his wife clouded the last years of his life, and he died in London on 13 March, 1883.

The influence of Marx, so narrow during his lifetime, expanded enormously after his death. This influence was at first evident in the growth of the Social Democratic Party in Germany, but reached world-wide dimensions following the success of the Bolsheviks in Russia in 1917. Paradoxically, although the main thrust of Marx's thought was to anticipate that a proletarian revolution would inaugurate the transition to socialism in advanced industrial countries, Marxism was most successful in developing or Third World countries, such as Russia or China. Since the problems of these countries are primarily agrarian and the initial development of an industrial base, they are necessarily far removed from what were Marx's immediate concerns. On a more general level, over the whole range of the social sciences, Marx's materialist conception of history and his analysis of capitalist society have made him probably the most influential figure of the twentieth century.

David McLellan
University of Kent

Further Reading

Avineri, S. (1968), *The Social and Political Thought of Karl Marx*, Cambridge.

Cohen, G. (1978), *Karl Marx's Theory of History: A Defence*, Oxford.

Marx, K. (1977), *Selected Writings*, ed. D. McLellan, Oxford.

McLellan, D. (1974), *Karl Marx: His Life and Thought*, New York.

Ollman, B. (1971), *Alienation, Marx's Conception of Man in Capitalist Society*, Cambridge.

Plamenatz, J. (1975), *Karl Marx's Philosophy of Man*, Oxford.

Suchting, W. (1983), *Marx: An Introduction*, Brighton.

Mill, John Stuart (1806–73)

John Stuart Mill, the classic exponent of liberalism, was brought up in utilitarian principles by his father, James Mill, a close friend and associate of Bentham. His rigorous childhood education, described in his *Autobiography* (1873), involved a brilliant and precocious mastery of classical languages by the age of seven. For most of his working life he was a clerk at India House in London, though briefly a Member of Parliament. He married Harriet Taylor whom he always claimed as his inspiration and intellectual partner.

Mill was a many-sided thinker and writer – a philosopher,

social scientist and humanist. Amongst the subjects he treated were politics, ethics, logic and scientific method. Particular topics on which he wrote included the position of women (*The Subjection of Women*, 1869), constitutional reform (*Considerations on Representative Government*, 1861), and economics (*Principles of Political Economy*, 1848).

In *Utilitarianism* (1861) Mill expounded and defended the principle that the tendency of actions to promote happiness or its reverse is the standard of right and wrong. His version of utilitarianism was from a logical point of view flawed, and from a moral point of view enhanced, by the notion that some forms of happiness are more worthwhile than others. *On Liberty* (1859) is the classic argument for the claims of the individual against the state, and in it Mill makes an impassioned defence of the principles of liberty and toleration. This is sometimes seen as inconsistent with his basic utilitarianism, but Mill believed that principles like liberty and justice were themselves important social instruments for utility. This follows from his view of human nature, and in particular from his belief that self-determination and the exercise of choice are themselves part of a higher concept of happiness. Regarding toleration, Mill argued in favour of liberty of thought, speech and association, as well as for freedom to cultivate whatever lifestyle one chooses, subject only to the constraint of not harming others. It is often disputed whether there are any actions which do not affect other people in some way, but the distinction between other-regarding and self-regarding actions is an essential element of liberalism.

Mill applied these principles to education, defending a liberal and secular education. He considered compulsory education not an invasion of liberty but essential to it. However, he believed strongly that there should not be a 'state monopoly of education' but that state education should be one amongst a number of competing systems.

In *A System of Logic, Ratiocinative and Deductive* (1843), Mill defended a classical view of induction as empirical generalization and held that this can supply a model for both logical deduction and scientific method. In some respects this may be seen as a classic version of British empiricism, but because Mill was prepared to accept the uniformity of nature as a basic postulate, it is free from the sceptical consequences that this position sometimes seems to involve. Mill extended his discussion of methodology to cover the application of exper- imental method to social science and set out to provide 'a general science of man in society'. His argument is to be found in Book VI of *A System of Logic*, which has been called the most important contribution to the making of modern sociology until Durkheim's *Rules of Sociological Method*.

Brenda Cohen
University of Surrey

Further Reading
Gray, J. (1983), *Mill on Liberty: A Defence*, London.
Ryan, A. (1974), *J. S. Mill*, London.
Ten, C. L. (1980), *Mill on Liberty*, Oxford.

Montesquieu, Charles Louis de Secondat (1689–1755)

Charles Louis de Secondat, Baron de Montesquieu was one of the major precursors of sociological thought. Born at La Brede near Bordeaux, he inherited the family vineyard estates and was able to use his wealth and training as a lawyer to travel widely both in France and abroad, and to ingratiate himself with the influential Parisian intellectual society of the first half of the eighteenth century. He became a major figure of Enlight- enment thought and a perceptive critic of the society of the time.

His major works, the *Lettres Persanes* (1721), the *Considérations sur les causes de la grandeur des Romains et de leur décadence (1734)* and the *De l'esprit des lois* (1748) ostensibly deal with very different topics, but beneath the surface these can be shown to have a seriousness of purpose and concatenation of subject matter not easily detected. The *Lettres Persanes*, a novel about two Persian princes visiting Paris in the early years of the eighteenth century are, on closer examination, also a critical investigation into the major institutions of *ancien régime* society. The *Considérations*, a study which foreshadows Gibbons's *Decline and Fall of the Roman Empire*, is important in the history of ideas for its revolutionary historical methodology – *histoire raisonnée*, as it was called – making use of an embryonic ideal-type construct.

His third work, and by far his most important, the *De l'esprit des lois* is best known for its contribution to political thought. It continues the critique first developed in the *Lettres Persanes* of the social structure of the *ancien régime*: Montesquieu makes a powerful case for strengthening the role of the nobility and commercial interests as 'intermediate powers' between the absolutist monarchy and the mass of the people. Together with the argument for a 'separation of powers' which Montesquieu adapted from the British constitution, this provided a formula which, if it had been heeded, might have helped save France from the cataclysm that was to occur later in the century.

However, there has been perhaps too great an emphasis on the political aspects of the *Esprit*. Montesquieu, in the Preface to the work, asks the reader to 'approve or condemn the work as a whole', and if one reads beyond the introductory chapters, one finds a wealth of comparative data on all the major institutions of society – economic, belief and value systems, family and kinship systems – with evidence drawn both from his and others' researches on a wide range of societies, plus considerable historical and anthropological material. In this sense, it is true to say that the *De l'esprit des lois* is the first major essay in comparative sociology. Montesquieu brought to the fore the idea that each society, each social system, has its own natural law of development, and it follows that the objective of every student of society is to discover the real nature of that law. By viewing society as a set of interrelated elements, Montesquieu was putting forward an holistic interpretation of social structure akin to contemporary functionalism.

Functionalism is essentially a conservative doctrine, and Montesquieu is remembered as a founder of the conservative tradition in sociological thought. Through the works of Ferguson and Robertson, Bonald and de Maistre, Fustel de

Coulanges and Durkheim, his ideas have passed into the main-stream of sociological thought.

John Alan Baum
Middlesex Polytechnic

Further Reading
Baum, J. A. (1979), *Montesquieu and Social Theory*, Oxford.
Shackleton, R. (1961), *Montesquieu: A Critical Biography*, Oxford.

Nationalism

Nationalism is the belief that each nation has both the right and the duty to constitute itself as a state. There are many difficulties in specifying what a nation is – in Europe, for example, the candidates range from the Welsh and the Basques to Occitanians and Northumbrians – but some common culture is indispensable and a shared language highly desirable. The Swiss have so far got by without a common language, but its lack has sorely tried the rulers of Belgium. Nationalist theory usually attributes conflict to cross-national oppression, and thus offers a promise of world peace when self-determination has become a global reality.

Nationalism emerged in the hatred of cosmopolitanism which registered the resentment of Germans and other Europeans who were coming to feeling marginal in terms of the universalistic rationalism of the French Enlightenment. The romantic idea that true humanity must be mediated by a deep involvement in one's own unique culture led to an admiration for songs, poems, stories, plays and other creations understood as emanations of the national soul. The language of a people was accorded a unique value, no less as the medium of cultural self-expression than as a practical rule of thumb about how far the boundaries of a putative nation might stretch. The conquests of Napoleon turned these particularistic passions in a practical direction, and Fichte's *Addresses to the German Nation* delivered at Berlin in 1807–8 struck a responsive chord throughout Germany. Italy and Germany were both plausible candidates for state creation and both duly became states, though Italy remains imperfectly national to this day, while German unity owed more to Bismarck than to popular passion for nationhood.

The spread of nationalist ideas to Eastern Europe and beyond, where very different peoples were inextricably intertwined, was bound to create difficulties. Doctrinal diffusion was facilitated by the growth of industry, and of cities. Teachers, journalists, clergymen and other intellectuals found in nationalist ideas an identity for the present and a vision for the future. Some set to work writing down languages previously purely oral; others constructed a literature and elicited a suitable history. Opera and the novel were favourite vehicles of nationalist feeling. The politics of these endeavours triumphed with the Treaty of Versailles in 1918, which settled Europe in terms of the principle of national self-determination.

Throughout Africa and Asia, nationalist ideas fuelled the campaigns to replace the old European empires with home grown rulers, but since there were few plausible nations in this area, successor states which had been constructed on a variety of principles claimed freedom in order to *begin* the process of cultural homogenization which might lead to nationhood. Pakistan, based upon the religious identity of Islam, attempted to hold together two separated areas inherited from the British raj, and could not be sustained in that form; the eastern region broke off as Bangladesh in 1971. The artificial boundaries of imperial Africa have, however, been a surprisingly successful container of the often chaotic mixture of tribes they contained, though virtually all have had to compensate for lack of homogeneity by centralizing and frequently tyrannizing governments.

Political scientists often find in nationalism an attractive form of explanation because it promises to explain the hidden causes of conflict between different ethnic groups. In this usage, nationalism is not a belief, but rather a force supposed to move people to both action and belief. Such a concept provokes a search for the conditions under which the force is triggered. The promise of this research programme, like many another in political science, far exceeds the performance. Nationalism is better treated as a complex of ideas and sentiments which respond flexibly, decade by decade, to new situations, usually situations of grievance, in which peoples may find themselves.

Kenneth Minogue
London School of Economics and Political Science

Further Reading
Hertz, F. (1944), *Nationality in History and Politics*, London.
Kedourie, E. (1960), *Nationalism*, London.
Minogue, K. R. (1963), *Nationalism*, London.
Smith, A. D. (1971), *Theories of Nationalism*, London.

Parties, Political

Scholars who have specialized in the study of political parties have found it difficult to agree on a definition of the term. The oldest definition, which emerged in the nineteenth century, may still be the best one: political parties are organizations that try to win public office in electoral competition with one or more similar organizations. The problem with this definition is that it is a narrow one. As Schlesinger (1968) points out, it excludes several kinds of organizations that are also usually referred to as parties: (1) those that are too small to have a realistic chance to win public office, especially executive office, but that do nominate candidates and participate in election campaigns; (2) revolutionary parties that aim to abolish competitive elections; and (3) the governing groups in totalitarian and other authoritarian one-party states. However, the inclusion of these three additional categories makes the definition overly broad. This difficulty may be solved partly by distinguishing two very different types of parties: the governing parties in one-party states and the competitive parties in two-party and multiparty democracies or near-democracies (that is, countries that are not fully democratic but that do allow free electoral competition).

The principal problem that remains is how to draw a distinction, in two-party and multiparty systems, between political parties and interest groups. Interest groups may sometimes also nominate candidates for public office without *ipso facto* changing their character from interest group to political party. Hence two further criteria have been proposed. One concerns the breadth of the interests represented by parties and interest groups. The typical function of interest groups is to 'articulate' interests, whereas political parties serve the broader function of 'aggregating' the articulated interests (Almond, 1960). This distinction is obviously one of degree rather than of a sharp dividing line. It also applies more clearly to two-party systems with broadly aggregative parties than to multiparty situations.

The second criterion, suggested by Blondel (1969), entails a combination of the kinds of goals that parties and interest groups pursue and the types of membership that they have. Interest groups tend to have either a 'promotional' or 'protective' character. Promotional associations tend to advance specific points of view (such as environmentalism or the abolition of capital punishment) and are in principle open to all citizens. Protective associations (such as trade unions or veterans' associations) defend certain groups of people; their membership is therefore more limited, but their goals are broader and may extend over the entire range of public policy issues. Political parties can now be distinguished from both promotional and protective groups: their goals are general (like those of protective associations), but their membership is open (like that of promotional groups). The borderline cases are single-issue parties, which resemble promotional groups, and cultural or ethnic minority parties, which are similar to protective groups.

Parties can be classified according to three principal dimensions: (1) Their form of organization, which distinguishes between 'mass' and 'cadre' parties. The former have relatively many formal members and are centralized, disciplined, and highly oligarchical. The latter have a much smaller formal membership and lower degrees of centralization, discipline, and oligarchy. (2) The parties' programmes, which may be ideological or pragmatic, and which may reflect a leftist, centrist, or rightist outlook. (3) The parties' supporters: these may be mainly working class or mainly middle class, or they may be defined in terms other than the socio-economic spectrum, such as religion and ethnicity.

Duverger (1963) has shown that these dimensions are empirically related: socialists and other parties of the left tend to be based on working-class support, and are ideological mass parties; conservative and centre parties tend to be supported more by middle-class voters, and are pragmatic cadre parties. The link between party organizations and programmes in Western democracies was stronger in the period before the Second World War than in the post-war era. The general post-war trend has been for parties to assume the character of mass parties but also to become more pragmatic. The relationship between programmes and supporters has also grown somewhat weaker, but it is still true that the parties of the left tend to be supported by working-class voters to a greater extent than the parties of the right. Social class is a good predictor of party choice in virtually all democracies, but in religiously or linguistically divided countries voting behaviour is more strongly determined by religion and language (Lijphart, 1979).

The way in which a political party operates in a democracy depends not only on its own characteristics but also on its interaction with other parties. In this respect, the literature on political parties has emphasized the difference between two-party and multiparty systems. Here another definitional problem arises. How should we determine the number of parties in a party system? For instance, Britain is usually said to have a two-party system, although no less than ten different parties were elected to the House of Commons in the 1979 election. The usual practice is to count only the large and 'important' parties and to ignore the small parties. But how large does a party have to be in order to be included in the count?

Sartori (1976) has proposed that only those parties should be counted that have either 'coalition potential' or 'blackmail potential'. A party possesses coalition potential if it has participated in cabinet coalitions (or in one-party cabinets) or if it is regarded as a possible coalition partner by the other major parties. A party without coalition potential may have 'blackmail' potential: it may be ideologically unacceptable as a coalition partner, but it may be so large that it still exerts considerable influence (such as a large Communist party).

Sartori's counting rules therefore appear to be based on the two variables of size and ideological compatibility, but it should be pointed out that the size factor is the crucial one. A very small party with only a few parliamentary seats may be quite moderate and ideologically acceptable, but it will generally not have coalition potential simply because the support it can give to a cabinet is not sufficiently substantial. Hence the parties that Sartori counts are mainly the larger ones, regardless of their ideological compatibility. Moreover, although size is the dominant factor, he does not use it to make further distinctions among larger and smaller parties: they are all counted equally.

Blondel (1969) has tried to use both the number of parties and their relative sizes in classifying party systems. His four categories are two-party systems, 'two-and-a-half' party systems, multiparty systems with a dominant party, and multiparty systems without a dominant party. Two-party systems, like those of Britain and New Zealand, are dominated by two large parties, although a few small parties may also have seats in parliament. A two-and-a-half party system consists of two large parties and one that, although considerably smaller, does have coalition potential and does play a significant role, such as the German Free Democrats and the Irish Labour Party. Multiparty systems have more than two-and-a-half significant parties. These may or may not include a dominant party. Examples of the former are the Christian Democrats in the Italian multiparty system and the Social Democrats in the Scandinavian countries. The French Fourth Republic offers a good example of a multiparty system without a dominant party.

The concepts of a 'dominant' party and a 'half' party serve the useful function of distinguishing between parties of different sizes, but they only offer a rough measurement. A more precise index has been developed by Laakso and Taagepera (1979). This 'effective number of parties' index is calculated according to a simple formula that takes the exact share of parliamentary seats of each party into consideration. For a pure two-party system with two equally strong parties, the effective number of parties is 2.0. If the two parties are highly unequal in size – for instance, if they have 65 and 35 per cent of the seats – the effective number of parties is 1.8. This is in agreement with the view that such a party system deviates from a pure two-party system in the direction of a one-party system. If there are three parties of equal strength, the index is 3.0. In a two-and-a-half party system in which the parliamentary seats are distributed in a 45:43:12 ratio, the effective number of parties is exactly 2.5.

Party systems have a strong empirical relationship with electoral systems and with cabinet coalitions and cabinet stability (Lijphart, 1984). In four countries using plurality methods of election (Canada, New Zealand, the United Kingdom, and the United States), the average effective number of parties in the 1945–1980 period was 2.1; in fifteen, mainly West-European, countries with proportional representation, the average effective number of parties was 3.8, almost twice as many. Moreover, as the effective number of parties increases, the probability that a coalition cabinet will be formed also increases, but the longevity of cabinets decreases.

Arend Lijphart
University of California, San Diego

References

Almond, G. A. (1960), 'Introduction: a functional approach to comparative politics', in G. A. Almond and J. S. Coleman (eds), *The Politics of the Developing Areas*, Princeton.

Blondel, J. (1969), *An Introduction to Comparative Government*, London.

Duverger, M. (1963), *Political Parties: Their Organisation and Activity in the Modern State*, trans. B. and R. North, New York.

Laakso, M. and Taagepera, R. (1979), 'The "effective" number of parties: a measure with application to West Europe', *Comparative Political Studies*, 12, 1.

Lijphart, A. (1979), 'Religious vs. linguistic vs. class voting: the "crucial experiment" of comparing Belgium, Canada, South Africa, and Switzerland', *American Political Science Review*, 73.

Lijphart, A. (1984), *Democracies: Patterns of Majoritarian and Consensus Government in Twenty-One Countries*, New Haven.

Sartori, G. (1976), *Parties and Party Systems: A Framework for Analysis*, Vol. 1, Cambridge.

Schlesinger, J. A. (1968), 'Party units', in D. L. Sills (ed.), *International Encyclopedia of the Social Sciences*, 11, New York.

Further Reading

Butler, D., Penniman, H. R. and Ranney, A. (eds) (1981), *Democracy at the Polls: A Comparative Study of Competitive National Elections*, Washington, DC.

Epstein, L. D. (1980), *Political Parties in Western Democracies*, 2nd edn, New Brunswick, N.J.

Merkl, P. H. (ed.) (1980), *Western European Party Systems: Trends and Prospects*, New York.

Janda, K. (1980), *Political Parties: A Cross-National Survey*, New York.

La Palombara, J. and Weiner, M. (eds) (1966), *Political Parties and Political Development*, Princeton.

Lipset, S. M. and Rokkan, S. (eds) (1967), *Party Systems and Voter Alignments: Cross-National Perspectives*, New York.

Von Beyme, K. (1982), *Parteien in westlichen Demokratien*, Munich.

See also: *coalitions*; *democracy*; *elections*; *voting*.

Peace

Historically a number of peace concepts can be identified. They are carriers of different ideas, which could be joined together to yield a richer concept of peace than that usually found. Most important in the Western tradition is the Roman 'pax', *absentia belli* – in other words, a negative concept of peace, defined as the absence of war among countries. The Greek *eirene*, the Arabic/Hebrew *sala'am/shalom* and the Japanese/Chinese *heiwa/chowa* point in another direction which can be better understood by such terms as 'justice' and 'harmony'. In the Hindu, Gandhian and Jainist/Buddhist traditions, *shanti* would be more of a harmony concept, while *ahimsa* (the negation of *himsa*, violence) would emphasize the element of nonviolence.

These differences are important, for in all cultures 'peace' (or that which tends to be translated into 'peace') stands for something positive, the name of a goal, perhaps one of the deepest and highest goals.

The concept of 'peace' becomes a part of social ideology, embraced by everybody. As such it will also attain a class character. Who benefits from 'absence of war'? Not those with just grievances, fighting for a more just world, but possibly merchants and others who can profit from peaceful relations among states. 'Peace' becomes that which makes inter-state trade possible. And who is served by 'harmony', if not precisely those at the top of a structure which distributes power and privilege very unequally? Moreover, 'nonviolence' may mean pacification rather than peace in a more positive sense. 'Harmony' may also be interpreted as 'justice' – but that may be a synonym for equality, or it may mean giving more to the more worthy, the aristocrats or meritocrats.

In peace research, as it took shape at the end of the 1950s, the debate about the meaning of that very concept proved to be fruitful. It was evident from the beginning that there were two classes of meanings: 'negative peace', meaning absence of war and violence (any type of destruction); and 'positive peace', coming closer to integration, or union – with connotations of harmony and justice. But then violence, destruction, that which should be absent for a peace certificate to be issued (as a minimum condition) also has to be subdivided. On the one hand there is the *direct* violence most people think of: violence which destroys quickly and which is usually directed by a person who intends that destruction. On the other hand there is *structural* violence, built into the social structure, which is also capable of killing, but then usually slowly (through hunger, misery, and disease), but which is as a rule not steered by some clear intention – it just *is*. Structural violence is not the same as institutionalized violence – that is, direct violence which has become an institution, like the vendetta. It is very closely linked to social hierarchy in general, and to the class structure of a society in particular. It can be measured, much as direct violence is measured, by counting casualties. Structural violence can be measured in numbers of years not lived relative to the potential, given the knowledge, technology and resources at our disposal, on the assumption that all parts of the population can benefit fully from them. A life destroyed at the age of thirty through malnutrition is at least half a murder. One might add qualitative measures, to cope with the effect of morbidity on the quality of life. Other measures might be devised to deal with the cost of repression and/or alienation, tying freedom and identity to the concept of peace – in the tradition of non-Western peace theories.

The concept of negative peace is extended through the concept of structural violence. 'Absence of violence' is more than absence of direct violence; it also implies the absence of repression and alienation and exploitation, and other forms of verticality in the social structure. These considerations suggest the two main strategies for a peace process: policies based on maintaining distance (dissociation) and fostering closeness (association), or the pursuit of peace by positive and negative approaches.

Best known in the theory of peace is the policy of dissociation, whose aim it is to achieve 'security' (another word for negative peace), or the absence of direct violence, through the maintenance of distance. This may be achieved by securing natural borders (rivers, mountain chains), keeping great distances (oceans, deserts) between oneself and potential enemies, or fostering social distance (by prejudice and discrimination), and social borders, protected by force. Combining these four approaches, we arrive at the nation-state, built into a balance-of-power system. The system can be said to date from the Peace of Westphalia in 1648. Today its weaknesses are manifold: natural borders and distances become ludicrous in the age of rockets; nationalist prejudices tend to break down in the age of extended interaction; and the balance of power may break down in the age of multidimensional weapon systems, where there is no agreement as to how much of this weapon is equivalent to how much of that, and because weapons that can be potentially used for an attack look offensive, although the intention behind their deployment may be purely defensive – and consequently, they are inevitably provocative.

The closeness, or associative, approach is based on exactly the opposite idea: that a peace structure can be built by bringing the parties together, not by keeping them apart. Such a policy can succeed only when the parties are relatively equal, bound together in a relationship not only of interdependence but also of equity, and where ties proliferate in all directions and at all levels (governmental, public, private, élite, and popular), and so on. The difference between the two strategies is starkly evident if one compares the relation between Germany and France before the Second World War, and today.

For structural violence, there are also dissociative and associative approaches. Distance may be created through 'decoupling', selective or more complete, for example by means of a violent or nonviolent struggle for liberation. The closeness approach, 'recoupling', is again only possible on the basis of equality. The history of the Nordic countries illustrates a relatively solid and equitable process of recoupling. Recoupling has not so far been achieved successfully inside a society, reducing to zero structural violence between classes within a country. This is possibly because decoupling easily leads to separatism and the formation of a new state.

Johan Galtung
International Peace Research Institute, Oslo

Further Reading
Galtung, J. (1975–80), *Essays in Peace Research*, vols I–V, Copenhagen.
See also: *war*.

Plato (428/7–348/7 B.C.)

Plato was born into a wealthy, well-connected family of the old Athenian aristocracy (Davies, 1971). He and his elder brothers Adeimantos and Glaukon (both of whom figure in the *Republic*) belonged to the circle of young men attached to Socrates, as did his cousins Kritias and Charmides, who played a leading part in the oligarchic junta of the Thirty which seized power at the end of the Peloponnesian War in 404/3. In the seventh Letter (a sort of *apologia pro vita sua* by Plato himself or a disciple) Plato claims to have been quickly shocked by the tyrannous behaviour of the Thirty, and equally disgusted with the restored democracy when it condemned Socrates to death in 399; but his chances of playing any prominent part in Athenian politics had in any case been fatally compromised by his close connections with the junta. He settled down to the 'theoretical life' of a philosopher and teacher which he praises (for example, *Theaetetus* 172–6) as the highest form of human activity. In 367, however, after thirty years of highly productive theoretical activity, he attempted to put some of the political ideas of the *Republic* into practice by training the young ruler of Syracuse, Dionysius II, for the role of philosopher-king. Not surprisingly, he failed; one of Plato's most obvious weaknesses as a political analyst was his neglect of external factors and relations with other powers, which in the fourth century B.C. constituted in fact the main problem for the Greek cities. While there are problems of detail in dating Plato's dialogues, one can perhaps say that in his work before the Sicilian episode he is still engaged in a vivacious debate with ideas current in the Athens of his youth, whereas in his later works (*Sophist, Statesman, Philebus, Timaeus, Critias, Laws*) he is addressing himself more specifically to fellow-philosophers, present and future. The philosophical centre he founded in the Academy – a sort of Institute for Advanced Studies in rural surroundings – continued after his death.

The influences which shaped Plato's thought are thus the aristocratic milieu in which he grew up and the political events of his lifetime, the personality of Socrates, and the standards of systematic reasoning associated with the role of philosopher. His contributions to social thought as we would now define it lie mainly in the fields of political and moral philosophy, psychology and education; but these aspects of his thought cannot be detached from his epistemology and cosmology.

Part of the fascination of reading Plato comes from the dialogue form in which he presented his ideas. He was no doubt influenced in this choice by Socrates, who communicated his own ideas solely through argument and left no written works. More generally, the Athenians were used to hearing different points of view upheld by opposing speakers in political assemblies, in law courts and in drama. Socrates takes the leading part in Plato's earlier dialogues, and this enabled the author both to acknowledge his debt to his teacher and, perhaps, to avoid taking full responsibility for the ideas he was putting forward. Plato never figures in his own dialogues. The dialogue form also suited his gifts as a brilliantly natural and graceful writer, a skilful parodist and master of characterization and light-hearted conversation. The introductory scenes of his dialogues provide the historian with lively sketches of upper-class manners and mores in the late fifth century B.C.

The key element in Plato's thought as it concerned social life was a widening of the gap between body and spirit. This enabled him to preserve an essential core of religious belief from the criticisms which had been directed against traditional religion, to ground Socrates' argument that virtue is a kind of knowledge in a general theory of epistemology which offered solutions to logical problems raised by earlier philosophers, and to provide a foundation for belief in the immortality of the soul. At the same time it formalized a psychological split between lower and higher elements in the personality, and linked this to a justification of social hierarchy, and to a theory of education in which censorship played an essential part.

Plato's early dialogues show Socrates attacking a traditional, unreflective upper-class practice of virtue as a routine response of the gentleman to predictable situations. When asked to define courage (*Laches*), piety (*Euthyphro*), or moderation (*Charmides*), his interlocutors give specific examples of brave, pious or self-controlled behaviour, and Socrates then proves to them that such acts would not in all circumstances be considered virtuous. Echoes of the same attitude can be found in Xenophon and Euripides.

Some of Plato's contemporaries went on from this criticism of traditional conceptions of virtue to deny its existence altogether: in the *Republic*, Thrasymachus argues that values and virtues are defined by the ruling class to suit their own interests, and Glaukon argues that they represent the interests of the majority. Plato therefore needed a concept of virtue which was flexible and abstract enough to satisfy Socratic criticism but nevertheless safe against relativist attack. His response was the theory of Forms or Ideas, existing at a level of ultimate, abstract reality which was only imperfectly reflected in the material world but of which the human mind could gradually acquire better knowledge through philosophical training.

Coming closer to the world of Ideas thus becomes both the highest aim of human life and the standard by which all kinds of knowledge are judged; it follows that human societies should be directed by philosophers or by laws formulated by philosophers. The human personality is divided into three elements: intelligence, *amour-propre* (*Thumos*) and the physical appetites. Education aims to train the first to dominate the other two.

Thumos refers to a set of qualities regarded somewhat ambiguously in Plato's culture (Dover, 1974). It was the basis of man's pursuit of prestige and honour and thus – like the appetites – beneficial when exercised in moderation but dangerous when obsessive. Too eager a pursuit of honour led to tyranny or to a tendency to take offence for no reason. Thus there was a popular basis for the view that even ambition for what the ordinary man in the street considered the supreme good had to be controlled. This point was particularly important for Plato, because his belief that the good society was a society ruled by good and wise men meant that the essential problem of political organization was to prevent the ruling élite from becoming corrupted. This led him to formulate the idea of the 'mixed constitution', later to influence Polybius, Montesquieu and the Constitution of the United States.

Because a philosophical education involved training in subjects like astronomy and mathematics for which not all had equal interest or aptitude, and because the philosopher had to detach himself from activities and preoccupations likely to strengthen the influence of his *Thumos* and bodily appetites, the hierarchy of faculties in the psyche led to a hierarchy of groups in the ideal city. Philosophers would have supreme authority, semi-educated 'watch-dogs' would act as a military and police force on their behalf, and those who supplied the economic needs of the city would have the lowest status of all. Education was to be carefully adjusted to the reproduction of the system; the lower class were to be trained to obedience and persuaded by a political 'myth' that their status was due to natural causes; poets should only represent socially commendable behaviour; knowledge of alternative forms of society was to be carefully suppressed, except in the case of selected members of the ruling élite.

Such views have in our century led to attacks on Plato as a proto-Fascist or -Stalinist (Crossman, 1937; Popper, 1945). In the *Laws* the more extreme proposals of the *Republic* (in particular, the abolition of private property and the family) were dropped; it is interesting to see Plato grappling here with detailed problems of law-drafting, and the text is a key piece of evidence on Greek legal thought. Return to law as a source of authority was a capitulation to the rigid type of definition of virtue which Socrates had attacked (see the *Statesman*); but the argument which had seemed valid when applied to individuals would not work for collectivities. There was something wrong with the analogy between parts of the city and parts of the human psyche.

S. C. Humphreys
University of Michigan

References
Crossman, R. H. (1937), *Plato Today*, London.
Davies, J. K. (1971), *Athenian Propertied Families*, Oxford.
Dover, K. J. (1974), *Greek Popular Morality in the Time of Plato and Aristotle*, Oxford.
Popper, K. (1945), *The Open Society and its Enemies*, London.

Further Reading
Gouldner, A. W. (1966), *Enter Plato: Classical Greece and the Origins of Social Theory*, New York.

Guthrie, W. K. C. (1975–8), *A History of Greek Philosophy*, vols IV–V, Cambridge.

Ryle, G. (1966), *Plato's Progress*, Cambridge.

Shorey, P. (1933), *What Plato Said*, Chicago.

Taylor, A. E. (1926), *Plato. The Man and his Work*, London.

Wood, E. M. and Wood, N. (1978), *Class Ideology and Ancient Political Theory: Socrates, Plato and Aristotle in Social Context*, Oxford.

Pluralism, Political

Political pluralism is a normative perspective in modern politics that emphasizes the importance for democracy and liberty of maintaining a plurality of relatively autonomous political and economic organizations. The political pluralist believes that in large-scale societies competing economic interests and differences of political opinion are unavoidable. In opposition to Marxists, the political pluralist does not believe that these significant political cleavages are primarily or necessarily related to class. Nor does he believe that these sources of political conflict can be eliminated by bringing the means of production under public ownership. For the governmental system of large-scale societies to be democratic, the political pluralist insists that there must be institutions through which divergent interests can articulate their views and compete for power. A system of competitive political parties is a hallmark of pluralist democracies. Such democratic polities are often referred to as liberal democracies.

Some political pluralists recognize that inequality in the distribution of political resources may mean that some social interests or groups in a liberal democracy have much more power and influence than others. Thus a political pluralist may advocate redistributive policies to reduce political inequalities (Dahl, 1982). However much inequalities are reduced, the democratic pluralist is still faced with the dilemma of how much autonomy should be extended to groups whose views differ from those of the majority. Federalism is one solution to this dilemma where significant societal differences coincide with territorial divisions. Another approach is consociational democracy in which national policy is arrived at through a consensus of élites drawn from the country's major cultural or ideological segments (Lijphart, 1977).

Peter H. Russell
University of Toronto

References
Dahl, R. A. (1982), *Dilemmas of Pluralist Democracy*, New Haven.
Lijphart, A. (1977), *Democracy in Plural Societies*, New Haven.

Further Reading
Connolly, W. E. (ed.) (1969), *The Bias of Pluralism*, New York.
Lipset, S. M. (1960), *Political Man: The Social Bases of Politics*, Garden City, New York.

Policy Sciences

The policy sciences are concerned with understanding the decision processes of public and private institutions, and with assessing the significance of all knowledge for purposes of decision. The term policy sciences was introduced after World War II (Lerner and Lasswell, 1951) to refer to the emergence of this common frame of reference among specialists in many disciplines. Subsequent development of the policy sciences has been marked by the refinement of conceptual tools, their application to a variety of policy problems, and by the establishment of policy sciences centres in universities, government agencies and the private sector. Policy scientists in the aggregate have only begun to develop a distinctive professional identity and an understanding of the roles they may play in the evolution of our civilization.

Policy scientists are traditionally graduates from academic schools or departments of public or business administration, political science, political economy, jurisprudence, and the like. In recent decades, the physical and natural sciences, as well as the cultural sciences, have also produced policy scientists. These disciplines have had little contact with traditional policy theory but a great deal to do with the policy problems of our time. In a typical career pattern, a scientist in a laboratory or research institute discovers latent interests and talents in an initial attempt to relate his specialized knowledge to the broader environment. The political and social environment may nurture and reinforce these initiatives to the extent that knowledge is expected to pay. The budding policy scientist soon learns to sustain this expectation through delivery of partial results, and to justify further science and scholarship in terms that the environment rewards: security, profits, political advantage, health and social welfare, prestige and many other objectives. This career pattern broadens the attention frame and the circle of contacts beyond one's disciplinary origins.

Policy scientists tend to converge on a common outlook, despite their diversity of origins. One element of the common outlook is contextuality. Scholarship that restricts considerations of realism and worth to those of a single discipline may be acceptable to manuscript editors who enforce disciplinary standards. However, it is less likely to be acceptable to a decision maker who must grapple with a broader range of considerations and is unimpressed by the traditional academic division of labour. In the search for knowledge pertinent to the decision process and problem at hand, partial approaches tend to become more contextual. A second element is a problem orientation, which includes all the intellectual tasks logically entailed in the solution of any problem. For example, a choice among policy alternatives entails the postulation of goal values. The 'value free' connotation of 'science', as propagated in some disciplines, gradually becomes attenuated as policy scientists discover the value implications of their research and develop competence in normative analysis. (The connotation of 'science' as the 'pursuit of verifiable knowledge' is retained.) Conversely, philosophers and other specialists in normative analysis learn to describe trends, to clarify factors conditioning trends, and to project future possibilities in the process of relating normative principles to specific decisions. A third element is the synthesis of diverse methods. Each method of observation or analysis tends to divert attention from some potentially important aspects of the problem at hand. The use of multiple methods is an important means of compensating for such blind spots.

Evidence of convergence can be found in the development of concepts for contextual, problem-oriented, and multi-method research. Lasswell (1956; 1971) and his collaborators (Lasswell and Kaplan, 1950; Lasswell and McDougal, 1971) have refined the most comprehensive set of conceptual tools, but approximate equivalents are persistently rediscovered, often independently, by others. A contextual approach leads to an explicit conception of the decision process as a whole. Among other things, it identifies the multiple points at which decision outcomes might be affected, and thereby facilitates the rational allocation of analytical and political resources. Workable conceptions have been proposed by Anderson (1975), May and Wildavsky (1978), and Brewer and deLeon (1983). A contextual approach also leads to an explicit conception of the broader social process. Among other things, it directs attention to the otherwise unnoticed or discounted costs and benefits of decisions that impact on society. The social indicator movement (Bauer, 1966) and general systems theory (Isard, 1969) have spawned a number of social process models. The intellectual tasks entailed in problem-oriented research have been conceptualized in nearly equivalent ways by Simon (1968), Allison (1971), and many others. Finally, conceptions of 'economic man' and invariant 'behavioural laws' have turned out to be limited for purposes of the policy sciences. The explanation or interpretation of human acts requires attention to the simplified cognitive 'maps' used by the actors in question to respond to their environments. Essentially equivalent concepts for this purpose are Lasswell's 'maximization postulate' and Simon's (1957) elaboration of the 'principle of bounded rationality'.

Such conceptual tools ideally formulate and conveniently label the principal distinctions that have turned out to be useful across broad ranges of experience. They do not provide general answers to particular problems, as theory is sometimes purported to do. Rather, they provide principles of procedure (or heuristics) to guide a systematic search for data and insights pertinent to a specific decision problem; and they provide principles of content that outline elements of a satisfactory solution and help bring to bear the knowledge cumulated from different times, places, and cultural contexts. As short lists of interrelated concepts, they anticipate or implement findings of cognitive psychology showing how information can be processed efficiently (Simon, 1969; 1979). Command of these conceptual tools enables a policy scientist to maximize the potential for rational decision within the constraints of time, resources and the nature of the situation.

Applications of the policy sciences approach are numerous and diverse. Good examples illustrating the range of applications have addressed problems of administration and governance in a psychiatric hospital; public services for handicapped children; social development at the community level; defence analysis; income redistribution at the national level; public order of the world community, and global political transformations. Among authors of these studies alone, the disciplinary origins include anthropology, economics, law, medicine, political science, public administration and psychiatry.

The professional identity of the policy scientist tends to be in flux. Ideally, the policy scientist perceives himself as an integrator of knowledge and action. Complications arise, however, when other scientists perceive him as an ex-scientist and current politician. Moreover, decision makers may not know what to make of a scientist who nevertheless appears to know how to operate in the policy arena. Further complications arise from the question of whose interests are served. The rich and powerful are in a position to acquire his services, but knowledge may also be used to improve the position of the weak, the poor, and others who are disadvantaged. The situation is complex, and the policy scientist may share the ambivalences he perceives in his relationships with others.

From a broader perspective, there is little doubt that the scientific revolution has failed to modify the political structure of a militant and divided world, or to abolish zones of poverty amidst prosperity. In principle, the fruits of knowledge are available to all. In practice, knowledge is often selectively introduced and used for the benefit of the few. One of the continuing tasks of the policy sciences is to appraise its own impact on policy and society. The search for authoritative criteria can be guided by the Universal Declaration of Human Rights.

Ronald D. Brunner
University of Colorado, Boulder

References

Allison, G. (1971), *Essence of Decision: Explaining the Cuban Missile Crisis*, Boston.

Anderson, J. E. (1975), *Public Policy-Making*, New York.

Bauer, R. A. (ed.) (1966), *Social Indicators*, Cambridge, Mass.

Brewer, G. D. and deLeon, P. (1983), *The Foundations of Policy Analysis*, Homewood, Ill.

Isard, W. (1969), *General Theory: Social, Political, and Regional with Particular Reference to Decision-Making Analysis*, Cambridge, Mass.

Lasswell, H. D. (1956), *The Decision Process: Seven Categories of Functional Analysis*, College Park, Maryland.

Lasswell, H. D. (1971), *A Pre-View of Policy Sciences*, New York.

Lasswell, H. D. and Kaplan, A. (1950), *Power and Society*, New Haven.

Lasswell, H. D. and McDougal, M. S. (1971), 'Criteria for a theory about law', *Southern California Law Review*, 44.

Lerner, D. and Lasswell, H. D. (eds) (1951), *The Policy Sciences*, Stanford.

May, J. V. and Wildavsky, A. B. (eds) (1978), *The Policy Cycle*, Beverly Hills.

Simon, H. A. (1957), 'Rationality and administrative decision making', in H. A. Simon (ed.), *Models of Man*, New York.

Simon, H.A. (1968), 'Research for choice', in W.R. Ewald (ed.), *Environment and Policy: The Next Fifty Years*, Bloomington.

Simon, H. A. (1969), *The Sciences of the Artificial*, Cambridge, Mass.

Simon, H. A. (1979), *Models of Thought*, New Haven.

See also: *decision making*.

Political Culture

Though some of the themes evoked by the concept of political culture were not unknown to classical political thought, the term political culture appears to have been first used in the late eighteenth century by Herder (Barnard, 1969) and its elaboration and development as a concept of modern political science dates from the 1950s (especially Almond, 1956). Substantive empirical research organized around the concept began to appear in the 1960s (for example, Almond and Verba, 1963; Pye and Verba, 1965). These early applications of the concept were linked to questionable theories of 'political development', but more recent studies have demonstrated that the value of the concept of political culture in no way depends upon its incorporation in a particular type of developmental, structure-functionalist or systems analysis.

There have been numerous definitions of political culture, but they can be classified into two broad categories: (1) those which confine the scope of political culture to the subjective orientation of nations, social groups or individuals to politics; and (2) those which broaden the concept to include patterns of political behaviour. Most political scientists have favoured the more restrictive category. Representative definitions in this first group include those which see political culture as 'the system of empirical beliefs, expressive symbols, and values which defines the situation in which political action takes place' (Verba, 1965), or as 'the subjective perception of history and politics, the fundamental beliefs and values, the foci of identification and loyalty, and the political knowledge and expectations which are the product of the specific historical experience of nations and groups' (Brown, 1977).

Scholars who prefer the second, and broader, type of definition of the concept have suggested that in characterizing political culture in subjective or psychological terms, 'political scientists have parted company with the great majority of anthropologists' (Tucker, 1973), although that view has recently been questioned (Brown, 1984). There is a minority of political scientists employing the concept who prefer the more anthropological approach, whereby political culture can be defined as 'the attitudinal and behavioural matrix within which the political system is located' (White, 1979).

Those who favour a 'subjective' definition argue that quite enough has already been brought under the umbrella of political culture and that to broaden its scope further reduces its analytical usefulness. Specifically, it makes it difficult, if not imposible, to examine what part the particular perceptions, beliefs and values to be found in different societies may play in explanation of political conduct if no clear conceptual distinction is made between behaviour and subjective beliefs. Accepting that this criticism has some force, a prominent proponent of the 'anthropological' approach has questioned whether the scholarly value of the concept of political culture actually depends upon its 'explanatory potency' and suggests that its central importance lies rather in the fact that 'it assists us to take our bearings in the study of the political life of a society . . . to describe and analyse and order many significant data, and to raise fruitful questions for thought and research – *without explaining anything*' (Tucker, 1973).

The study of the political cultures and subcultures of societies ruled by authoritarian governments brings out acutely the definitional dilemma. On the one hand, political behaviour (for instance, voting behaviour in Communist systems) may – as a result of coercion or more subtle pressures – bear only a tenuous relationship to citizens' real beliefs and values. Thus, a more restrictive definition may, in principle, permit useful investigation of lack of congruence between the 'dominant' (as distinct from 'official') political culture and the political system. On the other hand, it is precisely in authoritarian regimes that it is hardest to get reliable quantified data on fundamental political beliefs and values, political knowledge and expectations, and so on, because of the difficulties not only of conducting surveys on such politically sensitive themes but also of getting honest answers from respondents. Behaviour, including deviant behaviour, may be more readily observable.

Yet, whereas early political culture studies concentrated on the First World and the Third World (where the frequent failure of transplanted Western-style political institutions to work in anything like the manner expected by the constitution-writers was a stimulus to the study of political culture), more recently increasing attention has been paid to the Second, or Communist, world (Brown and Gray, 1977; White, 1979; Almond and Verba, 1980). The special interest of these societies lies in the fact that unusually elaborate and conscious efforts have been made by the political power-holders to effect a radical transformation of political culture. Recent evidence indicates a much more limited success in this endeavour than might have been predicted, given Communist leaders' substantially tighter control over most of the major agencies of political socialization than that wielded by their counterparts in more pluralistic political systems. This, in turn, is now leading political scientists to examine more carefully the transmission and evocation of political beliefs and values, and to treat with equal seriousness both the psychological and historical dimensions of the study of political culture.

Archie Brown
St Antony's College, Oxford

References

Almond, G. A. (1956), 'Comparative political systems', *Journal of Politics*, 18.

Almond, G. A. and Verba, S. (eds) (1963), *The Civic Culture: Political Attitudes and Democracy in Five Nations*, Princeton, N.J.

Almond, G. A. and Verba, S. (eds) (1980), *The Civic Culture Revisited*, Boston.

Barnard, F. M. (1969), 'Culture and political development: Herder's suggestive insights', *American Political Science Review*, LXIII.

Brown, A. (ed.) (1984), *Political Culture and Communist Studies*, London.

Brown, A. and Gray, J. (eds) (1977), *Political Culture and Political Change in Communist States*, London.

Pye, L. W. and Verba, S. (eds) (1965), *Political Culture and Political Development*, Princeton, N.J.

Tucker, R. C. (1973), 'Culture, political culture, and
  Communist society', *Political Science Quarterly*, 88.
White, S. (1979), *Political Culture and Soviet Politics*, London.

Political Economy

Economic science was first called political economy by an unim-
portant mercantilist writer, Montchrétien de Watteville, in 1615
(*Traicté de l'oeconomie politique*). The word 'economy' dates back
to ancient Greeks for whom it meant principles of household
management (οἶκος = house, νόμος = law). Montchrétien
argued that 'the science of wealth acquisition is common to the
state as well as the family' and therefore added the adjective
'political'.

The term had not been accepted immediately, and it was
only in 1767 that it reappeared in the *Inquiry into the Principles of
Political Economy* by James Steuart, the last precursor of classical
economists. With the advent of classical economics, the term
came into general use and remained so throughout the entire
nineteenth century. It meant economics as it had just emerged
as one of the social sciences. English and French authors used
the term almost exclusively, while German authors vacillated
between *Staatswirtschaft* (Schlözer, 1805–7; Hermann, 1832),
Nationalökonomie (von Soden, 1804: Hildebrand, 1848) or *Volk-
swirtschaft* (Eiselen, 1843; Roscher, 1854–94; Menger, 1871;
Schmoller, 1900–4), *Politische Ökonomie* (Rau, 1826; List, 1840;
Knies, 1855) and *Sozialökonomie* (Dietzel, 1895; M. Weber).

Like any new discipline, political economy included both
theoretical principles and practical policies, scientific proofs and
political advocacies; it was a combination of science, philosophy
and art. In his *Wealth of Nations* (1776, Book IV) Adam Smith
wrote: 'Political economy, considered as a branch of the science
of a statesman or legislator, proposes two distinct objects: first,
to provide a plentiful revenue or subsistence for the people . . .
and secondly, to supply the state . . . with a revenue sufficient
for the public services.' The titles of some of the later treatises
reflect similar ideas (Hufeland, *Neue Grundlagen der Staatswirtsch-
aftskunst*, 1807–13; J. S. Mill, *Principles of Political Economy with
Some of Their Applications to Social Philosophy*, 1848). Also, like

many other sciences in the nineteenth century, political economy passed through a process of catharsis: it gradually liberated itself from the political and ideological baggage, the concepts used became more rigorously defined, the analysis and proofs imitated procedures in exact sciences, and art (which advises, prescribes and directs) was separated from science (which observes, describes and explains). Commenting a century later (1874) on Smith's definition, Leon Walras observed that 'to say that the object of political economy is to provide a plentiful revenue . . . is like saying that the object of geometry is to build strong houses . . .'.

This development proceeded in two different directions: towards pure economic theory unrelated to social relations, and towards social economics stressing production relations as the main task of analysis. The former is sometimes (very conditionally) denoted as bourgeois economics, the latter (equally conditionally) as Marxist economics. Both were equally critical of inherited doctrines, but from different perspectives. Bourgeois economists took capitalism as an established social order (as data exogenously given) and tried to develop economic science by reducing the immense complexity of social phenomena to some manageable proportions. Marx and the socialists, on the other hand, questioned the established social order itself (and treated production relations as endogenous variables).

Nasau Senior (*An Outline of Political Economy*, 1836) was probably the first to stress explicitly the abstract and hypothetical character of economic theory and to distinguish theoretical economics from policy advice useful for the statesmen. J. B. Say provided the definition of political economy in the title of his book *Traité d'économie politique, ou simple exposition de la manière dont se forment, se distribuent et se consomment les richesses* (1803). While Smith's definition referred to an art, 'from Say's definition it would seem that the *production*, *distribution* and *consumption* of wealth take place, if not spontaneously, at least in the *manner* somehow independent of the will of man' which means treating political economy as a 'natural science' (Walras). Marx also talks of natural laws in economics, though, unlike Say, he also subsumes production relations under the governance of these laws. Although the econometricians – as Schumpeter calls them – of the seventeenth and eighteenth century, Petty, Boisguillebert, Cantillon and Quesnay, tried to measure economic phenomena, it was only Cournot (*Recherches sur les principes mathématiques de la théorie des richesses*, 1838) who successfully introduced mathematics into economics. And 'a science becomes really developed only when it can use mathematics' (Marx). The marginalist revolution of the 1870s gave the purification tendencies full swing. In the last great work under the title of political economy – *Manuale di economia politica* by Pareto, 1906 – the author scorns 'literary economists and metaphysicians' and defines his discipline by enumerating its three component parts: the study of tastes, the study of obstacles and the study of the way in which these two elements combine to reach equilibrium. This type of reasoning led to the most popular definition of economics in the first of the two intellectual traditions: economics as the study of the allocation of scarce resources among competing uses. Starting from this definition, it is logical to conclude, as L. Robbins did, that 'the generalizations of the theory of value are applicable to the behaviour of isolated men or the executive authority of a communist society as they are to the behaviour of men in an exchange economy' (*An Essay on the Nature and Significance of Economic Science*, 1932). Economics has thus become applied praxiology (study of rational behaviour). Most of what goes for the contemporary economic theory is in fact not theory but analysis. The difference between the two consists in economic analysis being *identically* true: if the rules of logic are observed, the conclusions follow with certainty and cannot be refuted. Economic theory, like any other theory, cannot be proved but can be refuted. As a result of these developments, political economy disappeared from the titles of economic treatises and also from Western encyclopaedias.

The Marxist tradition uses the following definition: political economy is the science of the laws governing the production, exchange and distribution of material means for living in the human society (Engels, *Anti-Dühring*, 1878). Since the conditions under which people produce and exchange are different in different epochs, there must be different political economies. Political economy is basically an historical science. Marx's chief work, *Das Kapital. Kritik der Politischen Oekonomie* (1867), was a critique of bourgeois society and was intended to 'discover the law of economic development' of this society. In an earlier work he links political economy with the dominant class in a particular society and draws attention to the 'blind laws of demand and supply, of which consists the political economy of bourgeoisie, and social production governed by social forecast, of which consists the political economy of the working class' (1864). Political economists of Marxist persuasion start from the observation that means of production together with appropriately skilled labour power make up the forces of production. The latter, together with the corresponding relations of production, determine modes of production which represent the proper subject of study for political economy. Marxist economists have preserved the term and the approach, but have not contributed much to the development of political economy after the master's death.

After the Second World War, the emergence of many new nations, substantial political and social changes, and widening gaps in economic development made the usefulness of pure economic theory rather questionable. Models that implied Western *Homo economicus* proved inapplicable in many parts of the world and, increasingly so, in the West itself. The interest in political economy was revived. The subject was reintroduced into curricula, and studies bearing the title began to reappear (A. Lindbeck, *The Political Economy of the Left*, 1971; H. Sherman, *Radical Political Economy*, 1972). The current tendency is to bridge the gap between the two strands of thought: the most sophisticated analytical techniques are applied to analyse social relations. The term 'political economy' came to denote that part of economic theory which deals with the functioning of entire socioeconomic systems. In a somewhat looser sense it is also used to denote political-economic doctrines or comprehensive sets of economic policies such as liberal, conservative and radical. The increasing exactness of economics and the development of other social sciences make it possible to extend the task of political economy from merely explaining the functioning of economic systems to the design of basically new economic systems. In order to achieve this, an attempt has been made to integrate economic and political theory into one single theory of political economy (Horvat, 1982).

Branko Horvat
University of Zagreb

Reference
Horvat, B. (1982), *Political Economy of Socialism*, New York.

Further Reading
Lange, O. (1963), *Political Economy*, New York.

Political Participation

In earlier studies of political participation the focus was on *psephology*, or the study of electoral behaviour. However, since the 1960s the emergence and rise of political sociology has contributed not only to the study of conventional politics but to unconventional forms of political participation as well, such as protests, movements, revolutions, power and the like.

Every citizen can, theoretically, participate and influence the political process; in reality, however, there is an unequal degree of political participation and influence. Alford and Friedland (1975) note that participation without power is more characteristic of the poor and working classes, while power with or without participation is characteristic of the rich and upper classes.

Political participation includes all those activities by private citizens that seek to influence or to support the government and politics, including the selection of governmental personnel and/or actions they take (Milbrath and Goel, 1977; Verba and Nie, 1972). Booth and Seligson (1978) define it in terms of 'behaviour influencing the distribution of public goods'.

The empirical indicators include voluntary actions and/or behaviour by citizens in support of the regime; intentionality of participants that these activities are political and efficacious;

the element of conventionality or legality, and efforts to oppose the policies of government as a matter of right and privilege.

Most citizens are spectators of politics. In the US, about one-third are politically apathetic, and only a small percentage are activists. In most of the studies of why people do or do not participate in the political process, political sociologists and psychologists have pointed to the various agents of political socialization, including family, socioeconomic status, school, mass media, group/organizational identity, political and civic culture and the like. Lasswell (1951) lists eight reasons for participation: power, wealth, well-being, skill, enlightenment, affection, rectitude, and respect. Likewise, Lane (1959) thinks that a number of conscious and unconscious needs and motives are served by participation in politics, including economic and material gain, friendship and affection, relief from intrapsychic tensions, a need to understand the world, power, and self-esteem.

Any theory of political participation must consider both the individual action (motivation, needs, goals) and the constraints of participation (variable resource, psychological/cognitive and the contextual/environmental) (Booth and Seligson, 1978).

George Kourvetaris
Northern Illinois University

References

Alford, R. R. and Friedland, R. (1975), 'Political participation and public policy', *Annual Review of Sociology*, Palo Alto, Calif.

Booth, J. A. and Seligson, M. (1978), 'Images of political participation in Latin America', in J. A. Booth, M. A. Seligson *et al.* (eds), *Political Participation in Latin America*, New York.

Kourvetaris, G. and Dobratz, B. (1982), 'Political power and conventional political participation', *Annual Review of Sociology*, Palo Alto, Calif.

Lane, R. (1959), *Political Life*, Glencoe, Ill.

Lasswell, H. D. (1951), 'Psychopathology and politics', in *The Political Writings of Harold D. Lasswell*, Glencoe, Ill.

Milbrath, L. W. and Goel, M. L. (1977), *Political Participation*, Chicago.

Verba, S. and Nie, N. (1972), *Participation in America*, New York.

See also: *elections; political recruitment and careers; representation, political; social movements; voting.*

Political Recruitment and Careers

To study recruitment is to look at political events with an eye to how the participants got there, where they came from and by what pathways, and what ideas, skills, and contacts they acquired or discarded along the way. Knowing their abilities, sensitivities, aims and credentials, one is better able to anticipate and interpret what they say and do. In turn, better evaluations can be made of the key consideration: performance, by élites and by the institutions and systems they run.

Everywhere political recruitment is a system maintenance process that is only partly institutionalized. The trade of politics is largely learned through an apprenticeship system. The career perspectives of each generation are moulded both by new priorities placed on skills and knowledge appropriate to meet changing needs and by the performance examples, good and bad, of men and women ahead of them on the political ladder. It is not uncommon to note that, even at early stages in their careers, tomorrow's leaders are being screened for capacities their elders never had to possess. At the same time, élites persistently search for successors who are like themselves in style, judgement, temperament, beliefs and outlook. Élites are self-perpetuating.

The classic theorists, Mosca, Pareto and Michels, each explored the stultifying implications of incumbency. Governing élites are not necessarily adequate to the task. Too often, incumbency is a brake on efforts to update an institution's functional rationality, since performance norms and leadership objectives tend to be set by incumbents themselves.

Patterns of incumbency are called careers. Subjectively,

career perspectives are moving vantage points from which men and women in politics appraise their duties and opportunities, whether they treat public life as a calling or as a livelihood, or both. Objectively, an individual's life path through the communal and corporate infrastructure of his society never ceases to be an apprenticeship that equips him with crucial skills and typical attitudes as well as with material resources and organizational sponsors – which are often necessary as credentials at subsequent major career thresholds.

Opportunities in politics are almost inevitably characterized by elements of co-optation. Aspirants for political careers cross an unmarked threshold when they are taken seriously for a given job by those who control the necessary political resources to get it and keep it. The intramural screening system for a neophyte legislator, official, or party functionary is often a searching and unnerving process. Formal recruitment processes in politics – whether by election, examination, sponsorship, or other credentialing procedures – seldom bestow much interpersonal influence; rather, such influence comes when one can show special prowess, rally a following, claim inside knowledge, or otherwise impress one's colleagues.

Schlesinger (1966) has stressed the notion of a political opportunity structure. In different polities, the realistic routes to significant office can be identified, and both traffic flow and casualty rates can be calculated. For Seligman (1971) it is not offices but roles that define the opportunity structure. Both the supply of eligibles and the demand for people to fill political roles must be considered. Not only one's birth chances but one's access to education, wealth, or other avenues of mobility affect eligibility. Eligibles for any given role are those with appropriate resources and skills who are socialized, motivated, and certified to fill it.

Careers also depend on the kind of sponsorship available and credentialing mechanisms involved. A minor position can often be seized successfully with no more than makeshift and temporary team efforts. To sustain a significant career of office-holding, on the other hand, implies sustained organizational support. Political career opportunities, as contrasted with *ad hoc* chances to play roles or even briefly to hold formal posts, tend to be controlled by parties; cliques may help one start a career, or may cut it short, but rarely can they suffice to sustain one.

Typically, political parties control the high-risk thresholds that distinguish a local notable from a translocal functionary, a legislative career from a ministerial one. Once those who control the jobs and roles available at a given organizational node, in a given institutional setting, or at a given geographic locale, have taken an eligible aspirant seriously enough to invest organizational resources by sponsoring him formally, the aspirant is probably certified for at least a modest career in the same orbit. To put the same person in transit to a different career orbit, however, takes venture capital – party resources more difficult to secure and more jealously husbanded.

If a number of rivals contend for a party's nomination, the pattern of risks – financial, programmatic, organizational, and personal – for each contender is a function of the field against him. Some candidates change the risks significantly for others but not for themselves; they may need the exposure and experience, and they and their backers may view the effort as a long-term investment rather than a demonstrable loss.

Using an opportunity structure/political risk schema prompts certain key questions. Who are the gatekeepers? What selection criteria do they use? What quasi-automatic credentialing practices narrow the field? Is self-promotion encouraged? Are aspirants sometimes conscripted? Is a job sought for its own sake, or as a stepping stone, or as a seasoning experience? Career opportunities are probably more agglutinated, more commingled and more presumptively closed to outsiders than the opportunity-structure schema suggest.

Motivations have been much studied also. Lasswell's displacement formula (1930) (see Marvick, 1977) is concerned with personality dynamics: private motives are displaced onto public objects and rationalized in terms of public purposes. Eldersveld (1964) has demonstrated the labile and complex patterns of activist motivations. Wilson (1962) argues that leaders can grant or withhold various incentives, and thus nurture distinctive kinds of organizations. The political pros in 'machine politics' are accommodationist and success-minded. Quite different are the amateur volunteers, whose participation is principled and programmatic.

Dwaine Marvick
University of California, Los Angeles

References
Eldersveld, S. J. (1964), *Political Parties: A Behavioral Analysis*, New York.
Marvick, D. (ed.) (1977), *Harold D. Lasswell on Political Sociology*, Chicago.
Schlesinger, J. (1966), *Ambition and Politics*, Chicago.
Seligman, L. (1971), *Recruiting Political Elites*, Morristown, N.J.
Wilson, J. Q. (1962), *The Amateur Democrat*, Chicago.

Further Reading
Aberbach, J., Putnam, R. and Rockman, B. (1982), *Bureaucrats and Politicians*, Cambridge, Mass.
Eulau, H. and Czudnowski, M. (eds) (1976), *Elite Recruitment in Democratic Polities*, New York.
Eulau, H. and Prewitt, K. (1973), *Labyrinths of Democracy*, New York.
Prewitt, K. (1970), *The Recruitment of Political Leaders*, New York.
Putnam, R. (1976), *The Comparative Study of Political Elites*, Englewood Cliffs, N.J.
See also: *élites; political participation; parties, political.*

Populism

Populism is one of the least precise terms in the vocabulary of social science. It is used to refer to a wide variety of political phenomena, and students of these populisms continue to disagree about what, if any, features they share. It is possible to identify at least seven different types of political phenomena, each considered populist by some political scientists. Three of these are radical movements based on or oriented towards the countryside:

(1) Radical farmers' movements, of which the paradigm case is the US People's Party of the 1890s. This movement, whose adherents coined the label 'Populist', grew out of the economic grievances of farmers in the Western and Southern states, and for a time appeared to threaten the American two-party system. The Populists, whose manifesto declared, 'We seek to restore the government of the Republic to the hands of "the plain people"', demanded a variety of reforms, including monetary inflation by increased coinage of silver. The movement collapsed after the defeat in the 1896 Presidential election of W. J. Bryan, a Democrat who fought on a largely Populist platform. Other examples of a comparable 'farmers' radicalism' include the rise of Social Credit in Alberta and of the Co-operative Commonwealth Federation in Saskatchewan.

(2) Movements of radical intellectuals, aiming at agrarian socialism and romanticizing the peasantry. The type-case here is *Narodnichestvo* (Populism), a phase of the nineteenth-century Russian revolutionary movement during which disaffected intellectuals 'went to the people' to try to provoke them to revolution. At the height of the movement, in 1874, thousands of young people, girls as well as young men, risked imprisonment by flocking to the countryside to preach the gospel of agrarian socialism. They believed that since communal cultivation of land still survived in the Russian village, a new socialist society could be constructed upon this rural foundation once the state was destroyed. The peasantry proved unresponsive, however, and some of the *Narodniki* took to terrorism instead, even managing to assassinate Tsar Alexander II.

(3) Spontaneous grassroots peasant movements, aimed at control of the land and freedom from élite domination. Unlike the two previous categories, in this case there is no acknowledged paradigm movement, but examples include the Zapatistas in the Mexican Revolution, the Peasant Parties of Eastern Europe after the First World War, and the Russian Revolution before its capture by the Bolsheviks. Third-World revolutionary movements with a peasant base, such as Maoism, are often thought of as a fusion of Marxism with populism.

While these three categories all relate to political movements, and are all more or less agrarian, the term populism is also applied to several other diverse phenomena.

(4) Populist dictatorship – cases in which a charismatic leader appeals beyond conventional politicians to the masses, and gains unconstitutional power by giving them 'bread and circuses'. Juan Peron, who (with the help of his wife Eva) built up a loyal popular following in Argentina in the 1940s, is an obvious case; 'Southern Demagogues' in the US, such as Huey Long of Alabama, provide other examples. It is sometimes suggested that this kind of populist leader can gain a mass following only where the masses in question are either rural or else recent migrants from the countryside (like many of the first generation of *Peronistas*).

(5) If populism can be used to describe mass-based dictatorship, it can also indicate a form of democracy. 'Populist democracy' is hostile to representation, and seeks to keep as much power as possible in the hands of the people. Its characteristic institutional devices are the popular referendum on legislation passed by the representative assembly; popular initiative, whereby voters can bypass the assembly and initiate legislation to be voted on in a referendum; and the recall, whereby representatives can be forced to undergo an extra election in the course of their term of office if a certain number of voters express dissatisfaction with their performance. Populist democracy is taken to its furthest extreme in Switzerland, but, as a result of its adoption by American Progressives in the early years of this century, many US states (notably California) have constitutional procedures for referenda.

(6) A further sense of populism, which one might call 'reactionary populism', is its use to describe politicians who play to the reactionary prejudices of the masses against the enlightened views of the political élite in democratic countries. Politicians who gain popularity by playing on ethnic hostilities or right-wing views about law and order are particularly liable to the charge of 'populism' in this sense.

(7) Finally, the term is also applied to a particular political style. 'Politicians' populism' is the style of politicians who avoid ideological commitments and claim to speak for the whole

people rather than for any faction; of 'catch-all people's parties' that are short on principles, eclectic in their policies and prepared to accept all comers.

Although different social scientists apply the label populism to all these seven types, these types are obviously too diverse to be regarded as different varieties of a single political phenomenon. The only feature all of them share is a rhetoric making great use of appeals to 'the people'. However, since 'the people' can mean either the whole nation or some lower section of it (such as the peasants or the urban masses) this rhetoric is highly versatile and does not in itself indicate any particular programme or constituency.

Theorists who wish to explain 'populism' as a social phenomenon are necessarily selective, focusing on certain of the types listed above and denying that the others are really populist. Many theorists make their selection on sociological grounds, relating populist radicalism to the strains of modernization, and seeing populist movements as a kind of alternative to socialism, either in rural areas or among urban masses recently drawn from the countryside. According to these theories, populists, though politically radical, are characteristically traditionalist in their values and concerned to resist modernization. Many students of politics in the Third World find this type of theory illuminating. Attempts to interpret other populist phenomena (such as the US Populist movement) in these terms are highly controversial.

M. Canovan
University of Keele

Further Reading
Canovan, M. (1981), *Populism*, New York.
Ionescu, G. and Gellner, E. (eds) (1969), *Populism: Its Meanings and National Characteristics*, London.

Power

Definitions of power are legion. To the extent that there is any commonly accepted formulation, power is understood as concerned with the bringing about of consequences. But attempts to specify the concept more rigorously have been fraught with disagreements. There are three main sources of these disagreements: different disciplines within the social sciences emphasize different bases of power (for example, wealth, status, knowledge, charisma, force, authority); different forms of power (such as influence, coercion, control); and different uses of power (such as individual or community ends, political ends, economic ends). Consequently, they emphasize different aspects of the concept, according to their theoretical and practical interests. Definitions of power have also been deeply implicated in debates in social and political theory on the essentially conflicting or consensual nature of social and political order. Further complications are introduced by the essentially messy nature of the term. It is not clear if power is a zero-sum concept (Mills, 1956; Parsons, 1960); if it refers to a property of an agent (or system), or to a relationship between agents (or systems) (Arendt, 1970; Parsons, 1963; Lukes, 1974); if it can be a potential or a resource (Wrong, 1979; Barry, 1976); if it is reflexive or irreflexive, transitive or intransitive (Cartwright, 1959); nor is it clear if power can only describe a property of, or relationship between, individual agents, or if it can be used to describe systems, structures or institutions (Parsons, 1963; Lukes, 1978; Poulantzas, 1979); furthermore, it is not clear whether power necessarily rests on coercion (Cartwright, 1959) or if it can equally rest on shared values and beliefs (Parsons, 1963; Giddens, 1977). Nor is it at all clear that such disputes can be rationally resolved, since it has been argued that power is a theory-dependent term and that there are few, if any, convincing metatheoretical grounds for resolving disputes between competing theoretical paradigms (Lukes, 1974, 1978; Gray, 1983).

In the 1950s discussions of power were dominated by the conflicting perspectives offered by 'power-élite' theories (Mills, 1956), which stressed power as a form of domination (Weber, 1978) exercised by one group over another in the presence of fundamental conflicts of interests; and structural-functionalism (Parsons) which saw power as the 'generalized capacity of a

social system to get things done in the interests of collective
goals' (Parsons, 1960). Parsons thus emphasized power as a
systems *property*, as a *capacity* to achieve ends; whereas Mills
viewed power as a relationship in which one side prevailed *over*
the other. Mills's views were also attacked by pluralists who
argued that he assumed that some group necessarily dominates
a community; rather, they argued, power is exercised by voluntary groups representing coalitions of interests which are often
united for a single issue and which vary considerably in their
permanence (Dahl, 1957, 1961; Polsby, 1963). Against class
and élite theorists the pluralists posed a view of American
society as 'fragmented into congeries of small special-interest
groups with incompletely overlapping memberships, widely
differing power bases, and a multitude of techniques for
exercising influence on decisions salient to them' (Polsby, 1963).
Their perspective was rooted in a commitment to the study of
observable decision making, in that it rejected talk of power in
relation to nondecisions (Merelman, 1968; Wolfinger, 1971),
the mobilization of bias, or to such disputable entities as 'real
interests'. It was precisely this focus on observable decision
making which was criticized by neo-élite and conflict theorists
(Bachrach and Baratz, 1970; Connolly, 1974; Lukes, 1974),
who accused the pluralists of failing to recognize that conflict
is frequently managed in such a way that public decision-
making processes mask the real struggles and exercises of
power; both the selection and formulation of issues for public
debate and the mobilization of bias within the community
should be recognized as involving power. Lukes (1974) further
extended the analysis of covert exercises of power to include
cases where A affects B contrary to B's real interests – where
B's interests may not be obtainable in the form of held preferences, but where they can be stated in terms of the preferences
B would hold in a situation where he exercises autonomous
judgement. Radical theorists of power have also engaged with
structural-Marxist accounts of class power over questions of
whether it makes sense to talk of power without reference to
agency (Lukes, 1974; Poulantzas, 1973, 1979). Although these
debates have rather dominated recent discussions of power in

social and political theory, we should not ignore the work on power in exchange and rational-choice theory (Barry, 1976), nor the further criticisms of stratification theories of power which have been developed from positions as diverse as Luhmann's neo-functionalism (Luhmann, 1979), and Foucault's rather elusive post-structuralism (Foucault, 1980).

Definitional problems seem to be endemic to discussions of power. One major problem is that all accounts of power have to take a stand on whether power is exercised over B whether or not the respect in which B suffers is intended by A. A similar problem concerns whether power is properly restricted to a particular sort of effect which A has on B, or whether it applies in any case in which A has some effect on B. These two elements, intentionality and the significance of effects, allow us to identify four basic views on power and to reveal some of the principal tensions in the concept (White, 1972):

(1) This makes no distinction between A's intended and unintended effects on B; nor does it restrict the term power to a particular set of effects which A has on B. Power thus covers phenomena as diverse as force, influence, education, socialization and ideology. Failing to distinguish a set of significant effects means that power does not identify a specific range of especially important ways in which A is causally responsible for changes in B's environment, experience or behaviour. This view is pessimistically neutral in that it characteristically assumes that power is an ineradicable feature of all social relations, while it makes no presumption that being affected by others in one way or in one area of life is any more significant than being affected in any other. One plausible version of this view is to see power as the medium through which the social world is produced and reproduced, and where power is not simply a repressive force, but is also productive (Foucault, 1980). Note that with this conception there is no requirement that A could have behaved otherwise. Although this is an odd perspective, it is not incoherent, since it simply uses power to refer to causality in social and interpersonal relations.

(2) This isolates a set of significant effects. Thus, A exercises power over B when A affects B in a manner contrary to B's

preferences, interests, needs, and so on. However, there is no requirement that A affect B intentionally, nor that A could have foreseen the effect on B (and thus be said to have obliquely intended it). Poulantzas's Marxism provides one such view by seeing power in terms of 'the capacity of a social class to realize its specific objective interests' (Poulantzas, 1973). Any intentional connotations are eradicated by his insistence that this capacity is determined by structural factors. The capacity of a class to realize its interests 'depends on the struggle of another class, depends thereby on the structures of a social formation, in so far as.they delimit the field of class practices' (1973). As agency slips out of the picture, so too does any idea of A intentionally affecting B. Although idiosyncratic, this view does tackle the problem of whether we can talk meaningfully of collectivities exercising power. If we want to recognize the impact which the unintended consequences of one social group's activities have over another, or if we want to recognize that some group systematically prospers while others do not, without attributing to the first group the intention of doing the others down, then we will be pushed towards a view of power which is not restricted solely to those effects A intended or could have foreseen. The pressures against this restriction are evident in Lukes's and Connolly's work. Both accept unintended consequences so as to 'capture conceptually some of the most subtle and oppressive ways in which the actions of some can contribute to the limits and troubles faced by others' (Connolly, 1974). Both writers, however, also recognize that attributions of power are also often attributions of responsibility, and that to allow unintended effects might involve abandoning the possibility of attributing to A responsibility for B's disbenefits. Consequently both equivocate over how far unintended effects can be admitted, and they place weight on notions of A's negligence with regard to B's interests, and on counterfactual conditionals to the effect that A could have done otherwise. Stressing 'significant effects' also raises problems, since the criteria for identifying such effects are hotly disputed. Thus radical theorists criticize pluralists for specifying effects in terms of overridden policy preferences, on the grounds that power is also used to shape or suppress the formation of preferences and the articulation of interests. Again, two pressures operate, in that it seems sociologically naive to suppose that preferences are always autonomous, yet it is very difficult to identify appropriate criteria for distinguishing autonomous and heteronomous preferences. Taking expressed preferences allows us to work with clearly observable phenomena since B can share the investigator's ascription of power to A – it thus has the advantage of methodological simplicity and congruence with the dependent actor's interpretation. However, taking 'repressed' preferences or real interests can be justified, since it provides a more theoretically persuasive account of the complexities of social life and of the multiple ways in which potential conflicts are prevented from erupting into crisis. Yet this more complex theoretical account is under pressure to identify a set of real interests, and the temptation is to identify them in terms of autonomous/ rational preferences; the problem with this is that it often carries the underlying implication that power would not exist in a society in which all agents pursued their real interests. Power is thus used to decribe our deviation from utopia (Gray, 1983).

(3) The second view is primarily concerned with identifying the victims of power – not the agents. The focus is on A's power *over* B. The third view, which attributes power only when A intends to affect B, but which does not place any restrictions on the manner in which A affects B, switches the focus from A's power *over* B to A's power *to* achieve certain ends (Russell, 1938; Wrong, 1979). Power is concerned with the agent's ability to bring about desired consequences – 'even' but not necessarily 'against the resistance of others' (Weber, 1978). This view has a long pedigree (Hobbes, 1651), and it satisfies some important theoretical interests. In so far as we are interested in using A's power as a predictor of A's behaviour, it is clearly in our interests to see A's power in terms of A's ability to secure high net profit from an action – the greater the anticipated profit, the more likely A is to act (Barry, 1976). Another reason for focusing on A's intention is the difficulty in identifying a range of significant effects which is not obviously stipulative. Concen-

trating on A's intended outcomes allows us to acknowledge that there are a number of ways in which A can secure B's compliance and thereby attain his ends. Thus force, persuasion, manipulation, influence, threats, throffers, offers, and even strategic positioning in decision procedures may all play a role in A's ordering of his social world in a way that maximally secures A's ends. But seeing power solely in terms of A's intentions often degenerates into an analysis where all action is understood in power terms, with behaviour being tactical or strategic to the agent's ends. On this view agents become, literally, game-players or actors, and we are left with a highly reductive account of social structures and institutions (Rogers, 1980).

(4) The last perspective analyses power in terms of both intentional action and significant effects. It concentrates on cases where A gets B to do something A wants which B would not otherwise do. Two sets of difficulties arise here. The first concerns the extensiveness of the concept of power and its relationship with its companion terms, authority, influence, manipulation, coercion, and force. On some accounts power is a covering term for all these phenomena (Russell, 1938); on others it refers to a distinct field of events (Bachrach and Baratz, 1974). Getting B to do something he would not otherwise do may involve mobilizing commitments or activating obligations, and it is common to refer to such compliance as secured through authority. We may also be able to get B to do something by changing B's interpretation of a situation and of the possibilities open to him – using means ranging from influence and persuasion to manipulation. Or we may achieve our will through physical restraint, or force. Finally, we may use threats and throffers in order to secure B's compliance – that is, we may coerce B (Nozick, 1969). In each case A gets B to do something A wants which B would not otherwise do, although each uses different resources (agreements, information, strength, or the control of resources which B either wants or wants to avoid), and each evidences a different mode of compliance (consent, belief, physical compliance, or rational choice). Although exchange and rational-choice theorists have attempted to focus the analysis of power on the final group of

cases, to claim that the others are not cases of power is clearly stipulative. Yet it is these other cases which introduce some of the pressures to move away from a focus solely on intended effects and significant affecting. Where A's effect on B is intended, instrumental to A's ends and contrary to B's preferences, and where B complies to avoid threatened costs, we have a case which firmly ties together A's intention and the set of effects identified as significant (B's recognized costs are intended by A and functional to A's objectives). But the other cases all invite extensions, either in the direction of covering cases in which A secures his will, disregarding the nature of the effects on B, or towards cases where B's options or activities are curtailed by others, either unintentionally, or unconditionally. Also, this view of power risks focusing on A's *exercise* of power over B, to the detriment of the alternative and less tautological view (Barry, 1976) that power is a possession, that it may exist without being exercised, and that a crucial dimension of power is where A does not secure B's compliance, but is in a position to do so should he choose. Wealth, status, and so on, are not forms of power, but they are resources which can be used by A to secure B's compliance. And an adequate understanding of power in a given society will include an account of any systematic inequalities and monopolies of such resources, whether they are being used to capacity or not. The pressure, once again, is against exclusive concentration on A's actual exercise and towards a recognition of A's potential. But once we make this step we are also likely to include cases of anticipatory surrender, and acknowledging these cases places further pressure on us to move beyond easily attributable, or even oblique, intention on A's part. These pressures are resisted mainly by those who seek to construct a clear and rigorous, if stipulative, theoretical model of power. But there is also some equivocation from those who seek to match ascriptions of power with ascriptions of moral responsibility. Part of the radical edge of Lukes's (1974) case stems precisely from the use of ascriptions of power as a basis for a moral critique. But much is problematic in this move. A may act intentionally without being sufficiently sane to be held morally responsible; A may intentionally affect

B to B's disbenefit without violating moral norms (as in a chess game, competitions, some exchange relations with asymmetrical results, and so on); and it is also important to recognize that B's compliance must maintain proportionality with A's threat in order for B to be absolved of moral responsibility (Reeve, 1982).

The theoretical and practical pressures which exist at the boundaries of these four possible interpretations of power account for much of the concept's messiness. Each has its attractions. The fourth view is most promising for model or theory building, the third for the prediction and explanation of action, the second for the study of powerlessness and dependency, and the first for the neutral analysis of the strategic but non-intentional logic of social dynamics. Although metatheoretical grounds for arbitration between competing conceptions of power seem largely absent, we can make a few comments on this issue. Although 'restrictivist' definitions of power may serve specific model and theory-building interests, they inevitably provide a much simplified analysis of social order and interaction. However, more encompassing definitions risk collapsing into confusion. Thus, while there are good theoretical grounds for moving beyond stated preferences to some notion of autonomous preferences – so as, for example, to give a fuller account of B's dependence – we should be cautious about claiming that A is as morally responsible for B's situation as when A intentionally disbenefits B. Indeed, depending on how we construe the relevant counterfactuals, we might deny that agents are liable for many of the effects of their actions. Thus, we might see social life as inevitably conflict ridden, and while we might recognize that some groups systematically lose out it might not be true that A (a member of the élite) intends to disadvantage any individual in particular, or that A could avoid harming B without allowing B to harm him (as in Hobbes's state of nature). Also, although we are free to use several different definitions of power (such as the three dimensions identified by Lukes, 1974), we should recognize that each definition satisfies different interests, produces different results and allows different conclusions, and we need to take great care to avoid confusing the results. Finally, we should recognize that although definitions of power are theory-dependent, they can be criticized in terms of the coherence of the theory, its use of empirical data, and the plausibility of its commitments to positions in the philosophies of mind and action.

Mark Philp
Oriel College, Oxford

References

Arendt, H. (1970), *On Violence*, London.

Bachrach, P. and Baratz, M. S. (1970), *Power and Poverty, Theory and Practice*, Oxford.

Barry, B. (1976), 'Power: an economic analysis', in B. Barry (ed.), *Power and Political Theory*, London.

Cartwright, D. (1959), 'A field theoretical conception of power', in D. Cartwright (ed.), *Studies in Social Power*, Ann Arbor.

Connolly, W. (1974), *The Terms of Political Discourse*, Lexington, Mass.

Dahl, R. (1957), 'The concept of power', *Behavioural Science*, 2.

Dahl, R. (1961), *Who Governs? Democracy and Power in an American City*, New Haven.

Foucault, M. (1980), *Power/Knowledge*, Brighton.

Giddens, A. (1977), ' "Power" in the writings of Talcott Parsons', in *Studies in Social and Political Theory*, London.

Gray, J. N. (1983), 'Political power, social theory, and essential contestibility', in D. Miller and L. Siedentop (eds), *The Nature of Political Theory*, Oxford.

Luhmann, N. (1979), *Trust and Power*, London.

Lukes, S. (1974), *Power, A Radical View*, London.

Lukes, S. (1978), 'Power and authority', in T. Bottomore and R. Nisbet, (eds), *A History of Sociological Analysis*, London.

Merelman, R. M. (1968), 'On the neo-élitist critique of community power', *American Political Science Review*, 62.

Mills, C. W. (1956), *The Power Elite*, London.

Nozick, R. (1969), 'Coercion', in S. Morgenbesser *et al.* (eds), *Philosophy, Science and Method*, New York.

Parsons, T. (1960), 'The distribution of power in American society', in *Structure and Process in Modern Societies*, Glencoe, Ill.

Parsons, T. (1963), 'On the concept of political power', *Proceedings of the American Philosophical Society*, 107.

Polsby, N. (1963), *Community Power and Political Theory*, New Haven.

Poulantzas, N. (1973), *Political Power and Social Classes*, London.

Poulantzas, N. (1979), *State, Power, Socialism*, London.

Reeve, A. (1982), 'Power without responsibility', *Political Studies*, 3.

Rogers, M. F. (1980), 'Goffman on power hierarchy and status', in J. Ditton (ed.), *The View from Goffman*, London.

Russell, B. (1938), *Power*, London.

Weber, M. (1978 [1922]), *Economy and Society*, eds G. Roth and G. Wittich, Berkeley and Los Angeles. (Original German, *Wirtschaft und Gesellschaft*, Tubingen.)

White, D. M. (1972), 'The problem of power', *British Journal of Political Science*, 2.

Wolfinger, R. E. (1971), 'Nondecisions and the study of local politics', *American Political Science Review*, 65.

Wrong, D. (1979), *Power, its Forms, Bases and Uses*, Oxford.

See also: *authority; leadership*.

Public Choice

Public choice, or the economic theory of politics, is the application of the economist's way of thinking to politics. It studies those areas in which economic and political forces interact, and is one of the few successful interdisciplinary topics. The behaviour of the individual is taken to be rational, an assumption which political scientists and sociologists have also found to be fruitful.

While the term public choice was coined in the late 1960s, the type of politico-economic analysis has a long history. Condorcet was the first to recognize the existence of a voting paradox: in a system of majority voting, the individual preferences cannot generally be aggregated into a social decision without logical inconsistencies. Italian and Scandinavian public finance scholars have also explicitly dealt with political processes, in particular in the presence of public goods. Another forerunner is Schumpeter, who regarded the competition between parties as the essence of democracy.

The following four areas are central to public choice:

(1) *Preference aggregation.* Condorcet's finding of a voting paradox has been generalized to all possible methods of aggregating individual preferences. The impossibility result remains in force, in particular when many issue-dimensions are allowed for.

(2) *Party competition.* Under quite general conditions, the competition of two vote maximizing parties leads to an equilibrium: both parties offer the same policies in the median of the distribution of voters' preferences. The programmes proposed differ substantially when there are more than two parties competing, and when they can form coalitions.

(3) *Interest groups.* The product of the activity of a pressure group is a public good, because even those not participating in its finance may benefit from it. Consequently, economic interests are in general not organized. An exception is when the group is small, when members only receive a private good from the organization, or when it is enforced by government decree.

(4) *Public bureaucracy.* Due to its monopoly power in the supply of public services, the public administrations tend to extend government activity beyond the level desired by the population.

In recent years, the theories developed have been empirically tested on a wide scale. The demand for publicly provided goods and services has been econometrically estimated for a great variety of goods, periods and countries. An important empirical application is *politico-economic models* which explicitly study the interaction of the economic and political sectors. A vote maximizing government, which has to take into account the trade-off between inflation and unemployment, willingly produces a political business cycle. More inclusive politico-economic models have been constructed and empirically tested for various representative democracies: economic conditions such as unemployment, inflation and growth influence the government's re-election requirement, which induces in turn the government to manipulate the economy to secure re-election.

Viewing government as an endogenous part of a politico-economic system has far-reaching consequences for the theory of economic policy. The traditional idea of government maximizing the welfare of society has to be replaced by an emphasis on the consensual choice of the appropriate rules and institutions.

Bruno S. Frey
University of Zurich

Further Reading
Frey, B. S (1978), *Modern Political Economy*, Oxford.
Mueller, D. (1979), *Public Choice*, Cambridge.
See also: *interest groups and lobbying; voting*.

Radicalism

Though social theories and philosophical analyses may be termed radical, the primary modern usage of the word radicalism is to designate basic or extreme political challenges to established order. The term (with an upper-case R) came into use in the late eighteenth and early nineteenth centuries to refer to an élite political faction which sought parliamentary and other 'rationalizing' reforms, and became a key root of the Liberal Party in England. Almost immediately, a lower-case usage developed to describe all sorts of political orientations which shared either an analysis of current troubles claiming to go to their roots, or a programme deduced from first principles. Under pressure of the French Revolution and various English popular agitations, attention came increasingly to focus on actual mobilizations – radical actions – rather than merely radical ideas.

Social scientists are still divided in the extent of their emphasis on the importance of rationalistic analyses (for example Marxist class consciousness) compared to other more directly social sources of radical actions. There are two conventional views among the latter group. One, now nearly discredited, holds that social atomization and marginalization dispose those cut off from the social mainstream to engage in protests which reveal more of their psychological troubles than any serious programme for social change. The other stresses the underlying interests which a common position in relation to some external factor, such as markets or means of production, gives to individuals. Both positions are challenged by empirical findings that a great deal of organization and internal cohesion are necessary to radical collective action. Common 'objective' interests are not necessarily enough to produce concerted action. Activists can hope to achieve this coalescence through further organizational efforts, and they often see trade unions and similar organizations as way-stations on the road to class organization.

Traditional communities, however, have been the basis of more radical movements than class or any other abstract bonds and formal organizations. The popular radical movements (as opposed to élite radicals) of early industrial Britain acted on radical social roots in reaction to the disruptions of the Industrial Revolution. Though the members of these communities often lacked sophisticated radical analyses, they had visions profoundly at odds with conditions around them. Perhaps even more importantly, they had the social strength in their communal relations to carry out concerted action against great odds for long periods of time; few compromise positions were open to them, unlike the members of the 'modern' working class. These sorts of social foundations continue to be central to radical movements around the world. Peasants and other traditional farmers along with artisans and craft workers form the mainstay of these radical movements.

Social revolutions, the most radical of actual political transformations, certainly have many causes besides anti-governmental radical movements. A state structure weakened by external conflicts or internal disunity may, for example, be essential to the success of a revolutionary movement. Where revolutions succeed, and transform societies rather than only change regimes, two sorts of radical groups have generally been involved. On the one hand, there has usually been a tightly organized, forward-looking, relatively sophisticated group of revolutionaries. On the other hand, there has also generally been a broad mass of protesters and rebels acting on the basis of strong local communities and traditional grievances. The latter are essential to making the revolution happen, to destabilizing the state. The former, however, are much better positioned to seize power during the transformation.

At least in the contemporary world of states and other large-scale abstract social organizations, there is a paradox to radicalism (which may of course be of the 'right' as well as the 'left'). Most radicalism is based on local bonds and tradition, yet, when successful, it both disrupts tradition and displaces power towards the centre of society and its large-scale systems of control. This is true even of radical movements aimed at less extreme goals than revolutions. The US civil rights movement could succeed in ending local intolerance and oppression only by forcing an increase of central state power and its penetration into local life. But it could not at the same time make local communities democratic and preserve their autonomy as free realms of direct participation.

Craig Calhoun
University of North Carolina, Chapel Hill

Further Reading
Calhoun, C. (1983), 'The radicalism of tradition', *American Journal of Sociology*, 88.
Moore, B., Jr (1979), *Injustice: The Social Bases of Obedience and Revolt*, White Plains, New York.
See also: *populism; revolutions; social movements.*

Representation, Political
The history of political representation is that of the rise of European parliaments, through the transformation of the sovereign's councillors into a sovereign assembly.

The medieval monarch used to seek advice from persons chosen at his discretion for their competence and trust, but since he wanted them to report from all the land and then to convey his orders and tax demands back to 'their' people, he tended to pattern his selection after the actual social hierarchy, choosing those in the nobility and high clergy, whose fiefs and dioceses constituted his kingdom, and (as early as the thirteenth century in England) among important commoners.

During crises, when the king most needed their co-operation, the councillors demanded and obtained the right to be convened periodically and to be masters of their agenda; also, instead of answering individually to the king for their particular community (which was soon to be reapportioned into electoral districts), they made collective deliberations and rendered them obligatory and compelling. They were now acting as one single assembly (whose number, election, immunity and so on had to be formalized) and speaking for the people as a whole; thus the king, who had been seen as the head, and natural representative, of his people, implicitly began to speak only for himself.

Not only political legitimacy, but also power, had shifted: in the name of political representation they had in fact established their rule. For example, the slogan of the American Revolution did not mean 'no taxation without our spokesman to the king' but 'without our share of power', indeed 'without governing ourselves'. Parliament, instead of the king, was sovereign.

Whatever its constitutional formula, representative government is an awkward proposition, (1) because the more faithful the representation, the less the ability to rule, that is, to make choices or even compromises or coercions; and (2) because the demands of modern politics have both glorified government (the rise everywhere of the executive branch which executes always less and rules always more) and diminished the role of parliaments based on territorial representation. When the representational logic of the former royal councillors came to its democratic triumph with their election according to the principle 'one man, one vote', it appeared that one vote is too little to be correctly represented: every man wants to press for his multifaceted interests through specific spokesmen or organizations which will fight the suppressions, amalgamations and distortions that territorial representation implies in each electoral district and then at the legislative level, whatever the endeavours of special and minority groups to force their 'quotas' into elected or appointed bodies.

Political representation takes an ironical turn when (1) advocates of functional representation criticize parliaments for disregarding obvious demands of the people and arbitrarily imposing their idea of the common interest (much like the kings had been criticized as unrepresentative); (2) when parliamentary elections often become geared to the nomination of a government rather than of representatives; and (3) when the executive branch surrounds itself more and more formally with 'councillors' drawn from the most important interest groups in the country and whose 'advice' tends to become obligatory and compelling.

Jean Tournon
University of Grenoble

Further Reading
Birch, A. H. (1971), *Representation*, London.
Eulau, H. (1978), *The Politics of Representation*, London.
Eysenck, H. J. (1954), *The Psychology of Politics*, London.
Pennock, J. and Chapman, J. (1968), *Representation*, New York.
Pitkin, H. (1967), *The Concept of Representation*, Berkeley and Los Angeles.
See also: *democracy; interest groups and lobbying; political participation.*

Revolutions

A revolutionary crisis, or revolution, is any political crisis propelled by illegal (usually violent) actions by subordinate groups which threatens to change the political institutions or social structure of a society.

Some revolutionary crises result in great changes in politics and society, as the Russian and Chinese Revolutions; some result in great political changes but few changes in social life outside of politics, as the English Revolution; some result in hardly any change at all and are hence considered unsuccessful revolutions, as the Revolutions of 1848 in Germany.

The word 'revolution' first appeared in political writing in fourteenth-century Italy and denoted any 'overturning' of a government; such events were seen as part of a cycle in the transfer of power between competing parties, with no great changes in institutions implied. However, since the French Revolution, revolution has become associated with sudden and far-reaching change. It is this particular sense of the word that has been carried to fields other than politics, as in the Industrial Revolution, or scientific revolutions.

Revolutions have causes, participants, processes of development and outcomes. No two revolutions are exactly alike in all these respects, thus no general theory of 'revolutions' has proven satisfactory. Understanding revolutions requires theories of causes, of participants, of processes and of outcomes of revolutions that stress the variations in each element and how they combine in specific historical cases.

Many of the key issues in current studies of revolution were set out in the nineteenth century by Marx and Engels (1968). Marx viewed Europe's history since the Middle Ages as a progression through various modes of production, each one more fruitful than the last. 'Bourgeois' revolutions, exemplified by the French Revolution of 1789, were necessary to destroy the privileged feudal aristocracy and the agrarian society over which it presided. However, the resulting political freedom and material benefits would extend only to the class of professionals and businessmen who controlled the succeeding capitalist society; thus a further revolution in the name of labourers remained necessary to extend self-determination and the material benefits of modern industrial technology to all. The major elements of this view – that revolution is a necessary agent of change; that such change is progressive and beneficial; and that revolutions, in both cause and effect, are intimately related to great historical transitions – pose the articles of faith for practising revolutionaries and the chief research problems for academic analysis.

In recent years, the work of Tocqueville (1856) has assumed increasing importance. Tocqueville's analysis of the French Revolution stressed the continuity of the Old Regime and the post-Revolutionary state, and the greater centralization of state power that followed from the Revolution. Similar continuities have occurred elsewhere: The Russian Imperial bureaucracy and secret police, the Chinese Imperial bureaucracy, and the Iranian personal authoritarian state have been replaced by similar, albeit more powerful, post-revolutionary versions. Thus the extent of the historical transformation associated with revolutions appears less striking in practice than in Marxist theory.

In the last two decades, social scientists seeking the causes of revolutions first focused on changes in people's expectations and attitudes, but later moved to an emphasis on institutions and the resources of states. Gurr (1970) argued that when people's social opportunities no longer accorded with their expectations, either because expectations were rising too quickly, or welfare was falling, feelings of 'relative deprivation' would make fertile ground for popular opposition to governments. Johnson (1966) suggested that any large and sustained 'disequilibrium' between the economic, political and cultural sectors of a society – such as education increasing more rapidly than economic output, or economic organization changing more rapidly than political organization – could lead many individuals to withdraw their allegiance to the current regime. Huntington (1968) emphasized expectations in the political sphere, arguing that if popular expectations for participation in politics came to exceed a country's institutional procedures for political participation, unmet demands for political participation could lead to an explosion of popular activity directed against the current regime. However, Tilly and his collaborators (1975), in empirical studies of collective violence, found that strikes and riots did not occur most frequently during times of deprivation, such as periods of falling real wages or falls in economic output. Nor were strikes and riots especially common during times of 'disequilibrium', such as periods of rapid urbanization or industrialization. Instead workers acted to protect and defend their interests whenever the opportunity was available; those opportunities depended on shifts in the balance of power between workers and the employers and states that they faced. Tilly's 'resource mobilization' view argued that whenever conflict arose over economic or political issues, the incidence of popular protest depended chiefly on how the abilities and the range of actions open to those at odds with the current regime compared with the resources of the regime and its supporters. Recently, Skocpol (1979), emphasizing the differences between states and the importance of international competition, has led the way in developing a 'social-structural' perspective on revolutions, which views revolutions as a consequence of state weaknesses combined with institutions that provide aggrieved élites and popular groups with opportunities for effective collective action.

The origins of revolutions do not appear to reside in an exceptional level of 'deprivation' or 'disequilibrium'. Instead, revolutions occur when difficulties that are successfully coped with in other times and places – wars and state fiscal crises – occur in states with institutions particularly vulnerable to revolution. Skocpol has identified three institutional features that make for such vulnerability: (1) a state military machine considerably inferior to those of nations with which the state is normally in competition; (2) an autonomous élite able to challenge or block implementation of policies sought by the central administration; (3) a peasantry with autonomous village organization. One could also add a fourth: large concentrations of artisans and labourers in and near inadequately policed political centres. These elements, in various combinations, have played a role in the origins of the major revolutions of modern times: England 1640 (1, 2, 4); France 1789 (1, 2, 3, 4); Mexico 1910 (1, 2, 3); China 1911 (1, 2); Russia 1917 (1, 3, 4); Iran 1979 (2, 4). In recent years, peasant organization has often been supplied by a revolutionary party, rather than automonous village organization. This functional substitution has led to different, characteristically peasant-party-based, revolutions: China 1949, Vietnam 1972, Nicaragua 1979.

A military or fiscal crisis in an institutionally vulnerable state may begin a revolution; however, the process of revolution and the roles of various participants vary greatly. Certain processes appear to be, if not universal, extremely common: an initial alliance between moderates seeking reform and radicals seeking far-reaching change; involvement in international war (in part because nearby states fear the revolution spreading, in part because revolutionary leaders find the nationalist fervour generated by external wars useful); a gradual fission between moderates and radicals, with the latter triumphing; a civil war as leaders of the revolutionary parties seek to extend their control throughout the nation and eliminate opposition; the emergence of authoritarian rule by a single dominant leader. Other variables – the extent and autonomy of popular participation, the extent of civil war, the degree and permanence of radical triumph, and the duration of autocratic rule – range from high to low across revolutions, depending on the resources available to various groups, the skills of individuals, and the luck of political and military battles.

The outcomes of revolutions are equally diverse. These depend not only on the factors that caused the revolution, but also on the vagaries of the revolutionary process, the influence wielded by external countries and the problems and resources faced by the eventual victors in the revolutionary struggle. The French and English Revolutions, though differing greatly in the level of popular uprisings, resulted eventually in similar regimes: monarchies in which possession of private property was the key to political participation and social status. By contrast, the Russian and Chinese (1949) Revolutions, the former with a level of autonomous popular participation, both rural and urban, akin to that of France, the latter with a chiefly rural peasant-party revolution, both resulted eventually in socialist party-states, in which membership and rank in the state party are the keys to political participation and social status. Mexico's revolution led to a hybrid capitalist party-state, in which political participation is directed by and through the state party, but private wealth is the chief criterion of social status.

Evaluations of the material progress made under post-revolutionary regimes are also mixed. There are cases of great progress in health and literacy, such as Cuba; but the ability of post-revolutionary regimes to provide a generally higher material standard of living than similarly situated non-revolutionary regimes is yet to be demonstrated (Eckstein, 1982).

The role of ideological changes in causing revolutions and shaping their outcomes is hotly debated. Most revolutionaries have proven quite pragmatic in modifying revolutionary programmes as seemed necessary; Russia under the New Economic Plan of the 1920s, and China in the 1980s, have embarked on such pragmatic paths. At other times ideological fervour has taken precedence, as in the Jacobin years of the French Revolution, and the Great Leap Forward and Cultural Revolution in China. Ideological programmes are thus a rather unpredictable, if far from dominant, element in shaping revolutions.

Ideology in a broader sense, as an overall cultural perspective, has been a more uniformly important factor. Eisenstadt (1978) has noted that the key to revolution lies in the coalescence, in a time of political crisis, of diverse movements – peasant uprisings, élite political revolts, religious heterodoxies – into a widespread attack on the institutions of the old regime. Thus the main role of ideologies in revolutions has been to bring together diverse grievances and interests under a simple and appealing set of symbols of opposition. For this purpose, any ideology that features a strong tension between good and evil, emphasizes the importance of combating evil in this world through active remaking of the world, and sees politics as simply one more battlefield between good and evil, may serve as the foundation for a revolutionary ideology. Thus puritanism, liberalism, communism, anti-colonialism, and, most recently, Islam, have all proved adaptable to providing symbols for revolutions. Studies of peasants' and workers' revolts have stressed that traditional ideologies – the communal ideology of 'members' against 'outsiders' of the peasant village and the craft guild – can also motivate actors in revolutionary crises. None of these ideologies of themselves brought down governments; but they were crucial in providing a basis for uniting diverse existing grievances under one banner and encouraging their active resolution.

In the past, major revolutions have occurred only in preindustrial or early industrializing nations with small élites. If this pattern continues, the arena of major revolutions in the future will be Africa, Southern Asia and Central America. The advanced industrial democracies may see strikes and mass demonstrations, but are unlikely to witness revolutions. An enigma for which there is little historical precedent appears in the developed South American nations and the Eastern European socialist states, with developed industrial economies and small highly dominant élites. These countries have faced incipient revolutionary crises (Hungary 1956, Czechoslovakia 1968, Poland 1980) and frequent *coups d'état* (Brazil 1964, Argentina 1966), but so far they have lacked the autonomous élite groups or popular organizations that made for revolutionary vulnerability in successful revolutions of the past. This is in large part because neighbouring superpowers, by backing specific élites in these countries, have actively shaped political struggles and their outcomes. Whether these nations' future development, and future super-power actions, will render them more similar to vulnerable states will be a crucial factor in the future incidence of revolutions.

Jack A. Goldstone
Northwestern University

References

Eckstein, S. (1982), 'The impact of revolution on social welfare in Latin America', *Theory and Society*, 11.

Eisenstadt, S. N. (1978), *Revolution and the Transformation of Societies*, New York.

Gurr, T. R. (1970), *Why Men Rebel*, Princeton, New Jersey.

Huntington, S. (1968), *Political Order in Changing Societies*, New Haven, Conn.

Johnson, C. (1966), *Revolutionary Change*, Boston.

Marx, K. and Engels, F. (1968 [1848]), *The Communist Manifesto*, London. (Original German edn, *Manifest der Kommunistischen Partei*, London.)

Skocpol, T. (1979), *States and Social Revolutions*, Cambridge.

Tilly, C., Tilly, L. and Tilly, R. (1975), *The Rebellious Century 1830–1930*, Cambridge, Mass.
Tocqueville, A. (1856), *The Old Regime and the French Revolution*, New York.

Further Reading
Goldstone, J. A. (1982), 'The comparative and historical study of revolutions', *Annual Review of Sociology*, 8.
Moore, B., Jr (1966), *Social Origins of Dictatorship and Democracy*, Boston.
Wolf, E. R. (1969), *Peasant Wars of the Twentieth Century*, New York.
See also: *radicalism; Tocqueville.*

Rousseau, Jean-Jacques (1712–78)

Rousseau's contribution to the social sciences has been a paradoxical one. In his first *Discours* (Discours sur les sciences et les arts, (1964 [1750]) ['On science and art'], Rousseau argued that scientific inquiry in general tends rather to corrupt than to enlighten, and that public virtue would be better served by ignorance than by systematic knowledge. On the other hand, in his second *Discours* ('Sur l'origine et les fondements de l'inégalité parmi les hommes', 1964 [1775]) ['On the origins of inequality']), Rousseau himself offered a pioneering work in social theory that generations of social scientists have considered crucial to the founding of such disciplines as sociology and social anthropology – the very sorts of theoretical inquiry that Rousseau had virtually ruled out in his first *Discours* as inimical to the public good (See Derathé, 1970; Durkheim, 1965; Lévi-Strauss, 1962.)

Furthermore, whereas Rousseau argued in the second *Discours* that man is not originally a social being and that sociability is fundamentally alien to man's nature, his argument in *Du contrat social* (1762) [*The Social Contract*, 1978], his main work of political philosophy, is that one can only conceive of a legitimate state where the members are wholeheartedly devoted to the good of the community and are able to identify their own interests with those of the whole society. It would seem that an author whose work is rooted in such basic contradictions would be incapable of producing a cogent and consistent social philosophy, and indeed many critics would dismiss Rousseau's achievement on just these grounds. However, one of the central claims of Rousseau's thought is that society itself is founded on irresolvable contradiction, and that therefore paradox may be the most appropriate medium in which to understand the essence of social life.

It is in his magnificent treatise on education, *Émile, ou de l'education* (1762) [*Émile*, 1979], that Rousseau states the basic insight of his social theory – the impossibility of reconciling the contradiction between nature and society: 'He who would preserve the supremacy of natural feelings in social life knows not what he asks. Ever at war with himself, hesitating between his wishes and his duties, he will be neither a man nor a citizen. He will be of no use to himself nor to others. He will be a man of our day, a Frenchman, an Englishman, one of the great middle class.' This insight is further developed in *The Social Contract* (published in the same year as *Émile*).

The core idea of *The Social Contract* is a very simple one: it is that no polity can be considered legitimate except in so far as its laws issue from the will of its members; that citizens are only entitled to renounce natural liberty for the sake of a superior freedom; and that the touchstones of politics based on right are law, democratic will and popular sovereignty. Rousseau managed to articulate a vision of politics as a moral community, even though he remained suspicious of all social relationships and held to the view that society as such is inevitably corrupting. His solution to the problem lay in substituting the power of law for the power of men, thus making men independent of one another by making them all equally dependent on the laws of the republic.

Although Rousseau categorically repudiated the conditions of political life in modernity, many of the fundamental ideas of liberal democracy are owed to him: the idea that the overarching function of government is legislation; the idea that political legitimacy flows from the will of the people; and the idea that formal equality and the rule of law are essential to democratic liberty.

From the first *Discours* onwards, Rousseau's work represented a lifelong battle against the assumptions and aspirations of the Enlightenment. Although Rousseau knew, and had been personally close to, many of the leading members of the French Enlightenment, his ideas led him into increasingly heated and passionate controversies with the champions of Enlightenment. Of these, the most significant product was Rousseau's *Lettre à d'Alembert sur les spectacles* (1758) [*Letter to D'Alembert*, 1968], debating the issue of whether the theatre should be introduced into Rousseau's native city of Geneva. In general, the spokesmen of the Enlightenment sought to refashion the nature of man and society by constructing scientific principles of social existence. Rousseau, by contrast, thought that man is best as he is by nature, that human nature is invariably deformed by life in society, and that such a science of society could only deepen the corruption and debasement of man. This was, in fact, the central insight of his social and moral philosophy, the foundation upon which all his political principles and psychological analyses are built.

Despite recurrent attempts to expose 'totalitarian' traits within Rousseau's political thought, the ever-present concern throughout his political writings was with republican liberty. Rousseau feared that without the sustaining nourishment of genuine citizenship and civic virtue, men in society would become slaves to social conformity, that they would (in the words of the second *Discours*) always live outside of themselves rather than within themselves, and that they would forfeit their natural liberty without attaining the higher condition of civil freedom, thus being worse off rather than better for having left nature to enter social existence. Notwithstanding the supposed romanticism attributed to Rousseau's thought, he possessed a sober and clear-headed insight into the possibility that post-Enlightenment science and technological civilization would pose an ever-greater threat to freedom and civic solidarity.

Even though Rousseau's literary and autobiographical writings have established the image of him as an unworldly and misanthropic dreamer, his political discernment is testified to by his acute diagnosis of the crumbling social order in Europe: In *Considérations sur le gouvernement de la Pologne* (1782) [The Government of Poland, 1972] Rousseau writes, 'I see all the states of Europe hastening to their doom'; in *Émile*, he predicts, 'The crisis is approaching, and we are on the edge of a revolution'; 'In my opinion it is impossible that the great kingdoms of Europe should last much longer.'

There remains, of course, the predictable complaint that Rousseau's social theory is irretrievably utopian, and cannot in any sense be applied to modern conditions. For Rousseau himself, given the conception of political philosophy that he adheres to, and steeped as he is in the classical utopianism of Plato, this does not necessarily count as a very telling objection. As he remarks in *Émile*, 'We dream and the dreams of a bad night are given to us as philosophy. You will say I too am a dreamer; I admit this, but I do what the others fail to do. I give my dreams as dreams, and leave the reader to discover whether there is anything in them which may prove useful to those who are awake.'

Ronald Beiner
University of Southampton and Queen's University,
Kingston, Ontario

References
Derathé, R. (1970), *Jean-Jacques Rousseau et la science politique de son temps*, Paris.
Durkheim, E. (1965 [1953]), *Montesquieu and Rousseau: Forerunners of Sociology*, trans. R. Manheim, Ann Arbor, Mich. (French edn, *Montesquieu et Rousseau, précursors de la sociologie*, Paris.)
Lévi-Strauss, C. (1962), 'Jean-Jacques Rousseau, fondateur des sciences de l'homme', in S. Baud-Bovy *et al.*, *Jean-Jacques Rousseau*, Neuchâtel.

Further Reading
Texts by Rousseau:
(1979), *Emile, or On Education*, trans. A. Bloom, New York.

(1964), *The First and Second Discourses*, ed. R. D. Masters, trans.
R. D. and J. R. Masters, New York.
(1972), *The Government of Poland*, trans. W. Kendall,
Indianapolis.
(1978) *On the Social Contract*, ed. R. D. Masters, trans. J. R.
Masters, New York.
(1968), *Politics and the Arts*, trans. A. Bloom, Ithaca, New York.
Other:
Masters, R. D. (1968), *The Political Philosophy of Rousseau*,
Princeton, New Jersey.
Shklar, J. N. (1969), *Men and Citizens: A Study of Rousseau's
Social Theory*, Cambridge.
See also: *social contract*.

Social Contract

The doctrine that government should be for and by the people
informs the constitution of all countries claiming to be democratic, even when the precept is not observed in practice. Democratic governments today rest their claims to legitimacy and
obedience on electoral consent, but the concept of consent itself
derived originally from contract theory which discovered the
origins of government in a primal act of consent, the social
contract. The foremost exponents of contract theory, Hobbes,
Locke and Rousseau, did not believe that savages had literally
congregated and agreed to set up governments; contract was,
rather, a hypothetical device. Its purpose was to show that
governments should be viewed *as if* they had been established
by the people and evaluated according to whether they served
the purpose of protection for which they were instituted. In
Hobbes's case the theory had illiberal implications: almost any
government, however bad, would serve to keep anarchy at bay.
But for Locke, the people had the right to resist a government
which failed to protect their lives and property. Whether the
conclusions of contract theory were reactionary or revolutionary
depended on its basic assumptions.

In *Leviathan* (1651), Hobbes, fresh from the horrors of civil
war, imagined men in an anarchic state of nature, living in fear
of sudden death. These men would eventually make a contract

to guarantee peace, for their own protection. But since none would trust their fellows, they would then appoint a sovereign, independent of the contract, to enforce it and maintain order by all necessary means, including coercion. Because Hobbes sees authorization as a blank cheque, imposing no account-ability on those in authority, his sovereign would have unquali-fied power over those who authorized him.

Locke's contract theory (1690) was developed partly in protest against Hobbes's absolutist conclusions, partly to vindi-cate the revolution of 1688 which replaced the Stuarts with a constitutional monarchy. His state of nature is peaceful and orderly; people follow natural, moral laws and cultivate land and acquire property. But the absence of laws to resolve disputes leads people to establish a government by agreement. In making the contract, individuals surrender their natural rights, receiving instead civil rights and protection. The govern-ment thus created has a limited, fiduciary role. Its duty is the preservation of 'life, liberty and estate', and if it reneges, the people have the right to overthrow it. Although Locke argued that the contract enforced consent to majority rule, his was not a theory of democracy but an argument for a balanced constitution with a people's legislature, an executive monarch and an independent judiciary. This innovatory constitution-alism was a far cry from Hobbes's axiom that sovereignty was necessarily indivisible. Locke's doctrine that post-contract generations must consent to government, either actively or tacitly, later gave rise to consent theory.

Contractualism is developed in a different direction by Rous-seau (1762), who argued that governments originally resulted from conspiracies of the rich to protect their property. But through an ideal social contract, individuals would freely consent to exchange their natural autonomy for a share in government. This could only be achieved by a direct, participa-tory democracy, which would be directed by the 'General Will'. The General Will is 'that which wills the common good', the decision which all citizens would accept if they laid aside personal interests. Dissenters from the General Will could be 'forced to be free', that is, compelled to obey laws for the public good which, if less self-interested, they would themselves freely have chosen. The General Will thus represents our 'better selves', but liberal theorists have often regarded it as a potential justification for authoritarianism or for totalitarian regimes claiming to act in the 'real interests' of the people (although undoubtedly this was not Rosseau's intention) and have therefore rejected Rousseau's contract theory.

Despite their differences, all three theories reflect the same desire to make the legitimacy of governments rest on the people's choice. The cultural environment which produced this desire was one of increasing individualism, secularization and legalism: the doctrine of individual free will dictated that nobody should be governed without his own consent, while the decline of the 'divine right of kings' dogma meant that a secular justification for political power was needed. The recourse to a contractual justification mirrored the growing reliance on contracts in the expanding commercial world, and a new, anti-feudal, legalistic attitude to public affairs.

The central fallacy of contract theories, as T. H. Green stated (1901), is that they presuppose 'savage' men with notions of rights and legality which could only be generated *within* a society. More damning for critics such as Hume, Bentham and Paine was the fact that existing governments were blatantly based on coercion, not consent, and operated largely for the benefit of the governors. History, too, suggested that most governments had been established through conquest and force. Such criticisms explain why contract theory was later replaced by the more plausible idea of democratic consent. However, contractarianism has recently been revived in Rawls's *Theory of Justice* (1971), which identifies the principles of justice as those to which people would consent, if deliberating in a state-of-nature-like vacuum. Rawls's work, which vindicates a broadly liberal view of justice, illustrates again how the original assumptions, especially those concerning human nature, determine the form and the contents of a hypothetical social contract. Contract theory is not abstract speculation, but a political myth tailored to prove a point.

Despite the logical and empirical shortcomings of contract

theory, it deserves serious attention because of its relation to central political ideas such as 'the will of the people', legitimacy and political obligation. All these have been employed manipulatively by regimes which have no basis in the people's choice. The 'social contract' which British politicians have recently resurrected seems neo-Hobbesian, requiring unconditional compliance from citizens. To avoid such ideological manoeuvres and sleights of hand, we now need to reject the rhetorical invocation of implicit, tacit or imaginary social contracts and to develop a doctrine of meaningful and participatory choice and consent.

Barbara Goodwin
Brunel University, Uxbridge

References
Green, T. H. (1901), *Lectures on the Principles of Political Obligation*, London.
Hobbes, T. (1968 [1651]), *Leviathan*, ed. C. B. Macpherson, London.
Locke, J. (1924 [1690]), *An Essay Concerning the True Original, Extent and End of Civil Government*, London.
Rawls, J. (1971), *A Theory of Justice*, Cambridge, Mass.
Rousseau, J. J. (1913 [1762]), *The Social Contract* (trans. G. D. H. Cole, London). (Original French, *Du contrat social*, Paris.)
Riley, P. (1982), *Will and Political Legitimacy: A Critical Exposition of Social Contract Theory in Hobbes, Locke, Rousseau, Kant and Hegel*, Cambridge, Mass.
See also: *Locke; Rousseau.*

Socialism

Socialism is the name for a varied group of political theories and movements. Socialist ideas and agitation began in the early nineteenth century in England and France. The period between the 1820s and the 1850s was marked by a plethora of diverse and distinguished theorists, among them, Saint-Simon, Fourier, Owen, Blanc and Proudhon, and also many lesser thinkers. It was also marked by the foundation of co-operative societies, model utopian communities and the advocacy – and in the case of Blanc's national workshops half-hearted adoption – of schemes to be put into action by governments.

Socialism was brought into existence by the rise of industrial production and the intensification of wage labour in handicraft enterprises alongside it. Prior to the large-scale existence of workshops, factories and machines, most radical conceptions of a reorganization of society were agrarian, as in Rousseau's constitution for an imaginary republic of Corsica. Socialist doctrines sought to 'organize' society in order to replace the anarchy of the market-place and large-scale poverty with an orderly system based on greater or lesser degrees of central control, co-operation and mutuality. Organization offered a rational solution to the 'social question' – the problems of mass poverty and poor urban living conditions. Most of the early socialists were middle-class reformers, concerned philanthropists who sought to better the lot of the poor by changes in social organization rather than charitable works.

The radical and revolutionary movements in this period were nationalist in countries like Hungary or Poland or Italy under foreign domination, and popular-democratic in England and France. Such political movements were not dominated by socialist ideas. Between 1848 and 1871 the popular democratic and revolutionary traditions exhausted themselves in the European countries in a series of political defeats, at the barricades in countries like France, or through political containment in the case of the Chartists in England.

In the period between 1848 and 1871, Marx and Engels made radical attempts to recast socialist theory. They attacked the utopianism of their predecessors, refusing to promulgate schemes of social reform. In essence they argued that:

(1) the class struggle is the objective basis of socialist victory, socialism is identified with the proletariat and its struggle to eliminate exploitation and oppression;
(2) the class struggle arises from the system of social production

and that the development of the forces of production would secure the objective basis for a planned economy;

(3) the overthrow of the exploiting class and its ruling machinery, the state, would usher in a new period of popular self-government in which the domination of man by man would be replaced by the administration of things.

Marx and Engels insisted on the necessity of revolution, and the seizure of power by the working class, but they did recognize that universal suffrage might facilitate the downfall of capitalism.

Actually, it did nothing of the sort. Between 1870 and 1914 the institutional foundations of modern socialism were developed in Britain and Germany. Universal suffrage created the modern political party – a permanent machine with paid officials whose task is to mobilize the mass electorate. The SPD became the dominant force in German socialism, not because it came to treat Marx's ideas as party orthodoxy, but because it started early and effectively to compete for votes in elections for the Reichstag. In Britain and Germany, large-scale industrialism was accompanied by the growth of trade unionism. The British Labour Party was created to facilitate the parliamentary representation of the trade unions, and the links between the SPD and the unions were similarly close.

As a mass electoral party and the political representative of unionized labour, any socialist movement in an advanced industrial country had to relegate to virtual impotence the popular insurrectionary politics of the old European 'left'. Even Engels conceded as much, and Eduard Bernstein did no more than carry the conclusion to its logical extreme. Bernstein's *Evolutionary Socialism* (1899) represented the first articulate advocacy of 'social democracy' as against socialism, and it displaced the goal of 'revolution' for a never-ending struggle for attainable reforms. Others, like Karl Kautsky, argued that by parliamentary and legal means the workers could engineer a revolutionary change in the social system.

To the mass party and the labour union must be added the rise of big government as a key institutional support of modern socialist movements. In the period 1870–1914 in Britain and Germany, central state and municipal authorities came to provide, administer and organize an increasing range of activities, mass schooling, social insurance, public health, sewerage and electric light, and so on. This administration of mass needs and utilities provided another base for socialist advocacy and practice. Fabian socialism consciously sought to intervene in central and local government's provision, to provide an organizing core of intellectuals equipped to shape the extent and character of 'big government'. The success of the Fabian position stands in stark contrast to the failure of the anti-statist doctrines of Guild Socialists and others. For all the forceful advocacy by able thinkers like G. D. H. Cole (1953–61), the Guild Socialist movement was dead by the early 1920s. Likewise, British syndicalism perished in the same period, while institutional unionism survived and flourished.

After 1914 the landscape of the socialist movement in Europe was changed by World War I, the split in socialism and the rise of Communism. The Communist Parties for a considerable period in the 1920s and early 1930s emphasized revolutionary insurrectionary politics, going so far as to stigmatize the still existent European socialist parties like the SPD as 'social fascist'. World War II, the consolidation of Soviet rule in Eastern Europe and the stabilization of parliamentary democracy in Western Europe led to a radical change in the Communist parties. Where legally permitted or successful, they became mass electoral parties and developed links with their own labour unions, as in France and Italy, for example, and sought to participate in government. The split between Communism and socialism in Europe, bitter into the 1950s, ceased to have much meaning with the rise of Eurocommunism.

Since 1945 socialist and social democratic parties have participated in government to a hitherto unprecedented degree. The post-war boom was a period of intensification of 'big government' and welfarism. In Scandinavia, the UK and Germany, socialist parties became accepted parties of government, and in the Swedish case ruled uninterruptedly for over thirty years. In this period, traditional socialist ideas, centring on publicly-owned planned production, suffered at the expense of social-democratic views of redistribution and welfare in a state-managed, full-employment, capitalist system. Anthony Crosland's *The Future of Socialism* (1964) advocated, like Bernstein, a change in British Labour Party doctrine to match the Party's practice.

Since the end of the post-war boom in 1973, social democratic ideas have had to compete with a revitalized socialist fundamentalism in the UK. At the same time throughout Europe many intellectuals have begun to rethink the goals of socialism. Many are chastened by the experience of centrally-planned production and distribution in the USSR, but also by the consequences of the growth of statist welfarism in Western Europe. Many favour the sort of anti-authoritarian, decentralizing and self-management views advocated by Cole and the Guild Socialists. The problem with much of this rethinking is the failure to provide a new political base comparable to that provided by the mass party, the union and big government. A good example of such views is André Gorz's *Farewell to the Working Class* (1982). Socialist doctrine has entered a period of diversity and productivity comparable to the 1820s–50s; its institutional supports, however, remain those developed in the period 1870–1914.

Socialism has been treated as an exclusively European phenomenon. Socialism in the United States, having grown spectacularly between the formation of the American Socialist Party in 1901 and 1912, thereafter underwent a process of decline such that in 1938 it had been reduced to a mere 7,000 members. This failure is attributable to many causes but most important is the character of American trade unionism which made it impossible to create the links between a united union movement and a socialist political party so important in Germany and England. Socialist doctrines in the Third World, where they are not modelled on those of Europe, have tried to offer a vision of social organization different from that based on large-scale industry, as in the case of 'African Socialism'. Julius Nyerere (1969) offers perhaps the most systematic version of this alternative to European ideas. Some commentators would contend that not only have such doctrines been a dismal failure in practice, but also that as a doctrine they are better conceived as a variant of agrarian populism. Socialism is an outgrowth of advanced industrialism but, as the United States shows, is by no means an inevitable one.

Paul Hirst
Birkbeck College
University of London

References
Berstein, E. (1961 [1899]), *Evolutionary Socialism*, New York.
Cole, G. D. H. (1953–61), *A History of Socialist Thought*, Vols I–V, London.
Crosland, A. (1964), *The Future of Socialism*, London.
Gorz, A. (1982), *Farewell to the Working Class*, London.
Nyerere, J. K. (1969), *Freedom and Socialism*, Dar-es-Salaam.

Further Reading
Wright, A. W. (1979), *G. D. H. Cole and Socialist Democracy*, Oxford.
See also: *communism; equality; welfare state.*

Social Movements

For Lorenz von Stein (1855) the social movement of the nineteenth century was the proletariat. Scholarship in the twentieth century has pluralized the term, removed its historical connotation and applied it to a variety of social phenomena, from unstructured collective behaviour, to cults and religious sects, to issue-oriented protest movements all the way to organized revolutionary groups. The only common denominators in the variety of definitions employed is that social movements are uninstitutionalized groups in some insurgent relationship to existing society, involving unmediated bonds between leaders and followers.

With so broad a focus, empirical richness has been gained but at the cost of both theoretical clarity and methodological consensus. Though organizational and statistical analyses are increasingly common, the typical research approach remains the descriptive case study. The mass of case studies available has led to a large number of typologies, based in part on the empirical properties of groups and in part on their relation to existing society.

Theoretically, the field has focused on three major questions: (1) What kind of people are recruited into social movement organizations? (2) How does the appearance of social movements relate to reversals in economic growth and changes in class relations? (3) How do relations between leaders and followers affect the outcomes of social movement activity?

Social movement theory and research have two main sources. In the conservative reaction against the French Revolution and its aftermath, a school of thought developed which emphasized the formlessness, rage and irrationality of the mob, contrasting it with the structure, calm and moderation of 'normal' (bourgeois) society (Oberschall, 1973). With less animus against mass unrest, Durkheim's concept of 'anomie' provided a theoretical rationale for such behaviour, providing a guide for the location of 'vulnerable' groups within the class structure, and connecting social movement research to the transition from traditional to industrial society.

With the rise of the Socialist movements of the late nineteenth century grew a belief in the underlying rationality, form and justice of lower-class unrest. The early twentieth century, with its institutionalization of the working-class movement, strengthened this 'rationalist' strand of research and theory. Michels shifted the theoretical emphasis to the relations between leaders and followers within movements, posing the question of the effect on unconventional movements of using conventional means. In Britain, a tradition of social history began which emphasized the rational bases of lower-class unrest and its relation to the market and the state.

The great cataclysms of the twentieth century – Fascism and the Bolshevik Revolution – had the reverse effect. Fuelled by a generation of exiles who brought with them nightmarish memories of what 'the mob' – especially when poisoned by revolutionary agitation – could become, these experiences were

the source of a new generation of theories relating social movements structurally to economic decline and to psychological
'relative deprivation'. In this new synthesis, culminating in the
work of Smelser (1963), social movements were regarded mainly
as signs of dysfunction in the social system, and social movement recruits were once again seen as atomized individuals set
adrift on the seas of social change.

The turbulence of the 1960s led to a resurgence of interest
in social movements, with one group developing multivariate
statistical models of violent behaviour to examine its relationship to deprivation, a second attempting to reshape and renew
a Marxist interpretation of social movements, and a third
blending the 'rationalist' perspective with new findings and
insights from economics and political science.

The multivariate approach, best represented by Gurr's work
(1980), though most innovative methodologically, was closest
in spirit to the 'breakdown' theories of the past. Like the
tradition, its findings about the effects of relative deprivation
and the psychological sources of social movements were divided
and inconclusive. The firmest findings of multivariate statistical
analysis come from an area tangential to social movement
research – strike waves and their relation to economic
fluctuations.

Recent Marxist and Marxist-influenced schools of social
movement research show great richness and internal variation.
From their perspective, Touraine (1971) and his followers
regard the social movement as a transcendent experience in
radical rupture with existing authority and therefore as a rare
form of collective action. In contrast, Tilly (1978) and his
collaborators are less exclusive. Closer to the spirit of British
social history than to French historical sociology, they focus on
all forms of 'challenge' to the polity on the part of groups whose
resources can be mobilized to gain entry to it. Though explicitly
comparative, Tilly's work has been most influential in the
United States, where it dovetails with a lively tradition of
research on protest in political science and a reawakening
interest in working-class history.

The 'resource mobilization' theories of the 1970s have

blended the 'rationality' approach with insights from economics. Mobilization is generally defined as collective action by actual or prospective movement leaders to gain control of the resources of previously unmobilized population groups on behalf of their actual or perceived interests or values, much as entrepreneurs combine the factors of production (McCarthy and Zald, 1977). In contrast to theorists of breakdown or deprivation, these students focus on leaders rather than followers and view leaders' success as the result, not of changes in deprivation, but of short-term or contingent factors that enable them to find a constituency to represent. In contrast to the more structural perspective of the Marxists, they focus on the organizational innovations and political advantages that social movements can employ to mobilize a following.

An important impact of the 1960s on social movement research has been to underscore the remarkable diffusion of social movement-like activity among population groups that have been historically moderate in their behaviour – for example, the salaried middle class, regional ethnic groups, women and minorities. There has also been observed a hybrid of 'interest-group movements' combining traditional organization and membership with a capacity for unconventional or disruptive action. In these groups – visible in both environmental and the anti-nuclear movements of the 1980s – we see radical action employed on behalf of politically legitimate goals, reversing the paradox first seen by Michels that groups with politically unacceptable goals frequently use politically institutionalized forms of action.

Sidney Tarrow
Cornell University

References

Gurr, T. R. (ed.) (1980), *Handbook of Political Conflict: Theory and Research*, New York.

McCarthy, J. and Zald, M. (1977), 'Resource mobilization and social movements: a partial theory', *American Journal of Sociology*, 82.

Oberschall, A. (1973), *Social Conflict and Social Movements*, Englewood Cliffs, NJ.

Smelser, N. (1963), *Theory of Collective Behavior*, New York.

Stein, L. von (1855), *Geschichte der Sozialen Bewegung Frankreichs von 1789 bis auf unsere Tage*, Berlin.

Tilly, C. (1978), *From Mobilization to Revolution*, Reading, Mass.

Touraine, A. (1971), *The Post-Industrial Society*, New York.

Further Reading

Marx, G. and Wood, J. L. (1975), 'Strands of theory and research in collective behavior', in *Annual Review of Sociology*, A. Inkeles (ed.), vol. I.

Piven, F. F. and Cloward, R. (1977), *Poor People's Movements: Why They Succeed and How They Fail*, New York.

See also: *political participation; radicalism*.

Social Welfare Policy

In the long boom succeeding World War II, social welfare policy was widely seen as the state's intervention in society to secure the well-being of its citizens. This progressivist interpretation of increasing social expenditure by the state was sustained by the writings of key post-war welfare theorists such as Titmuss (1950) and Marshall (1967). The former welcomed increasing collectivism as a necessary and desirable means of enhancing social integration; the latter saw in the developing British Welfare State the extension of citizenship through the acquisition of social rights. The Beveridge-Keynes Welfare State, which had been called into existence by the exigencies of war and the balance of social forces in the post-war situation, came to assume an ideological significance, both as the exemplar against which other Welfare States were to be assessed, and also as an explanation of the development of the Welfare State itself. This ideological construction had few means of accounting for developments in other countries such as the pioneering achievements in social policy in New Zealand, nor of specifically conservative political strategies such as those of Bismarck's Germany, in which social insurance was conceived of as a mechanism to weaken the working-class movement and inhibit the spread of socialist ideas. For that matter, its emphasis on the peculiarly British nature of the achievement led to difficulties in explaining the rather better performance by most indicators of Britain's new partners when she joined the European Community, a phenomenon which was received with some shock by British political culture.

Relatively early on in the post-war period, social democratic theorists such as Crosland (1964) acknowledged the significance of social welfare policy and the achievement of the full employment economy in modifying a basically capitalist social formation. Nonetheless, redistribution was to be secured through growth, thus avoiding the political opposition of the rich – a strategy which was thrown into question as economic growth faltered and even declined. The significance of these policies for structuring sex-gender relations within the home and within the labour market was grasped very much more slowly (Wilson, 1977). Nonetheless, the achievement of the Welfare State or welfare capitalism, as it has been variously termed, was aided by the discourse and practices of social policy in which 'need' was set as morally and administratively superior to the market as the distributive principle for welfare. Thus integral to the achievement of welfare capitalism and institutional welfare was a concept of need which stood as an antagonistic value to that of capitalism with its, at best, residual welfare.

Need was at the same moment emancipatory and constrained within the dominant social relations. In its emancipatory aspect, need fostered the language of rights, not only in theoretical writing but within the popular demands of the new social movements which rose during the late 1960s and early 1970s within North America and Europe (Piven and Cloward, 1971; Rose, 1973). Aided by the 'rediscovery of poverty' in the 1960s (Harrington, 1962; Abel-Smith and Townsend, 1965), large-scale mobilization around income maintenance and housing exerted substantial pressure on governments to offer more, and more responsive, welfare provision. Thus, the new social movements shared with institutional welfare an opposition to mere residual welfare, but continuously sought to go beyond not only the level of existing provisions but also the organizational forms through which they were realized. Instead – and this tendency was to become magnified as the welfare movements were joined by the 1970s wave of feminism – existing forms of welfare were seen as coercive, inadequate and statist. In contrast, the oppositional forms developed by the movements themselves emphasized democratic accountability, and nonhierarchical ways of working. Freire's (1972) thesis of conscientization as the politically creative strategy for the poor in the Third World was shared by the new social movements as they sought to develop an alternative practice of welfare to what was usual in the old industrialized societies. At their most radical the new movements sought that society itself should be organized around the meeting of human need.

While the boom lasted, this critique of institutional welfare as statist and bureaucratic made relatively little impact on either mainstream social welfare policy thinking or on political culture: ideological support for a more or less institutional welfare overlaid the deeper antagonism between need and the market. The separation of need from market values was further facilitated by the separation between economic and social policy discourses. Social policy felt able to ignore economic policy since it was confident that Keynesian demand management techniques had delivered and would continue to deliver the precondition of the Welfare State, namely the full employment economy. Economists largely ignored the discussion of social welfare policy as of no interest to other than social ameliorists, until the crisis of the mid-1970s during which the loss of confidence in Keynesian techniques fostered a return to an endorsement of the market and an increasingly open opposition to state welfare expenditure (Friedman, 1962). Where institutional welfare had seen expanded welfare policies as socially integrative, a radical political economy had emphasized their contribution to capital accumulation and social control (O'Connor, 1973; Gough, 1979); now monetarism and the advent of a new right saw such expenditures as harming individualism and competitiveness and thus weakening the central dynamic of capitalism. With considerable populist skill the new right acknowledged the critique of the coercive character of public welfare, and offered an increase in personal liberty through rolling back the (Welfare) State, restoring the market and the family as the paramount providers of welfare.

The very depth of the current crisis which has provided the conditions for the rise of the new right, nonetheless serves as a major constraint for its remedies. Global restructuring of manufacturing is associated with widespread and foreseeably long-term unemployment in the de-industrializing countries. Unemployment, averaging around 12 per cent in the OECD countries in 1982 and with few clear indications of a significant improvement, requires, even in the most residual conception of welfare, substantial expenditure for both maintenance and control of an expanding surplus population. This situation is aggravated by the large numbers of young people among the unemployed, among whom ethnic and racial minorities are over-represented.

Despite these political constraints, since 1975 most Western governments have reduced the rate of growth of their social welfare budgets. Thus, up to 1975 the real rate of social expenditure growth in the seven largest OECD countries was no less than 8 per cent per annum (15 per cent growth at current prices); between 1975 and 1981 the real rate was halved. While all countries have experienced difficulties in maintaining their social welfare budget in the face of the reduction of the growth of the overall economy, governments with a specifically anti-welfare ideology such as the US and Britain have made substantial inroads. Thus, in the case of Britain an institutional system of welfare moves increasingly towards a residual model, particularly in the area of social security. The Nordic countries stand apart as the last bastion of the most highly developed expression of the old Welfare State, although the mix of labour market and social policies through which they achieve this varies substantially between them. Given the double significance for women of the existence of the Welfare State, as potential provider of both employment and services, it is perhaps not by chance that those Nordic countries with a continuing commitment to welfare have also an unusually high proportion of women representatives in their parliaments and upper houses.

It is noteworthy that writers from these countries, such as Himmelstrand (1981) and his co-workers, are taking an active part in the current international debate concerning the possible future direction open to a post-Welfare State society. These writers seek to develop a theory which looks beyond welfare capitalism, to a new but very much more democratically based corporatism. Such post-Welfare State theorists are typically not unsympathetic to the claims of the new social movements (Gorz, 1982). However, they seem not to have fully appreciated the significance of feminist theorizing concerning the relationship between paid and unpaid labour within the development of the Welfare State, and thus the advantage to the dominant gender of retaining the present arrangements. Thus, even though the precondition of the old Welfare State, the full employment of one gender with welfare flowing through the man to the dependent family, no longer fits the actuality of either domestic or labour market structures, the ideological defence of those arrangements persists. Faced with the growing 'feminization of poverty' (Pearce, 1978), and the profoundly segregated (by both occupation and between full and part-time employment) labour market, there is a serious question concerning the extent to which the needs of women are met by the new post-Welfare State theorizing.

These are cautious, even sceptical reflections on the debate around the Welfare State and the place of social welfare policy (Glennister, 1983). How far any of the new theories can offer to serve as the new fusion of the social and the economic, the contemporary historical equivalent of the old Welfare State of Keynes and Beveridge is not yet clear. What is clear, however, is that social welfare policy having spent its years of greatest growth relatively detached from economic policy has now been forcibly rejoined by circumstance. Together they occupy the centre of an intensely debated political arena.

Hilary Rose
University of Bradford

References

Abel-Smith, B. and Townsend, P. (1965), *The Poor and the Poorest*, London.

Crosland, C. A. R. (1964), *The Future of Socialism*, London.

Freire, P. (1972), *Cultural Action for Freedom*, Harmondsworth.

Friedman, M. (1962), *Capitalism and Freedom*, Chicago.

Glennister, H. (ed.) (1983), *The Future of the Welfare State*, London.

Gorz, A. (1982), *Farewell to the Working Class*, London.

Gough, I. (1979), *The Political Economy of Welfare*, London.

Harrington, M. (1962), *The Other America*, Harmondsworth.

Himmelstrand, U., Ahrne, G., Lundberg, L. and Lundberg, L. (1981), *Beyond Welfare Capitalism; Issues Actors and Social Forces in Societal Change*, London.

Marshall, T. H. (1967), *Social Policy*, 2nd edn, London.

O'Connor, J. (1973), *The Fiscal Crisis of the State*, New York.

Pearce, D. (1978), 'The feminization of poverty: women, work and welfare', *Urban and Social Change Review*.

Piven, F. F. and Cloward, R. (1971), *Regulating the Poor: The Functions of Public Welfare*, New York.

Rose, H. (1973), 'Up against the Welfare State: the claimant unions', in R. Miliband and J. Saville (eds), *The Socialist Register*, London.

Titmuss, R. M. (1950), *Problems of Social Policy*, London.

Wilson, E. (1977), *Women and the Welfare State*, London.

See also: *welfare state*.

State

State refers, in its widest sense, to any self-governing set of people organized so that they deal with others as a unity. It is a territorial unit ordered by a sovereign power, and today involves officeholders, a home territory, soldiers distinctively equipped to distinguish them from others, ambassadors, flags, and so on. The inhabitable land of the world has for the last century been parcelled up into such units; before that, quite large areas had been either unclaimed and uninhabited, or inhabited by nomadic and wandering peoples who were not organized as states. Most states are now represented at the

United Nations, and they vary in size and significance from China and the United States at one extreme, to Nauru and the Seychelles at the other.

More specifically, however, the term state refers to the form of centralized civil rule developed in Europe since the sixteenth century. This model has been imitated, with varying success, by all other peoples in the modern world. What most distinguishes the state as an organizational entity is the freedom and fluency with which it makes and unmakes law. The empires of the East, by contrast, were predominantly bound by custom, while in Europe in the medieval period, authority to rule was dispersed among different institutions, and in any case took long to acquire the habits of fluent legislation.

The modern European state came into being gradually, and has never ceased to evolve. Its emergence can in part be traced in each of the major European realms by way of the growing currency of the word 'state', along with its analogues in other European languages: *stato, état, estado, Reich* and so on. The idea, however, has played a varying role in different countries – much less, for example, in Britain than in some continental countries. Machiavelli in the *Prince* (1513) exhibits a clear grasp of the emerging realities of central power, but while he sometimes talks of *lo stato*, he can also use expressions like *loro stato* (your state) which suggest that he is not altogether clear about the difference between a state and a régime. In Jean Bodin's *Six Livres de la République* (1578) later in the sixteenth century, the French state was explicitly theorized in terms of the idea of sovereignty, as the absolute and perpetual power of both making and unmaking laws. The *un*making of laws is important, because it constitutes one reason why the growth of absolute power could be welcomed as a liberation from the dead hand of inherited rules. A weariness with the civil strife of the sixteenth and seventeenth centuries further disposed many people to welcome absolute rulers as guarantors of peace. Monarchs were, of course, far from loathe to acquire this power, and set to work diminishing the co-ordinate powers and jurisdictions inherited from earlier times. The Church was perhaps the most important of these jurisdictions, and lost power no less in realms that remained Catholic than in those which became Protestant. Parliamentary institutions fell into desuetude everywhere except in England. The nobility, which had been turbulent in the exercise of its feudal powers, were domesticated as courtiers, most famously at the Versailles of Louis XIV. Monarchy became strictly hereditary and evolved mystiques both of blood and divine right. The absolute power thus generated was often used with a ruthless cynicism typified in the motto 'canons are the arguments of princes' and exemplified in the careers of spectactulary aggrandizing monarchs like Charles XII of Sweden and Frederick the Great of Prussia. But all states alike tried to expand their power both by mobilizing the resources available and by conquering new territory. It would be a mistake, however, to think that this early modern absolutism became indistinguishable from despotism. The sovereigns remained subject to myriad customary restrictions and had to operate for the most part in terms of law, whose abstractness limits its usefulness as an instrument of pure policy. Further, as the new system settled down in the later seventeenth century, the more powerful classes, such as the nobility, clergy and the bourgeoisie in the towns, solidified into corporations which sensibly limited the freedom of action exercised by monarchs who found in Enlightenment rationalism a doctrine highly conducive to their dreams of mobilizing national power. What emerged was the *ancien régime*, a social form so immobile it needed a French Revolution and a Napoleon to destroy it.

The issues raised by the emergence of this quite new form of civil association can best be grasped by their reflection in European political philosophy. A pure theory of the state was presented by Thomas Hobbes in *Leviathan* (1651). Hobbes argued that subjection to a sovereign ruling by law was the only alternative to the incessant discord created when proud and insecure individuals jostled together. Hobbes was clear, as Machiavelli was not, that the state (or *Leviathan*) is an abstract and impersonal structure of offices conditionally exercised by particular men. Men must, as subjects, rationally consent to the absolute power of the sovereign, but this consent lapses if the sovereign cannot protect them, or if he begins directly to threaten their lives. The boldness of the Hobbesian conception, which reflects the thoroughness with which Hobbes thought the issue through, lies in the extrusion of any external limitations on the sovereign power: what the sovereign declares to be just is *ipso facto* just, and he has the right to determine religious belief, and what may be taught in the schools. Liberty is the private enjoyment of the peace brought by civil association, a peace in which alone culture and material prosperity may be garnered.

Being a philosophical work, the *Leviathan* explained but did not justify, and fragments of its argument were appropriated by both sides in the English civil war. Both sides were offended by it. The *Leviathan* was publicly burned at Oxford in 1685. Immediately after the Revolution of 1688, John Locke published *Two Treatises on Government* which softened the intolerably austere picture of the state Hobbes gave. This was an occasional work which popularized the notion that governments rested upon the consent of their subjects, and were limited by natural rights (to life, liberty and property) with which men entered civil society. Their business was to protect such rights. Locke avoided the idea of sovereignty altogether and emphasized that the rulers *represented* the ruled. The spread of liberalism in the next two centuries extended this idea, both in theory and in practice.

In the course of the eighteenth century, it became clear that the modern European state raised quite new problems, both practical and theoretical. It was a free association of individuals claiming the power to legislate for themselves, without any necessary moral, religious or metaphysical commitments. Two ideas, potentially disharmonious, consequently dominated further development: community and freedom. The best formulation of the problem is in the sixth Chapter of Rousseau's *Social Contract* (1762):

How to find a form of association which will defend the person and goods of each member with the collective force of all, and under which each individual, while uniting himself with others, obeys no one but himself, and remains as free as before.

Rousseau's solution focused on a general will constituting a community of citizens devoted to the public interest. Such a conception clearly emerged from the ancient conception of the virtuous republic which had haunted European thought since Machiavelli's *Discourses on the First Ten Books of Livy* (1518), and which was unmistakably subversive of the European system of extended monarchies. Just how subversive it was soon became evident, both in the thought of Immanuel Kant, who argued that republics were the condition of perpetual peace, and in the French Revolution, whose protagonists adopted Rousseau posthumously as one of their own.

The problem was that the classical republic was possible only in a small city with a homogeneous population. Montesquieu had argued in *De l'esprit des lois* (1748) (*The Spirit of the Laws*) that no such thing was possible in the conditions of modern Europe. In the 1820s Hegel presented in the *Philosophy of Right* (1821) an account of the modern state as the objective embodiment of the fully-developed subjective freedom towards which the human spirit had always been tending. At the time, however, a whole group of writers emerged to emphasize the misery and repression, as they saw it, of modern life and the iniquity of the state. Marx and Engels argued that the state was an illusion masking the domination of the bourgeois class, and predicted that after a proletarian revolution the state would wither away. A newly homogeneous mankind would be able to surpass the unity and virtue of the classical republics on a world-wide scale.

The actual history of states has been one of a continuous growth, both in their claim to regulate the lives and property of their subjects, and in their physical capacity to enforce such claims. It is, for example, possible to regulate a literate society much more completely than an illiterate one. The propensity of European states to engage in war with one another has provided frequent emergencies in which necessity trained governments in how to regulate; and all states now have bureaucracies and other instruments of control. Yet, paradoxically, the increase in the state's range and power has produced countervailing decreases in effectiveness. When its functions were limited to guaranteeing order and security, the state was accorded immunity from some of the moral restraints binding on individuals. The doctrine called 'reason of state' authorized the breaking of treaties, deceit, and the employment of violence, when necessary. From the nineteenth century onwards, some extensions of state power (especially the redistributions of wealth which began to constitute the state as a system of welfare for all members of society) were justified on the ground that the state stood for a higher morality. Citizens thus came to believe that they had rights *against* the state. The state's claim to suspend law, to guard its own secrets, to the use of nonlegal measures in dealing with enemies who themselves resorted to terror – all the traditional apparatus of *raison d'état* – was challenged, and it was felt to be the duty of the state to represent the highest moral standards even against those who violated them. In developments such as this, and in the persistently transforming dynamism of the idea of democracy, will be found reasons for seeing the modern state, at least in its European heartland, not as an abstract idea, but as an institution ceaselessly responsive to the beliefs that move its subjects.

Kenneth Minogue
London School of Economics and Political Science

Further Reading
d'Entreves, A. P. (1967), *The Notion of the State*, London.
Mabbott, J. D. (1967), *The State and the Citizen*, 2nd edn, London.
Maritain, J. (1951), *Man and the State*, London.
See also: *government; social contract.*

Terrorism

Terrorism consists of a series of acts intended to spread intimidation, panic, and destruction in a population. These acts can be carried out by individuals and groups opposing a state, or

acting on its behalf. The amount of violence is often disproportionate, apparently random, deliberately symbolic: to hit a
target which would convey a message to the rest of the population. Violence perpetrated by the state or by right-wing
terrorist groups is anonymous. Its goals are to shift sectors of
public opinion to support the restoration of law and order and
repressive measures, at the same time physically destroying
political opponents and intimidating their actual and potential
supporters. Violence from left-wing groups is usually 'signed'.
Its goals are the awakening of public opinion to the injustices
of the 'system', the 'punishment' of hated representatives of the
system and their lackeys, and the expansion of political support
for, and/or the defence of, their organizations. The ultimate
goal is to muster enough support to overthrow the regime or,
at least, to produce a revolutionary situation. An intermediate
stage might be the unmasking of the 'fascist face' of the regime
and the revelation to the population of its repressive reality.

Terrorism by the state or against it must be considered
rational behaviour within the context of alternative options. It
is suggestive of the lack of vast support both for the state
and for terrorist organizations. Otherwise, both would utilize
different political means. It is indeed a short cut to the problem
of the creation of the necessary support. Sociopolitical terrorism
may arise both in democratic and non-democratic states. It is
more frequent in the former because of the relative ease with
which terrorist organizations can be created in an atmosphere
of freedom, when their appearance is unexpected. In non-democratic states, of course, it may be the state apparatus itself
which resorts to terrorist activities. In any event, the lack of
peaceful alternatives to change is likely to radicalize the situation and to push some opponents towards violent, clandestine
activities.

There is not a single cause of terrorism: several conditions
and determinants must be present. For state terrorism the most
important conditions are the willingness and determination of
the dominant groups to retain power against mounting opposition, even by violent means. For sociopolitical terrorism, it is
the inability to acquire sufficient support for radical changes in

the light of mass passivity and élite unresponsiveness. However, terrorism is never simply the response to socioeconomic conditions of marginality. It is always the product of a political project. Be they at the service of the state or against the state, the terrorists pursue political goals.

According to their goals, one can define and identify several types of terrorism: repressive, revolutionary, secessionist. It is also possible to speak of international terrorism – though somewhat inappropriately – for those groups staging their activities on the international scene. They want to dramatize their plight and obtain international visibility, recognition, and support (such as some sectors of the Palestine Liberation Organization (PLO), the Armenians, the Ustasha). However, most terrorist organizations are indigenous, such as the Irish Republican Army (IRA), the German Rote Armee Fraktion, the Italian Brigate Rosse and the neo-fascist Ordine Nuovo, the French Action Directe, the Basque ETA. They have roots and pursue goals that are inherently 'national', even though they might enjoy some (reciprocal) 'international' support.

On the basis of the superior technical strength of modern states and of the legitimacy of democratic ones, it is often said that political terrorism cannot win. However, terrorism by the state can achieve significant results, and political terrorism against non-democratic regimes can severely weaken them (though, in order to win, the terrorist group will have to transform itself into guerrilla bands).

Terrorism, even if it is defeated, is not without consequences. The dynamics of political competition, the structures of the state, the relationships between citizens and political-administrative bodies will be changed to an extent that has thus far not been assessed. Therefore, political terrorism will endure as the weapon of groups that have neither the capability, the possibility, nor the patience to utilize other instruments to pursue their goals and implement their strategies.

Gianfranco Pasquino
University of Bologna

Further Reading

Alexander, Y., Carlton, D. and Wilkinson, P. (eds) (1979), *Terrorism: Theory and Practice*, Boulder, Colorado.

Bell, R. (1975), *Transnational Terrorism*, Washington.

Crenshaw, M. (ed.) (1983), *Terrorism, Legitimacy and Power*, Middletown, Conn.

Eckstein, H. (1963), *Internal War*, New York.

Laqueur, W. (1977), *Terrorism: A Study of National and International Political Violence*, Boston.

Lodge, J. (ed.) (1981), *Terrorism: A Challenge to the State*, London.

Schmid, A. P. (1983), *Political Terrorism: A Research Guide to Concepts, Theories, Data Bases and Literature*, New Brunswick, NJ.

Stohl, M. (ed.) (1979), *The Politics of Terrorism*, New York.

Wardlaw, G. (1982), *Political Terrorism: Theory, Tactics, and Countermeasures*, Cambridge.

Third World

The division of the world into three categories is a very popular device among social scientists, and especially economists and sociologists of development. The distinction derives from a United Nations classification system, which distinguishes between developed, free market economies (The First World), centrally-planned economies (the Second), and undeveloped, free market economies (the Third). The criteria for this classification are an awkward mixture of economic and political indices, easier to describe than to define (or to defend). Western European countries, the United States of America and Japan, clearly fall into the First World; all socialist countries clearly fall into the Second; and the Third World is therefore a residual category which includes the very rich (such as Kuwait), the very poor (such as Bangladesh), some very complex (such as Brazil), and some starkly simple economies (such as Paraguay). Reduced to its simplest terms, the Third World consists of economies which are neither fully industrial nor centrally planned; this definition permits the inclusion of a great range, not only of economic, but also of social and political conditions.

Arbitrary as it may seem, the division has proved highly durable. All those economies which now belong to the First World were already relatively industrialized by the outbreak of World War I, when an invisible door was slammed in the face of all economies which had not yet achieved some measure of industrial sophistication. Many settler societies (notably Australia, New Zealand, Canada, Argentina, Uruguay, and perhaps Israel) have often enjoyed higher incomes per capita than Western European societies; but in spite of the availability of capital, skilled manpower, and natural resources, none has broken through to the charmed circle of industrial maturity. They commonly perceived the United States as the development model to follow, and therefore adopted essentially *laissez-faire* strategies. Japan has been the equally compelling model for several Asian governments, which have striven for industrialization through encouragement of industrial capital and the coercion of a domestic labour force. Brazil, Iran, South Africa, South Korea, and Taiwan are among the more 'arresting' instances of this strategy; and thus far the appalling human costs have not been matched by redeeming economic performance.

The term Third World is not only arbitrary: it is also pejorative. Nobody believes that the conditions it describes ought to be permitted. Where differences of opinion occur, they are about prescribing how the conditions are to be abolished. Economists commonly emphasize specific measures which individual governments might adopt, with a view to increasing national income or promoting industrial production. Sociologists and political scientists commonly insist that political and social reforms of various kinds must precede any major transformation of economic conditions. In point of fact there must be some question as to the ability of the world's resources, however benignly controlled, to sustain the level of industrial production which universal industrialization implies. If that doubt is valid, then the transformation of the First World may be as urgent as the abolition of the Third. In any event, this arbitrary, pejorative, and thoroughly irritating term seems destined to enjoy a long life, since the conditions it describes are evidently

profoundly entrenched in the political, social and economic
structure of the contemporary world.

Donald Denoon
Australian National University, Canberra

Further Reading
Goldthorpe, J. E. (1984), *The Sociology of the Third World*,
  Cambridge.
Worsley, P. (1964), *The Third World*, London.

Tocqueville, Alexis de (1805–59)

Alexis de Tocqueville, French statesman and political writer,
may be considered the founder of comparative historical sociology. He was one of the first to undertake the rigorous
comparison of social systems, studying France, England,
America and Algeria, and collecting information also on India
– his aim being to specify similarities and differences.

An aristocrat by birth, and a committed political animal, he
was also a nonpositivist sociologist: his approach was closer to
that of Weber than of Marx or Durkheim. 'Liberty,' he
remarked, 'is the foremost of my passions.' In the hope of
furthering the cause of liberty in France, he undertook the study
of democracy in America, where the role of the 'equality of
status' as the 'generating factor' attracted him. In America,
equality could be reconciled with liberty because democracy
preceded equalization and structured it. Men who enjoyed
identical civil rights rejected all pressures, and the importance
of associations and of local elections frustrated the development
of administrative centralization – which, like the threat of social
atomization, fostered despotism. In France, in contrast, the
Revolution of 1789 reduced the aristocratic society to rubble.
The extremely centralized state, rather than the society itself
as in the US, did try to foster the equality of civil status, but
the resistance to the aristocracy stimulated the development of
universalistic and radical theories, unknown in the US, which
legitimated the revolutionary process. From that point democracy became inceasingly vulnerable, and it confronted a state,

which, while supporting its development, nevertheless remained external to the society. Moreover, both in the US and in France, democracy was threatened by a new authoritarianism, that of industrial power, whose growth it fostered.

Tocqueville's two major works, *De la démocratie en Amérique*, vol. I–IV, (1835–40) (*Democracy in America*, 1945) and *L'Ancien régime et la révolution* (1856) (*The Ancient Regime*, 1952), form a logical unity. In his prolific correspondence with Beaumont, Gobineau, and Mill, as in his *Souvenirs*, Tocqueville was always careful to distinguish the multiple variables which organize different social systems: avoiding deterministic approaches, he always emphasized the essential significance of the values specific to the actors who fashioned consensus or turned revolutionary as a consequence of disappointed hopes.

Pierre Birnbaum
University of Paris

Further Reading
Birnbaum, P. (1970), *Sociologie de Tocqueville*, Paris.
Drescher, S. (1968), *Dilemmas of Democracy: Tocqueville and Modernization*, Pittsburgh.
Lively, J. (1965), *The Social and Political Thoughts of Alexis de Tocqueville*, London.

Utilitarianism

Utilitarianism is the doctrine that decisions should promote good consequences. It is a normative theory, meant to guide conduct and to serve as the basis of sound evaluations. It does not assume that actual decisions or judgements always satisfy that standard.

Like other important philosophical ideas, utilitarianism has many variations. The founders of modern utilitarianism, Bentham (1789) and J. S. Mill (1861), assumed that good consequences are, at bottom, desirable conditions of individuals (perhaps including animals other than humans). Bentham's 'hedonistic' utilitarianism called for the promotion of 'pleasure' and the prevention of 'pain'. Mill, who distinguished 'higher' and 'lower' pleasures, seems to have held that human good consists in the free development of individuals' distinctive, and distinctively human, capacities. 'Ideal' utilitarians believe that what is most fundamentally of value can include such things as beauty, which need not be defined in terms of human good or conscious states.

Utilitarianism in its various forms can be understood to combine a theory of intrinsic value with some notion of how stringently and directly it should be served, for example, whether good consequences must be maximized or need only be promoted to a lesser degree, and whether each and every decision should be so regulated ('act' utilitarianism) or rather that acts should conform to useful patterns ('rule' utilitarianism).

Utilitarians often claim as a virtue of their theory that it bases evaluations on ascertainable facts, such as how much 'pleasure' and 'pain' would result from alternative courses of action. But the calculations require 'interpersonal comparisons of utility', of which many are sceptical. This has led some theorists to develop normative standards in terms of less demanding notions of efficiency, as in welfare economics.

Utilitarians have generally favoured social reforms (because, for example, income transfers from rich to poor are supposed to promote welfare overall), and they have championed political rights and personal liberty (because, for example, 'paternalistic' interference is supposed to be counterproductive). Critics charge, however, that utilitarianism lacks principled commitment to all such values: it cares only how much good is produced, but not about equitable distribution, respect for personal desert, or the security of freedom and individual integrity.

Most generally, critics charge that utilitarianism distorts sound moral judgement: to promise to do something, for example, is deliberately to place oneself under an obligation, the demands of which (it is argued) are greater and more specifically directed than utilitarianism allows. They claim that utilitarianism fails to take obligations (or for that matter rights) seriously.

Utilitarianism nevertheless remains a widely accepted theory of central importance, though its status – like that of any normative principle – is uncertain. The idea that principles merely express more or less arbitrary attitudes seems largely based on an exaggerated contrast between ethics and science, which suffers from overly simple conceptions of empirical knowledge and discovery. Developments in the theory of reference and justification, along with the decline of logical positivism, have revived interest in moral realism (or cognitivism) and in the possibility of rationally defending either utilitarianism or some competing doctrine.

David Lyons
Cornell University

References
Bentham, J. (1789), *An Introduction to the Principles of Morals and Legislation*, London.
Mill, J. S. (1861), *Utilitarianism*, London.

Further Reading
Brandt, R. B. (1979), *A Theory of the Good and the Right*, Oxford.
Sen, A. and Williams, B. (eds) (1982), *Utilitarianism and Beyond*, Cambridge.
Smart, J. J. C. and Williams, B. (1973), *Utilitarianism, For and Against*, Cambridge.
See also: *Bentham; Mill*.

Utopianism

Utopianism is a form of social theory which attempts to promote certain desired values and practices by presenting them in an ideal state or society. Utopian writers do not normally think of such states as realizable, at least in anything like their perfectly portrayed form. But nor are they engaging in a merely fanciful or fantastic exercise, as the popular use of the term suggests. Often, as in Plato's *Republic*, the first true utopia, the aim is to show something of the essential nature of a concept – justice or freedom – by painting it large, in the form of an ideal community based on such a concept. At other times, as with

Sir Thomas More's *Utopia* (1516), the object is primarily critical or satirical, to scourge the vices of the writer's society by an artful contrast with the virtuous people of Utopia. Only rarely – Edward Bellamy's *Looking Backward* (1888) is a good example – do utopian writers seek to transform society according to the blueprint painstakingly drawn in their utopia. Essentially the function of utopias is heuristic.

Until the seventeenth century, utopias were generally located in geographically remote areas of the globe. The European voyages of discovery of the sixteenth and seventeenth centuries killed off this useful device by making the world too familiar. From then on utopias were spatially displaced: to outer space – journeys to the moon begin in the seventeenth century – or beneath the sea, as in the frequent discovery of the sunken civilization of Atlantis, or deep below the earth's crust. But increasingly too the displacement was temporal rather than spatial, a move encouraged first by the seventeenth-century idea of progress and later by the vastly expanded notion of time offered by the new geology and biology of Lyell and Darwin. Instead of utopia being the better place, it became the better time. H. G. Wells took his Time-Traveller billions of years into the future, and Olaf Stapledon in *Last and First Men* (1930) employed a time scale of 2,000 million years to show the ascent of man to full utopian stature.

The displacement of space by time also produced a new sociological realism in utopias. Utopias were now placed in history and, however distant the utopian consummation, it could at least be presented as something mankind was tending towards, perhaps inevitably. The link with science and technology in the seventeenth century – as in Bacon's *New Atlantis* (1627) and Campanella's *City of the Sun* (1637) – strengthened this development. With the rise of nineteenth-century socialism, itself heavily utopian, utopianism became increasingly a debate about the possible realization of socialism. The utopias of Bellamy and Wells (*A Modern Utopia*, 1905) were the most powerful pleas on behalf of orthodox socialism, but William Morris offered an attractive alternative version in *News from Nowhere* (1890). An alternative of a different kind came with the invention of the 'dystopia' or anti-utopia, an inversion and a savage critique of all utopian hopes. Foreshadowed in Samuel Butler's anti-Darwinian *Erewhon* (1872), it reached its apogee in the 1930s and 1940s, especially with Aldous Huxley's *Brave New World* (1932) and George Orwell's *Nineteen Eighty-Four* (1949). Only B. F. Skinner's *Walden Two* (1948) kept the utopian torch alight in these dark years, and there were many who saw in this utopia of behavioural engineering a nightmare worse than the blackest dystopia. Utopianism, however, revived strongly in the 1960s, in such works as Herbert Marcuse's *An Essay on Liberation* (1969), and is to be found alive and flourishing in the futurological and ecological movements.

Perhaps utopianism is inherent in the human condition, perhaps only in those cultures affected by the classical and Christian traditions; but one might well agree with Oscar Wilde that 'a map of the world that does not include Utopia is not worth even glancing at'.

Krishan Kumar
University of Kent

Further Reading
Manuel, F. E. and Manuel, F. P. (1979), *Utopian Thought in the Western World*, Cambridge, Mass.
Mumford, L. (1922), *The Story of Utopias*, New York.

Voting

Studies of electoral behaviour seek to account for the response of individuals and groups to, as well as their influence on, the body politic. Most of the studies have been carried out in Western democracies, where not only is voting by secret ballot but where respective governments and other political factions are thought not to interfere with the individual's vote choice. While different social science disciplines approach the study of voting from rather different vantage points, they have in common the need to interpret information obtained about a particular election within an historical or comparative frame-work. An historical approach relates given election results to those of previous elections, thereby seeking explanations for change in the country's, the parties' or the voters' history; a comparative approach seeks explanations across national boundaries for the rise and influence of similar voting trends or of similar political and social movements, as, for example, the Women's Movement, the environmental and anti-nuclear lobbies, as well as the growth of prejudice, anti-immigrant sentiments in Britain and anti-*Gastarbeiter* sentiments in West Germany. Other comparative studies examine the impact of the recession and of unemployment on the public's vote choice and on the parties' promises and performances.

Countries differ in the role assigned to the public in political decision making. In Britain this is limited to votes cast to elect a British and, more recently, also a European Member of Parliament, and to the election of local councillors. In the United States the public participates far more. There are elections at national, state and local levels including the election of a wide range of officials, even judges. Additionally, the public is asked to vote on policy, including some budgetary proposals put forward by the officials or – and this is an important extension of the public's right – by members of the public. Thus in the US the public votes for a wide range of officeholders, a wide range of policy proposals and can also affect the political agenda. In France and in some other countries, referenda are called to allow the public to vote in important policy issues.

Because of the bewildering range of vote opportunities across countries, most comparative analyses deal with general elections only, since these occur in every country, are judged the most important by the electorate and therefore yield a higher turnout compared with other elections.

Voting practices differ across countries in a number of important ways: (1) In the frequency and variety of occasions on which the electorate's views are sought. (2) In the number of parties that participate. (3) In the minimum voting age stipulated. (4) In the ease or difficulty of registration, once eligible. While all countries have general or national elections and require an election to be called after a fixed number of years (generally four or five), in some countries the date of the election is laid down, while in others, as in Britain, the government of the day can call an election at any time within the stipulated period of office when it judges its chances propitious for re-election.

To these differences must be added two other very important differences, namely the constitutional checks on the power conferred on the leader of the government of the day, and the electoral system itself. In the United States there are constitutional checks and balances restraining the power of the President; in Britain the power of the Prime Minister is directly proportional to the size of the majority of seats held by the Prime Minister's party in the House of Commons.

The electoral system of a country profoundly affects the extent to which the legislative chamber reflects the voters' preferences. Most European countries have accepted one or other form of proportional representation, of which the direct form is used in the Irish Republic, where the distribution of seats in parliament directly reflects the distribution of votes in the country for the different parties. Britain's 'first past the post' method is by now the exception and causes the most serious distortion in the representation of voters' preferences in parliament. This is because each individual casts the vote *within* his constituency in order to return one of the candidates as the constituency Member of Parliament. There are 650 constituencies. The government of the day is formed not necessarily from the party with the highest number of votes in the country, but from the party that has more Members of Parliament among the 650 than any other party. The 1983 election provides a particularly glaring example of the degree of distortion generated by this system. The figures presented below show the number of votes cast for each party, the number of seats gained and the number that would have been gained had there been proportional representation. While at present the Conservative government has a large absolute majority, with proportional representation it would not have a majority at all – a difference which, of course, has profound repercussions on the government's ability to bring about legislative changes where these are opposed by the other parties. (Or put another way, it took 33,000 votes to elect one Member of Parliament for the Conservative party and 339,000 votes for the Alliance party. This is because the Alliance candidates in most constituencies scored a high percentage of votes but since they did not come first, their votes were wasted.)

Other parties	No. of votes cast	Seats allocated	Seats allocated by proportional representation
Conservatives	13 mil.	396	280
Labour	8.5 mil	209	182
Alliance	7.8 mil	23	170

Types of Election Studies
While all aim to explain the antecedents and consequences of election results, studies differ in the level of analysis adopted (macro- or micro-level) and in the models of electoral decision making they employ. At the macro-level of analysis, aggregate statistics across elections are used to determine trends and to isolate the rare 'critical election' one which records a significant shift in vote choices which persists in subsequent elections. Studies of trends in the electorate's preference for parties of the right or left, changes in turnout (there has been a general downward trend sufficiently pronounced in the United States that now just over half the electorate votes in Presidential elections), in the share of the vote by the two major parties (which has steadily decreased) are examples of such analyses.

At the micro-level, interest focuses on the individual voter's process of decision making, both in a particular election and across elections. This latter approach only became possible once individual voters themselves were questioned and not as in the 1930s, when inferences about vote choice had to be drawn from relating election returns to known characteristics of the electorate in that district: the only ones available being demographic data (age, sex, social class and religious affiliation). The change came in the United States with the pioneering work of Lazarsfeld and Berelson who in the 1940s carried out the first surveys of voters in particular districts, followed by the first national election surveys in 1948 conducted by the Michigan Survey Research Center, which has since then continued to undertake such surveys at every subsequent election. Similar surveys of voters were subsequently conducted in Britain and in most European countries, seeking information from individual voters about their vote choice, reasons for that choice, their images of parties and candidates, and about their knowledge of the parties' stands and their attitudes towards the policy proposals put forward. Cross-sectional studies are periodically supplemented by panel studies, where respondents are re-interviewed at the next or even subsequent general elections. The two longest panel studies were conducted in Britain, one extending over fifteen years.

Campbell and his colleagues, analysing the Michigan surveys of the 1950s, found reality to be at variance with the picture of the ideal citizen in a democracy. Voters cared little about politics, were relatively ill informed about issues and often voted for parties whose policy proposals they did not like. Campbell developed a model of vote choice in which he explained these inconsistencies by suggesting that the voter early in life, through parental example, develops a party identification (seeing himself as a Democrat or Republican) which guides both vote choice and policy evaluations. A kind of 'standing decision', as Key suggests, facilitates vote choice apart from rare occasions where attitudes to particular candidates or the strength of feelings about a particular issue proves decisive, overriding party attachment (a phenomenon that is described as the result of short-term forces but not one which basically affects long-term party attachment, which if anything grows with the years). 'An individual thinks politically as he is socially' is an apt description, suggesting that it is group membership that affects party attachment.

The *rational model* of voting put forward by Downs, and elaborated since, views the voters' behaviour in making their choice as rational in this as in other decisions where the choice is made on the basis of summing preferences, a choice in this case based on evaluation of candidates, issues, and party images. A more recent elaboration of the rational model put forward by Himmelweit *et al.* (1985) is described as the *consumer model of voting*, in which the search for the best fit or less misfit between preferences and parties affects the voters' choice, tempered by the strength of party attachment and the persistent habit of voting for one rather than another party.

The consumer model does not require voters to be well informed, but does require them to have preferences for given candidates and/or policies and to perceive parties to take dissimilar stands on these policies. One further factor must be added, a factor which Lipset has developed in comparing twenty elections from 1979 into the 1980s in Western democracies. He compiled for each country a 'misery index' to do with inflation and unemployment rates and found that in countries where such an index was high, the party in office was defeated in 17 of these elections, with socialists and liberals replacing their more conservative rivals in half, while the more right-wing parties defeated left-of-centre incumbents in the other half. The point here is an extension of one made by Fiorina: that the incumbents are judged on their performance and that a change in vote may reflect simply a desire for change rather than a preference for the policies of the opposing party, a view substantiated by the increase in negative reasons of voting for a party.

The difference between the Michigan and the consumer model is not that one accords an important place to party attachment and the other does not, but that the former sees party attachment as the key to vote decision, while the latter sees it as an important factor interacting with other preferences which also affect the decision. Where voters' preferences are evenly balanced, party attachment will prove decisive, or alternatively as in the calmer period of the 1950s where few issues divided the electorate. That is, in the consumer model, the strength of party attachment in influencing the vote will have as much, if not more, to do with the characteristics of a particular election, the number of issues which divide the electorate and the degree to which parties offer alternate styles of government, as with the individuals' strength of attachment from whatever cause to one or other party.

In the last twenty years there is much evidence of the electorate's increased awareness of parties' stands, and increased readiness to evaluate policy choice. Above all, there is growing evidence of volatility in voting and of a decline, not only in the readiness to identify with one or other party but particularly in the strength of that identification and with it its influence on vote choice.

Discussions about the most appropriate model of vote choice will undoubtedly continue. With individuals in many other aspects of their lives seemingly less influenced and more critical of institutional norms than before, and with the rapid social, technological and economic changes affecting their lives, it seems likely that parties will be less and less able to rely on party loyalties, with policy proposals being accepted on trust, and will instead be judged more on past performance and on the realism of new policy proposals.

Hilde Himmelweit
London School of Economics and Political Science

Further Reading
Barnes, S. H. and Kasse, M. (1977), *Political Action: Mass Participation in Five Western Democracies*, Beverly Hills, Calif.
Himmelweit, H. T. and Jaeger, M. (1985), *How Voters Decide*, revised edn, Milton Keynes.
Budge, I and Fairlie, D. J. (1983), *Explaining and Predicting Elections*, London.
Särlvik, B. and Crewe, I. (1983), *Decades of Realignment: The Conservative Victory of 1979 and Electoral Trends in the 1970's*, Cambridge.
See also: *elections*.

War

War, as we know it, is a relatively new phenomenon in the history of humanity. That groups of people have inflicted damage on other groups is nothing new. But, as Quincy Wright showed (1942), the most common form of war, which he called 'social war', was a ritual. Groups might attack each other, but hostilities commonly ended when the first blood was spilt.

War waged in order to obtain economic and political goals, to rob and to dominate, is a more recent phenomenon, related to what is usually called 'civilization'. The more society is characterized by agriculture (as opposed to hunting-gathering or cattle), the more it is organized as a state (as opposed to clan, tribe, village), and the more internal division of labour there is (over and above what is found in all societies, based on gender and age), the more belligerent the societies seem to be, in the sense that they use aggressive wars to obtain economic and political goals. As these structural characteristics are typical of Western societies ('modern', 'developed'), one would expect them to be particularly predisposed to belligerence. But the significance of Western social cosmology, the deep ideological structure of Western society, should also be mentioned. There is the idea of being the centre of the world, and possessing social formulas which are valid for the whole world – expressed, for example, in the missionary command (Matthew, 28:18–20). Given such beliefs, war is not only a right but a duty. This view is shared in Islam and in the secular offspring of Christianity, liberalism, and Marxism.

War is getting more dangerous all the time. There is an increased risk for the belligerents of getting killed, and an ever-greater portion of those who are killed are civilians. No more than about 2 per cent of belligerents in war in the Middle Ages lost their lives. The proportion rose to about 40 per cent in the First World War. But, whereas only one quarter of those killed in the First World War were civilians, about half of those who died in the Second World War, and more than 75 per cent in the Indochina Wars were civilians. It should be noted that in the event of a major nuclear war there will be many casualties in nonbelligerent countries due to the new phenomemon of fall-out. In addition, there will be casualties after hostile action has ceased due to long-term effects on the environment.

In order to understand wars, it is not enough to focus on the arms used; equally or more important is the conflict formation within which the war is enacted. If we divide the world into Centre and Periphery countries depending on where they are located on the international division of labour, we get three major types of war:

1 Centre-Centre wars – the current East-West conflict would be of this type.
2 Centre-Periphery wars – the current North-South conflict is an example.
2 Periphery-Periphery wars – these are often, disparagingly, referred to as 'local wars'.

Characteristically, Centre countries, and particularly the superpowers, regard their own conflicts as the real ones, and see all other conflicts as derived from them, and not without some reason. However, in the post-Second World War period, the Centre-Periphery wars have been by far the most important. At least 70 per cent of belligerent activity in the roughly 150 wars which have been waged since 1945 can be said to fall into this category, among them all the national and people's wars of liberation. The problem has been how to escape the colonial or neocolonial grip which Centre countries have had and continue to have on Periphery countries. Typically, one Centre country is allied with a local bridgehead of economic and political élites. If one superpower or bloc is involved, the other one can usually be counted on to support the local opposition, but meticulously avoiding direct confrontation in order not to escalate the conflict into East-West confrontation with the risk of nuclear war. In terms of casualties, the sum of the modern Centre-Periphery and the Periphery-Periphery wars is already of the magnitude of a Third World War. However, it does not conform to the European formula for a world war, which is based on an action like Germany crossing the Rhine and the Oder, or a Blitz attack on one of the present superpowers (like the German Operation Barbarossa on the Soviet Union on 22 June 1941 and the Japanese on Pearl Harbor on 7 December 1941). It is this image which has disposed today's superpowers to adopt a Nevermore policy of guarding against a first strike through incessant quantitative and qualitative improvements in armaments, making arms both more destructive and less vulnerable.

If nuclear war is a *macro* war, and conventional war (without weapons of mass destruction such as nuclear, biological, chemical, environmental and radiological weapons) are termed *meso* wars, then what would be a *micro* war? Clearly such a term might be used to describe what is often referred to as terrorism (by those against whom it is directed). The target is more precise, such as selected individuals and places; the weapons have short range and small impact areas, such as hand-guns. Such micro wars may become part of any concrete pattern of warfare but are probably particularly important in Centre-Periphery contexts as the form of warfare chosen by the weak. Dialectically, terrorism leads to counter-terrorism, military-police action, torture, death squads, and so on. It would be artificial not to include such conflicts in the concept of modern warfare, just as the old distinction between external and internal wars ('civil wars') becomes meaningless with the international-ization of almost all major conflicts today.

There are two broad approaches in the fight against war. One is directed against the arms, the other is concerned with the conflict itself, with a view to solving its deeper-lying causes. The former approach has not been a success, as is apparent from the great number of disarmament conferences which have not reduced the total amount of destructive power, although they have sometimes possibly shifted its form, reflecting techno-logical changes. One possibility here might be to harness tech-nical changes for the development of purely defensive arms, which could be used to buttress a non-provocative military posture, somewhat along the lines of the policy of the Swiss, the Yugoslavs, the Austrians, and the Finns in Europe.

Conflict resolution, however, remains a basic condition, necessary, if not sufficient, for avoiding wars and warlike activi-ties. The problem is, as a rule, that conflict resolution presup-poses some kind of change, usually also some redistribution of power and privilege, and will be resisted by those interested in the status quo, a category which includes those with a generally

expansionist and domineering stance in world affairs, and with
material and political interests all over the world.

Johan Galtung
International Peace Research Institute, Oslo

Reference
Wright, Q. (1942), *A Study of War*, Chicago.

Further Reading
Sorokin, P. (1957), *Social and Cultural Dynamics*, Boston.
See also: *peace; terrorism.*

Weber, Max (1864–1920)

Max Weber, the son of a member of the Reichstag and an
activist Protestant mother, grew up in Berlin in an intellectually
lively home frequently visited by the Bismarckian era's leading
politicians and intellectuals. After receiving an outstanding
secondary education in languages, history, and the classics, he
studied law, economics, history, and philosophy at the Universities of Heidelberg, Strasbourg, Göttingen, and Berlin.
Although his first appointments, at the Universities of Freiburg
(1894) and Heidelberg (1897), were in the faculty of economics,
he is best known today as one of the major founders of modern
sociology and as one of the intellectual giants of interdisciplinary scholarship. As strange as it may sound, he ranged
freely across the entire palette of written history, from the
ancient Greeks to the early Hindus, from the Old Testament
prophets to the Confucian literati, from the economic organization of early Near-Eastern civilizations to the trading
companies of the Medieval West, and from the origins of Continental law to comparative analyses of the rise of the modern
state.

The diversity of these themes – only a small sampling –
should not lead us to view Weber as a scholar of unlimited
energies frantically leaping about for its own sake. Rather, when
looked at closely, a grand design becomes visible in his writings,
yet one that remained incomplete and whose inner coherence

can be plotted only against the inner torments of their author. Weber and others of his generation in Germany viewed the dawning of rapid industrialization and the modern age itself with profound ambivalence rather than as a first step toward a new era of progress. While welcoming the possibilities it offered for a burgeoning of individualism and an escape from the feudal chains of the past, he saw few firm guidelines in reference to which modern man might be able to establish a comprehensive meaning for his life or even his everyday action (1946). Moreover, the overtowering bureaucracies indispensable to the organization of industrial societies were endowed with the capacity to render persons politically powerless as well as to replace creative potential with stifling routine and merely functional relationships. These developments threatened to curtail the flowering of individualism.

Just such quandaries stood behind all of Weber's sociological writings, particularly those undertaken after 1903. In these studies he wished to define precisely the uniqueness of his own civilization and to understand on a universal scale the manner in which persons, influenced by social constellations, formulate *meaning* for their lives that guides action. A curiosity founded in such questions instilled in him an amazing capacity to place himself, once he had constructed a 'mental image' of another era and civilization, into the minds of persons quite unlike himself. This aim to understand how values and actions made sense to their beholders, however foreign they were to the social scientist investigating them, formed the foundation for Weber's *verstehende* sociology.

Perhaps it was this sensitivity, as well as a sheer respect for meanings formulated over centuries, that prompted Weber to construct one of his most famous axioms, one debated heatedly to this day. To him, all scientific judgements must be 'value-free': once researchers have selected their themes of inquiry, then personal values, preferences, and prejudices must not be allowed to interfere with the collection of empirical data and its 'objective' evaluation (1949). Everyone involved in scientific work should avoid an inadvertent intermixture of his values with those of the actors being studied. To Weber, even the scientist who happened to be a Calvinist was duty-bound – as long as he wished to pursue science – to describe, for example, tribal sexual practices accurately and to interpret them in reference to their indigenous 'cultural significance', however repugnant they seemed to him personally. This postulate also implied a strict division between that which *exists* (the question for scientific analysis) and that which *should be* (the realm of personal values).

In explicitly circumscribing the legitimate domain of science and denying it the right to produce norms, ideals, and values, Weber had a larger purpose in mind. He hoped to establish an inviolable realm within which individuals would be forced to confront themselves and autonomously formulate a set of personal values capable of guiding their actions and endowing them with meaning. Nothing less was required as a counterforce in an age in which bureaucratization and the scientific world view threatened to encroach upon decision making, thus upsetting the already tenuous character of individualism. Weber's own adherence to a value-free science, particularly in his studies of pre-modern and non-Western societies, the penetration of his insight into the diverse ways in which meaning could be formed and patterned action ensued, and the universal-historical scope of his investigations enabled him to write – however fragmented, incomplete, and poorly organized – a comparative historical sociology of civilizations unique in the history of sociology.

Even though his interest focused upon comparisons between civilizations, Weber's emphasis upon individual meaning prevented him from taking the Hegelian Absolute Spirit, the Marxian organization of production and class struggle, or the 'social facts' of Durkheim as his point of departure. Nor was he inclined, due to his continuous accentuation of the conflicts between diverse 'spheres of life' (religious, political, economic, legal, aesthetic) and the centrality of power and domination, to view societies, like Parsons, as basically integrated wholes. In fact, Weber's orientation to the individual and the meaning he attaches to his action would seem to carry him dangerously close to a radical subjectivism. Two procedures guarded against this possibility:

First, in his substantive studies, it was the patterned actions of individuals in groups, and not individuals acting alone, that captured his attention. It was only this regular action that, according to Weber, proved to be culturally significant and historically powerful. Individuals tended to become knit together into collectivities primarily in five ways: acknowledgement of common material interests (as occurred when classes were formed), recognition of common 'ideal interests' (as took place when status groups arose), adherence to a single world view (as occurred in religious groups), acknowledgement of affectual feelings (as found in person-oriented groups, such as the household, the clan, and the neighbourhood), and awareness of relations of domination (as took place in the charismatic, patriarchal, feudal, patrimonial, and bureaucratic forms of domination). However massive and enduring an institution might appear, it must not, according to Weber, be understood as more than the orientations of individuals acting in common.

The second means employed by Weber to avoid lapsing into a radical subjectivism involves his major methodological tool, one that reveals his indebtedness to Kant: the 'ideal type' (1949). Indeed, this heuristic construct so effectively guarded against this possibility that a number of commentators have accused Weber – particularly in his later work – of moving away from a *verstehende* sociology and of reifying the social phenomena he studies. In part, Weber himself is to blame. Instead of discussing, for example, 'bureaucratically-oriented action', he uses the term 'bureaucracy', and rather than using 'class-oriented action', he speaks of 'classes'.

Perhaps the ideal type can be best understood against the backdrop of Weber's view of social reality. For him, when examined at its basic level, social reality presents a ceaseless flow of occurrences and events, very few of which, although repeatedly interwoven, seem to fall together coherently. Due to its infinite complexity, no investigator can expect to capture reality exhaustively, nor even to render accurately all its contours.

Weber took over a nominalistic position to confront this conundrum and propounded the use of the ideal type. This purely analytic tool enables us to acquire a purchase upon reality through its 'simplification'. Far from arbitrary, however, the procedures for doing so involve a deliberate *exaggeration of the essence* of the phenomenon under study and its reconstruction in a form with greater internal unity than ever appeared in empirical reality. Thus, Weber's conceptualization, for example, of the bureaucracy or the Calvinist does not aim to portray accurately all bureaucracies or Calvinists, but to call attention only to essential aspects. As an artificial construct, the ideal type abstracts from reality and fails to define *any* particular phenomenon. Nonetheless, it serves two crucial purposes: it allows us, once an entire series of ideal types appropriate for a theme under investigation have been formed, to undertake comparisons across civilizations and epochs; and, when used as a heuristic yardstick in comparison to which a given bureaucracy or Calvinist church can be defined and its deviation assessed, it enables an isolation and clear conceptualization of distinctive attributes. Only after a number of ideal-typical 'experiments' have been conducted can we move on to questions regarding the purely empirical *causes* for the uniqueness of the particular case. For Weber, these questions were more interesting than ones of definition alone.

Although he outlined a methodology – only hinted at above – that would allow him to investigate the manner in which individuals formulated meaning in different civilizations and epochs as well as to define precisely the uniqueness of the modern West, it must be concluded that, when viewed in reference to these broad aims, his various writings constitute mere fragments. Most, including his comparative studies on the *Economic Ethics of the World Religions* (*EEWR*) (these include *The Religion of China* [1951], *The Religion of India* [1958] and *Ancient Judaism* [1952]), and *Economy and Society* (*E&S*), were published in incomplete form. Nonetheless, the discrete elements of the whole have stood on their own and become classics in their own right. Broadly speaking, Weber's works divide into more empirical investigations on the one hand and analytical models on the other.

By far his most famous, debated, and readable book, *The Protestant Ethic and the Spirit of Capitalism* (1930 [1922]), falls into the former category. In this classic, Weber sought to understand certain origins of modern capitalism. For him, this form of capitalism was distinguished by a systematic organization of work, the replacement of a 'traditional economic ethic' among workers as well as entrepreneurs by methodical labour, and a systematic search for profit. Thus, Weber saw an attitude toward work and profit – a 'spirit of capitalism' – as important, and denied that the influx of precious metals, technological advances, population increases, the universal desire for riches, or the Herculean efforts of 'economic supermen' (Carnegie, Rockefeller, Fugger) were adequate to explain the origin of modern capitalism.

Religious roots, according to Weber, anchored this 'spirit', namely the doctrines of the Protestant sects and churches, particularly the seventeenth-century pastoral exhortations of Calvinism. The deep anxiety introduced by this religion's predestination doctrine in respect to the overriding question of one's personal salvation proved more than believers could reasonably bear. Gradually, worldly success came to be viewed as a *sign* that God had bestowed his favour and, thus, as evidence of membership among the predestined elect. In this way, since it allowed the devout *to believe* they belonged among the chosen few and thereby alleviated intense anxiety, worldly success itself became endowed with a religious – indeed, a salvation – incentive, or 'psychological premium'. Methodical labour in a calling (*Beruf*) proved the surest pathway toward worldly success, as did the continuous reinvestment of one's wealth – an unintended consequence of this attitude – rather than its squandering on worldly pleasures. To Weber, the medi-eval monk's 'other-worldly asceticism' became, with Calvinism, transformed into an 'inner-worldly asceticism'.

In calling attention to this religiously-based cause of modern capitalism, Weber in no way sought to substitute an 'idealist' for a 'materialist' explanation (1930 [1922]). Rather, he aimed only to point out the heretofore neglected idealist side in order to emphasize that a comprehensive explanation of modern capitalism's origins must include consideration of the 'economic ethic' as well as the 'economic form'. Far from claiming that Calvinism led to modern capitalism in a monocausal fashion, Weber asserted that the rise of this type of capitalism can be explained adequately only through multidimensional models (1961 [1927]; Collins, 1980; Cohen, 1981; Kalberg, 1983). Indeed, as Weber noted in his discussion of 'backwoods Pennsylvania (1930 [1922]), and as Gordon Marshall has demonstrated in the case of Scotland (1980, 1982), a constellation of material factors must exist in a manner such that a conducive context is formulated, for without this context the 'spirit of capitalism' is powerless to introduce modern capitalism. On the other hand, once firmly entrenched, modern capitalism perpetuates itself on the basis of secularized socialization processes as well as coercive mechanisms and no longer requires its original 'spirit'.

While addressing the rise of modern capitalism in a novel manner, *The Protestant Ethic* failed to grapple with the larger, comparative issue: the distinctiveness of the Occident, Weber knew well, could be defined only through a series of comparisons with non-Western civilizations. In turning to China and India, he again took the issue of modern capitalism as his focus, though here he posed the negative question of why, in these civilizations, this type of capitalism had failed to develop. Moreover, far from attempting to assess only whether Confucian, Taoist, Hindu, and Buddhist teachings introduced or inhibited methodical economic action, these studies turned as well to the 'materialist' side and sought to discuss the economic ethics of non-Western world religions in the context of a whole series of social structural and organizational variables. This comparative procedure enabled Weber also to delineate the array of 'material' factors in the West that proved unique and conducive to the development of modern capitalism. These empirical studies, in addition to his investigations of ancient Judaism, carried him a giant step further as well in his attempt to understand the manner in which sociological configurations influence the formation of meaning.

Yet these studies remained, as Weber himself repeatedly emphasized (1972 [1920]; 1930 [1922]), drastically incomplete, especially if examined in reference to his overall goals. They are, furthermore, too poorly organized to provide us with a distinctly Weberian approach for an unlocking of the elusive relationship between ideas and interests. These empirical investigations must be read through the lens of the analytical categories and models Weber develops for the analysis of social action on a universal-historical scale in one of the genuine classics of modern social science, *E&S* (1968 [1922]).

At first glance, this tome seems to conceal thoroughly Weber's larger aims. Part One is concerned primarily with the articulation of a broad series of sociological concepts. Although empirically-based, each of these, since formulated on a universal-historical scale, remains at a high level of abstraction. Nonetheless, each one can be utilized as a heuristic yardstick that serves as a point of reference for the definition of particular cases. The ideal types in Part Two are less all-encompassing and relate generally to specific epochs and civilizations (Mommsen, 1974). This section reveals on every page how its author, in considering historical examples, extracted their essence and constructed ideal types. Just this perpetual movement between the historical and ideal-typical levels, as well as Weber's unwillingness to formulate an ideal type before scrutinizing innumerable cases, accounts for its exceedingly disjointed character. His failure to discuss his overriding themes in a synoptic fashion has also decreased the readability of *E&S*.

These problems have blinded most Weber specialists to the comprehensive 'analytic' of social action buried between the lines of this treatise and utilizable for the comparative and historical study even of entire civilizations (Kalberg, 1980, 1985). Consequently, each chapter has been read and debated apart from its broader purposes in the Weberian corpus and in an ahistorical fashion. Nonetheless, standing on their own, the separate chapters have attained classical status in a wide variety of sociology's subfields, such as the sociology of religion, urban sociology, stratification, economic sociology, modernization and development, the sociology of law, and political sociology. In each chapter, Weber lays out, in light of the specific problematic involved, a universal-historical analytic that includes a differentiated discussion of the ways in which, at each stage in each analytic, social action becomes patterned by diverse internal and external constraints and acquires its *locus* in specific status groups and organizations.

Only the typology of rulership (*Herrschaft*) can be given special attention here. (This translation has been suggested by Benjamin Nelson and appears to me preferable to either 'domination', which captures the element of force yet weakens the notion of legitimacy, or 'authority', which conveys legitimacy but downplays the component of force.) In this voluminous section Weber wished to define the major bases conceivable for the legitimation of rulership and to articulate, for each, the typical relationships between rulers, administrative bodies, and the ruled. Charismatic personalities derived a right to rule from their extraordinary personal qualities and the belief of the ruled in their transcendent inspiration; traditional rulership (patriarchal, feudal, and patrimonial) rested upon custom and the belief that 'time immemorial' itself provided a justification for continued rule; and rational-legal (bureaucratic) rulership was legitimated through laws, statutes, and regulations. Crucial for the endurance of all types is at least a minimum belief on the part of the ruled that the rulership is justified. While many interpreters have reified these concepts, Weber designed them exclusively as heuristic yardsticks.

Throughout *E&S*, as well as the *EEWR*, a subtle and dialectical view of the relationships between value-oriented, interest-oriented, and tradition-oriented action prevails. As opposed to the more empirically-based *EEWR* studies, these relationships in the *E&S* are dealt with more as models which, on the one hand, combine ideal types in relationships of 'elective affinities' and, on the other hand, chart the patterned 'relations of antagonisms' between discrete concepts and even differentiated spheres of life. At this point, Weber's sociology goes far beyond mere concept-formation and classification and moves to the level of the dynamic interaction of constellations. At this 'contextual' level, he shifts repeatedly back and forth between ideal types of varying range, all of which aim to articulate 'developmental sequences': entire series of ideal types that, on the basis of a developmental dimension as well as a focus upon spheres of life and types of rulership, seek to conceptualize epochal change. Whether the change hypothesized by these research instruments in fact took place in the history of a particular epoch and civilization remained for Weber an empirical question, one that involved, above all, the strength of 'carrier' strata, the success of new groups and organizations in establishing their rulership, and sheer power. Despite his awareness of the inflexibility of tradition and the manner in which millennia-long histories remained within civilizational 'tracks', or world views, Weber's conviction that power and unexpected historical 'accidents' could always introduce a chain-reaction realignment of configurations prevented him from constructing global formulas that promised to forecast the unfolding of societies. To Weber, the materialist interpretation of history, for example, provided a useful hypothesis rather than a scientific explanation.

This sketch of Weber's sociology has touched upon only a few of its major contours. The intensity of Weber's persistent struggle with the immense complexity, unresolved paradoxes, and even contradictory drifts of social reality, and his refusal to simplify on behalf of doctrinal or ideological positions, can be appreciated only by those who directly confront his writings. Fortunately, in turning toward systematic analyses of the major underlying themes in his corpus as a whole, the ongoing Weber renaissance in the Federal Republic of Germany (Kalberg, 1979), Great Britain, and the United States (Glassman, 1983) promises to knit together its fragments and to reveal the concerns that literally possessed one of our century's most remarkable scholars.

Stephen Kalberg
Harvard University

References

Cohen, I. J. (1981), 'Introduction to the Transaction Edition', in M. Weber, *General Economic History*, New Brunswick.

Collins, R. (1980), 'Weber's last theory of capitalism', *American Sociological Review*, 56.

Glassman, R. (1983), 'The Weber renaissance', in S. G. McNall (ed.), *Current Perspectives in Social Theory*, Greenwood, Connecticut.

Kalberg, S. (1979), 'The search for thematic orientations in a fragmented œuvre: the discussion of Max Weber in recent German sociological literature', *Sociology*, 13.

Kalberg, S. (1980), 'Max Weber's types of rationality: cornerstones for the analysis of rationalization processes in history', *American Journal of Sociology*, 85.

Kalberg, S. (1983), 'Max Weber's universal-historical architectonic of economically-oriented action: a preliminary reconstruction', in S. G. McNall (ed.), *Current Perspectives in Social Theory*, Greenwood, Connecticut.

Kalberg, S. (1986), *Max Weber's Comparative Historical Sociology of Reconstruction*, London.

Marshall, G. (1980), *Presbyteries and Profits: Calvinism and the Development of Capitalism in Scotland, 1560–1707*, Oxford.

Marshall, G. (1982), *In Search of the Spirit of Capitalism*, London.

Mommsen, W. (1974), *Max Weber: Gesellschaft, Politik und Geschichte*, Frankfurt.

Weber, M. (1972 [1920]), *Collected Papers on the Sociology of Religion*, London. (Original German edn, *Gesammelte Aufsatze zur Religionssoziologie*, vol. 1, Tübingen.)

Weber, M. (1961 [1927]), *General Economic History*, London. (Original German edn, *Wirtschaftsgeschichte*, Munich.)

Weber, M. (1930 [1922]), *The Protestant Ethic and the Spirit of Capitalism*, London. (Original German edn, *Die protestantische Ethik und der 'Geist' des Kapitalismus*, Tübingen.)

Weber, M. (1946), *From Max Weber*, eds H. H. Gerth and C. W. Mills, New York.

Weber, M. (1949), *The Methodology of the Social Sciences*, selection and translation of essays by E. Shils, New York.

Weber, M. (1951), *The Religion of China*, New York.

Weber, M. (1952), *Ancient Judaism*, New York.
Weber, M. (1958), *The Religion of India*, New York.
Weber, M. (1968 [1922]), *Economy and Society*, New York.
  (Original German edn, *Wirtschaft und Gesellschaft*,
  Tübingen.)

Further Reading
Bendix, R. (1960), *Max Weber: An Intellectual Portrait*, London.
Bendix, R. and Roth, G. (1971), *Scholarship and Partisanship:
  Essays on Max Weber*, Berkeley and Los Angeles.
Löwith, K. (1982), *Max Weber and Karl Marx*, London.
Nelson, B. (1981), *On the Roads to Modernity: Conscience, Science
  and Civilizations*, Totowa, NJ.

Welfare State

The term Welfare State was first used, according to some authorities, when the People's Budget of 1909 in Britain was styled the Welfare Budget, although in Germany *Wohlfahrstaat* had already been applied to the system of social insurance introduced by Bismarck in the 1980s. Welfare State only came into general use in the 1930s, however, when democratic governments in Europe and the US displayed a real concern for the welfare of their citizens suffering under the strains of economic depression. The Oxford scholar Alfred Zimmern used the phrase Welfare State to characterize the democratic states, in contrast to the states of the Fascist dictators. It gained wide currency with the publication of the Beveridge report in Britain in 1942, though Beveridge and many others objected to it and preferred the idea of a Social Service State.

The view that the Welfare State was created in Britain by the Labour Government which came to power after the Second World War in 1945 is nonsense, because for centuries in Britain, and later in Scandinavia, and, especially, New Zealand, statutory powers to provide welfare services had long been in force. The United States of America rapidly developed state welfare resources during President Roosevelt's New Deal in the 1930s. In Britain, the Beveridge report on 'Social Insurance and Allied Services', published in 1942, proposed a full and free national health service, a system of social insurance, and retirement pensions. These measures were implemented in a series of Acts passed between 1945 and 1948, and then extended by successive governments, and the Welfare State ceased to be a divisive party-political issue. The Conservative Party, which came to power in Britain in the 1970s no longer talks about dismantling the Welfare State as they once did in the 1950s.

Welfare State could well have applied to New Zealand in the 1890s, which, because of its progressive measures of social legislation such as the provision of old-age pensions and a variety of industrial conciliation schemes, was described by one writer as the 'social laboratory of the world'. These measures were adversely affected by the depression of the 1930s, but when the Labour Party first came to power in New Zealand in 1935, it embarked on even more ambitious measures, including a comprehensive social security system to protect citizens against the ill effects of unemployment, sickness, industrial injury and old age, and the provision of an almost free national health service. The Second World War delayed their implementation, but they were fully operational after the war ended, and still are.

A Welfare State is one in which there are conscious and deliberate policies to secure at least a minimum standard of living for all, and to promote equality of opportunity. There will no doubt be shifts of emphasis in the provision of services. For example, it has been suggested in recent years in Britain that there should be more private and less state spending on health and educational services. But there is little chance of a massive reversal of welfare policies in most democratic states in the near future.

D. C. Marsh
Formerly of the University of Nottingham

Further Reading
Bruce, M. (1981), *The Coming of the Welfare State*, London.
Marsh, David (1980), *The Welfare State*, London.

Robson, W. A. (1976), *Welfare State and Welfare Society: Illusion and Reality*, London.
See also: *policy; social welfare policy.*

World-System Theory

The sociologist Immanuel Wallerstein developed world-system theory in the early 1970s in an attempt to explain the origins of capitalism, the Industrial Revolution, and the complex inter-connections of the 'First', 'Second' and 'Third' Worlds. The multidisciplinary research of world-system theory focuses on historical studies of the growth of the world-system and on contemporary processes within it.

The 'modern world-system' arose in Western Europe about 500 years ago (Wallerstein, 1979). It was based on capitalist trade networks which transcended state boundaries, hence it is called the 'capitalist world-economy'. The drive for capital accumulation caused increasing competition among capitalist producers for labour, materials and markets. As competition waxed and waned through repeated 'crises of overproduction' various regions of the world were incorporated into the unevenly expanding world-economy.

Uneven expansion differentiates the world into three inter-related types of societies. The central, or 'core', societies specialize in industrial production and distribution, have rela-tively strong states, a strong bourgeoisie, a large wage-labour class, and are heavily involved in the affairs of non-core societies. At the other extreme, in the 'periphery', societies concentrate on the production of raw materials, have weak states, a small bourgeoisie, a large peasant class, and are heavily influenced by core societies. The remaining societies form the 'semi-periphery', which shares characteristics of both the core and periphery. Semi-peripheral societies are typically rising peripheral societies, or declining core societies. The semi-periphery blocks polarization between core and periphery, thus stabilizing the system. The economic and political interrelations of the core and periphery are the presumed sources of the development in the core, and the lack of development in the periphery.

A key assumption of world-system theory is that the world-economy must be studied as a whole. The study of social change in any component of the system – nations, states, regions, ethnic groups, classes – must begin by locating that component within the system. The typical component analysed is a state. Thus world-system theory has a dual research agenda. On the one hand, it examines the consequences of dynamic changes in its components (such as states) for the evolution of the system and for the movement of various components within the system. On the other hand, it examines the consequences of dynamic changes in the world-system for the internal dynamics and social structure of its various components.

Case studies investigating the emergence and evolution of the world-system offer finer-grained analyses of various components of the system and complement global analyses. Controversy surrounds the measurement and explanation of the system and explanation of the system and its parts, and centres on two major issues: (1) to what degree and how is 'underdevelopment' in the periphery necessary to the development of the core; and (2) whether market (exogenous) factors or social-structural (endogenous) factors, especially class, are the primary agents of change.

World-system literature is complicated by a number of inter-twined polemics, which focus on the role of socialist states in the contemporary world-system; the probability of a world socialist revolution; the degree to which underdevelopment is a necessary consequence of core development; the effects of various policies on the evolution of the world-system; and whether world-system theory is a useful extension or a crude distortion of Marxist theory.

Polemical debates notwithstanding, world-system theory has generated many studies of long-term social change. These studies use techniques from the various social sciences and appear in a variety of publications. In its first decade world-system theory has developed its own journal, *Review*, and has made a major contribution to the social sciences by focusing attention on the importance of both global and historical factors in understanding both changes and processes of contemporary social life.

Thomas D. Hall
University of Oklahoma

Reference
Wallerstein, I. (1979), *The Capitalist World-Economy*, Cambridge.

Further Reading
Bergesen, A. (ed.) (1980), *Studies of the Modern World-System*, New York.
Chirot, D. and Hall, T. (1982), 'World-system theory', *Annual Review of Sociology*, 8.
Nash, J. (1981), 'Ethnographic aspects of the world capitalist system', *Annual Review of Anthropology*, 10.
Wallerstein, I. (1974), *The Modern World-System, I*, New York.
Wallerstein, I. (1980), *The Modern World-System, II*, New York.
Wallerstein, I. (1984), *The Politics of the World-Economy*, Cambridge.
See also: *dependency theory; imperialism*.